A COMPARATIVE STUDY FOR YOUTH

CHRISTIAN THEOLOGY & ANCIENT POLYTHEISM

*A resource enabling parents
to discuss with their children
the differences between
Christian and Pagan beliefs.*

MARCIA HARRIS BRIM

A Comparative Study for Youth
VOLUME I

CHRISTIAN THEOLOGY & ANCIENT POLYTHEISM

FOR USE WITH

PUBLISHED BY

BrimWood Press

BRIMWOOD PRESS
1941 Larsen Drive
Camino, CA 95709

Copyright 2009 © by Marcia Harris Brim. All rights reserved including the right of reproduction in whole or in part, except by the original purchaser for family use following the permission prescribed within. All other reproduction rights must receive prior permission from BrimWood Press.

Cover Artwork: Jacob Wrestles with the Angel, Eugene Delacroix (1798-1863)
Graphic Design: Carmen Pereira Pucilowski
Editor: Anne Roundtree and Lori Hostetler
Writing Assistant: Madelaine Wheeler
ISBN: 978-0-9770704-7-3
Manufactured in the United States

Dedicated to

Madelaine Wheeler

WHOSE THOUGHTFUL
INSIGHTS AND KEEN
OBSERVATIONS
HAVE HONED THIS
WORK, AND WHOSE
ENCOURAGEMENT
HAS BEEN AN
INVALUABLE IMPETUS
TOWARDS FINISHING
THE COURSE.

·

WITH SPECIAL THANKS
TO CARMEN
WHOSE LABOR OF LOVE
CREATED THE VISUAL
APPEAL OF THIS WORK.

TABLE OF

INTRODUCTIONS......7
Parent/Teacher Introduction
Student Introduction

LESSON I......18
A Comparison of the Gods, Their Creations,
Their Creatures and the Beliefs They Birthed

LESSON II......25
All God's Creatures Great and Small,
or All Gods Great and Small

LESSON III......29
Gilgamesh's Flood versus the Genesis Flood

LESSON IV......34
Diving Deeper – the Flood Continued

LESSON V......41
Worship: Seven Days of Idolatry or Imitation

LESSON VI......47
The Sacrifices of Sumerian and Israelite Worship

LESSON VII......52
Pagan Sacrifices and the Eight Great Sacrifices of the Bible

LESSON VIII......62
To Obey is Better than Sacrifice

LESSON IX......67
Prayer – The Names have Changed to Deceive Worshippers

LESSON X......75
Prayer as Power or the Power of Prayer

LESSON XI......81
Modern Worship in Modern Culture

LESSON XII......85
The Consequences of Idolatry

LESSON XIII 91
The Men and the Purposes Behind Babylonian and Hebrew Law

CONTENTS

LESSON XIV......102
The Code of Hammurabi and the Laws of Moses

LESSON XV......126
Love – the Fulfillment of the Law

LESSON XVI......137
Israel's History and Our Lessons

LESSON XVII......146
The Bible's Main Characters – the Good, the Bad and the Ugly

LESSON XVIII......156
The Big Show-down – Is it God or is it Baal?

LESSON XIX......167
Judah's End and New Beginning and the
Never-Ending Faithfulness of God

LESSON XX......180
The Suffering of the Babylonian and Biblical Job

LESSON XXI......191
The Significance of Suffering

LESSON XXII......202
Suffering – Central to the Plan of God

LESSON XXIII......210
An Encounter with the Almighty

LESSON XXIV......221
The Afterlife and the Resurrection

LESSON XXV......243
A Course Summary of Christian Theology
and Ancient Polytheism

APPENDIX......250
Jacob Journal
Parent/Teacher Charts
Student Charts

Parent/Teacher Introduction

This HNET Christian Reader's Guide is not the typical ten-page companion that accompanies many works of historical fiction. While *Secret of the Scribe* has its own educational value and literary merits, it was commissioned to facilitate the five chief objectives of this Christian Reader's Guide:

1. To teach Christian worldview through teaching Christian theology

2. To teach Christian theology using literary methods

3. To juxtapose pagan belief against Christian belief

4. To fuel discussion about God's Word

5. To prepare children for the big ideas presented in great books, apart from the challenge of classical literature

FIRST OBJECTIVE:
Teaching Worldview through Theology

Our first purpose is to provide young people a fuller understanding of the Christian worldview. A worldview is based upon an integrated whole of presuppositions. The Christian's assumptions about the nature and meaning of reality are rooted in Scripture. An understanding of God's Word that provides an integrated and holistic view of the world comes from theology. Theology begins with the study of God, and encompasses His work in and through mankind. Thus a Christian's worldview is based upon his or her theology. *Teaching children a solid Christian theology develops a solid Christian worldview.*

After more than six years of teaching worldview classes to Christian homeschool students ages 10 to 13, I am troubled by significant gaps in their Christian theology. In general, Christian children lack a Christian worldview because they have an insufficient understanding of Christian theology. They know some things well: the plan of salvation, a stockpile of memorized verses, lots of Bible stories and an arsenal of arguments for the age of the earth. Nonetheless, this knowledge does not constitute the theological understanding necessary to have a Christian view of the world. Their most notable weaknesses are their understanding of the character and nature of God and His special creation of man. The basis of theology is the study of the character and nature of God and His purposes for His creation. This is the foundation upon which a Christian theology and worldview are built. The Bible does not begin with Scripture's climactic event. Genesis starts by addressing the worldview question "Who is God?" and "What is His purpose for mankind?" The question "How can I be saved?" – though critically important for humanity – must

Parent/Teacher Introduction · **7**

ultimately rest upon a solid understanding of God, His works and His purposes. Without such a foundation we lack the theology necessary to see the world through a Christian lens, let alone to live the fullness of the Christian life.

Nevertheless, God in His mercy has made the answer to "How can I be saved?" simple enough that a small child can experience salvation. But that child must be mentored and discipled in the understanding of the Christian faith so that he grows up to be a mature believer, producing fruit that will last. Statistics tell us that large numbers of young adults abandon their Christian worldview in college.

Many, I fear, are walking away because they have a deficient view of the world based on a partial Gospel. The Gospel begins in Genesis 1.

Let's look at this problem using an analogy. Imagine that a biblical worldview is like a beautiful country home, built of bricks and with a substantial wrap-around porch. The porch has a swing and a couple of rocking chairs and hanging baskets full of blossoms. This handsome, restful spot is the delight of the homeowners. On a warm summer's evening, there is no place they would rather be. This lovely porch represents the salvific work of Christ that gives rest to our souls. Our Christian young people's worldviews possess a beautiful front porch.

Now let's imagine that all the individual Bible verses they know represent red bricks. The more verses they know, the bigger their pile. But therein lies the problem – the pile. The bricks have not been mortared together to form a house. Their porch wraps around a jumble of bricks, not a secure brick home. Without mortared bricks, those Bible stories which should be windows through which they see both the porch and the world beyond, lie carefully stacked upon the ground. Here's where their knowledge about the age of the earth and other pieces of scientific apologetic information helps. It provides the windows with packing material for storing and protecting them from the guys who like to throw rocks.

Christian children may not have a house, but do they really need one when they have an amazing front porch? Some nights in spring are a little chilly, but there is no better place to smell the apple blossoms and listen to the song birds. Summer may be stifling in the heat of day, but the porch roof provides shade and the evenings are always so lovely. Autumn can be the most pleasant time of year, but the nip in the air forebodes a difficult season ahead. The winter is not at all pleasant spent on the porch. Indeed, a porch will not provide the shelter of a home. Our children are in great need of a home.

Why is it that we are constructing so many porches and so few homes? Perhaps it is because of our own insufficient worldview. Our own salvation theology is clear and we want our children to experience the forgiveness of Christ and eternal life. But Paul labored in the churches to see "Christ formed in them".[1] He recognized

---

1 GALATIANS 4:19

full well that the Gospel is not an end in itself; it is the beginning – an amazing beginning, what the Bible calls a new beginning in Christ. We are made new creations and are given again the same purpose that God gave Adam and Eve in the Garden – to become like God, to bear His image and to spread His image and likeness across the whole earth.[2] The wording has changed ever so slightly, while the meaning remains exactly the same: we are called to be like Christ, the image of the invisible God. Therefore, this Christian Reader's Guide and its subsequent companions seek to develop a child's understanding of the God who creates and saves and His singular purposes for both actions. In short, this guide builds Christian theology with the prayer that our children's "porches" will lead into houses that will remain.

SECOND OBJECTIVE:

Teaching Theology using Literary Methods

While my degree happens to be in theology, the method this work employs does not result in a systematic theology that dissects the various doctrines of Scripture. A typical theology may begin with the various attributes of God such as His omnipresence, omnipotence, omniscience, etc, etc. All are followed by a definition and a collection of verses supporting each facet of God's nature. While these and many other attributes of God spring right from the pages of Scripture, this fact-based approach – which is actually a scientific approach – is not the primary method God uses to teach us about Himself. God cannot be distilled into a collection of facts, even when those facts describe His nature. God is always more. God will not be reduced to a quantifiable level that the scientific method requires. God can be known, but He cannot be comprehended.

God has revealed Himself in three ways: through nature, through His Word and through the Incarnation. Scientific means are helpful in studying what God has revealed about Himself through His creation, but nature cannot display the personhood of God which is central to His Trinitarian being. So God came and lived among us and wrote His story through us. And God invites us to participate in this story with Him. We have been invited to share in the very life of the Trinity. This reality will *never* belong to the realm of science.

While the term *theology* (the study of God) is actually a field of science, the tools for accomplishing its aim are better found in the humanities. From beginning to end, God teaches us about Himself through stories. He uses the convention of language and the medium of culture to reveal Himself to mankind. He shows Himself to us in the context of a living narrative. Sometimes He is the leading character, other times He plays much more of a supporting role, other times His presence goes

give us a vision of the wonderful possibilities of "the exchanged life"!

---

2 GENESIS 1:28; MARK 16:15

completely undetected ... but He is there. With careful reading that is married to the understanding that each individual narrative is actually a part of the unfolding epic, we can uncover a picture of rich complexity and astounding beauty for those who will work to see it.

Stories demand effort on the part of the reader to extract their meaning. They require us to think and rethink, while facts can be filed away in memory. Gathering facts is a scientific skill, mining for meaning is a literary exercise. I often wonder if, living in a scientific world, we are tempted to value learning facts about God rather than striving to discover His Person within the pages of His narrative. Yet, this narrative approach is not nearly so tidy. It does not lend itself to worksheets or multiple choice tests. It looks more like journaling or poetry – more like a response to literature, less like a lab summary. God's unfolding narrative is a *love story* – not something that can be dissected or classified. Without a literary approach to Scripture, Bible stories may remain merely a collection of narratives that can stand alone but happen to cohere through historical progression and common ancestry. With this approach, the value of the story can be reduced to its ability to provide moral teaching and wisdom. Helping children see these stories as intricate pieces of God's grand narrative is as important to the formation of a Christian worldview as is the trowel to the work of a brick mason.

THIRD OBJECTIVE:

Juxtaposing Ancient Polytheism and Biblical Monotheism

While we are seeking to build theology using literary rather than scientific methods, that is not this guide's only novel approach. Through teaching worldview classes I have discovered how much Christian theology can be clearly taught when Christian ideas are compared and contrasted to the ideas of other worldviews. This is especially true when comparing the conflicting beliefs about the character and nature of God. Comparison and contrast becomes a powerful tool for teaching Christian theology. Thus, this guide unapologetically gives serious attention to polytheism or what the Bible calls paganism – the worship of many gods. Through examining polytheism closely we see more clearly what it looks like to worship one God. In the same way that the dark deepens one's appreciation for the light, the ramifications of falsehood make the truth that much more compelling.

It is especially appropriate that the first HNET novel, *Secret of the Scribe*, revolves around the worldview of polytheism. The central conflict of the Old Testament is the clash between ancient polytheism and biblical monotheism –– the choice between worshipping one God or worshipping many. Knowing Whom we worship, what worship is, and why we worship is foundational to the Gospel. Again, here is critical mortar that cements bricks together and allows a home to take shape.

The primary theology taught through this guide that springs from its juxtaposition of polytheism and monotheism could be summarized as follows: the purpose of our lives is worship. The chief expression of worship is obedience. Obedience is that which progressively moves us in cooperation with the Spirit of God towards the likeness of God. We were made to be like God. We have been called to be like Christ. Christ-likeness is a life of worship. Salvation is the means that makes this life possible. The understanding of this life is rooted in the Old Testament.

FOURTH OBJECTIVE:
Stimulating Discussion about God's Word

While this guide covers a lot of content, it has been structured to foster discussion. Thus, there is no workbook, answer key, or script to follow. Instead, the guide provides plenty of thought-provoking material from Scripture and from the texts of polytheistic religions, and discussion questions to get you talking about what you have read. Challenging students to think and interact stimulates learning. Conversations are valuable in and of themselves, regardless of the dialogue's result or its lack of tangible output. Learning to converse about important ideas is one of the most vital skills your student will gain. As your student practices articulating his own questions and engaging in a back-and-forth dialogue with you, his grasp of the subject will deepen and become personal. The ancient philosopher Socrates believed in this method of teaching for these very reasons. A student who works out an idea in dialogue instead of merely being lectured develops a much more comprehensive understanding of the idea itself and its implications.

This may all sound well and good, but what about the homeschool parent who is trying to create learning records? Do not despair. At the end of each unit a chart is provided, upon which the student will synthesize his or her learning about the given topic. Beyond the blank charts, a filled-in sample is available on each topic for the teacher. These samples are teaching aides for the parent, not check lists and certainly not answer sheets. The blank charts are a tool, aiding the child's ability to capture the similarities and differences between polytheism and monotheism. Your child's syntheses may vary. Children should record the ideas that impressed them; if the ideas are in the general ball park, parents must resist the desire to correct. The charts will be a concrete help in visualizing and grounding the big ideas you and your child discuss, and provide an enduring record of what the child learned. As you progress through the lessons, the guide provides instructions for when and where to fill in the charts. Each participating child should keep a separate set.

Parent/Teacher Introduction · **II**

We have talked about the value of discussion and tried to allay the teacher's concerns about tangible learning output, but we have not fully addressed the objective stated at the beginning of this introduction – "to foster rich discussion about God's Word". The discussion ideas that this guide gleans from Scripture are gathered using an atypical method. For Protestants the typical approach to Bible study is topical or expository. In a topical study, the student looks up a series of verses or passages on a particular subject – for instance stewardship or purity – in order to understand what the Bible teaches on this area of Christian living. In an expository study, the student looks deeply at the intent of a particular text, studying line by line, even word by word to "expose" the meaning and application of a particular passage of Scripture. Both approaches are used effectively in pulpits and Bible study books to build up the Body of Christ, but this guide uses a different approach. In viewing Scripture as God's literary masterpiece, this guide examines some of the great *themes* originating from the Word of God that run the breadth of the text from Genesis to Revelation. This guide covers great swaths of Scripture, rather than focusing on any particular passage, because our purpose is breadth not depth. We are striving to help the student gain *context* for the great volume of content he already knows. It is our prayer that through completing the course of all four HNET Study Guides, Christian students will gain a structural framework for Scripture's great ideas by discussing its great themes.

FIFTH OBJECTIVE:
Priming Students for the Great Books

The final purpose of this guide is to prepare children ages 10-13 for a high school study of the western great books. The approach already discussed in this introduction lays the groundwork for exploring the great works of Western literature. As noted, this guide aims to ground a child's worldview by expanding and anchoring his or her theology, by developing the ability to compare and contrast conflicting ideas and by fostering conversational/critical thinking skills. The student who is hit with a barrage of challenging ideas in Marx or Darwin will handle the challenge much better if he or she has the ability to compare these ideologies point by point with a scriptural worldview. In order to do this, the student's theology must be comprehensive enough to withstand the challenge. To withstand requires thinking, for which the fundamental skill of compare and contrast will be an invaluable aide in successfully reading the great books without being engulfed by their challenging ideas. This Guide and its subsequent companions teach compare/contrast skills while bolstering one side of the comparison – a biblical worldview.

A final preparation this guide offers the future "great books student" is the ability to "cut one's teeth" on great ideas, without having to choke on the advanced literary style of most classic work. *Secret of the Scribe* is intentionally written in simple, flowing prose, yet its narrative provides a platform for some of the same big ideas addressed by the classics. Learning to recognize and wrestle with big ideas as a prerequisite to wrestling with the classics will serve future scholars well.

HOW TO USE THIS GUIDE:

1. Read *Secret of the Scribe.*

Secret of the Scribe should be read prior to working through the context of this guide. As noted earlier, the novel was written to provide a pagan setting for contrast with the narrative of Scripture. In some exercises, you will be asked to look up and read portions from *Secret of the Scribe*. Thus it is important to have the book available for the entirety of the time spent in this guide.

The index provides a series of topics explored in this guide. Many of the topics spring from the pages of the historical novel. Those that do not are included because they are necessary to flesh out the monotheistic story of Israel, which this guide covers in some depth.

2. Be prepared to spend multiple days on each lesson.

Within each lesson you will find numerous logical breaks (provided through charting activities). You control the speed at which your family travels. Take your time and enjoy the journey! Stop the lesson as soon as your child is no longer engaged. Do not be surprised if working through a single guide takes six months or more. Ideally, work through all four guides while your children are between the ages of 10 and 13. Remember, your goal is not to provide a crash course in theology because you know "winter" is coming.

3. Create each child's notebook by photocopying the Student's Notebook Material found in the Appendix.

Before you begin your study, each child will need some form of notebook to contain all the charts he or she will be working on. You will need to photocopy all of the material in the appendix labeled "Student Charts" and three pages of "Jacob Journal" for each participating member in your family. If you are using this program in a classroom or co-op setting, you will need to pay a small copyright fee to BrimWood Press for written permission to legally photocopy materials for non-family members. Please contact Marcia@brimwoodpress.com.

Parent/Teacher Introduction · 13

4. Relax your expectations.

The Parent Charts encompass more material than a child should be epected to record. Celebrate each insight they are able to document. Remember, the charts are not a writing assignment in which grammar and sentence structure rule the day. The ideas they are recording are so much more important than grammar. Use other subjects to teach the mechanics of writing. You may wish to create your own notebook, capturing the ideas of the whole family.

5. Wait to write.

The Discussion Questions are intended for rich, free-flowing conversation. Resist the temptation to record your child's wonderful responses. Having to pause for an accounting scribe will destroy the art of conversation and hinder the development of thought. Again, it will burden the exercise and work against its effectiveness. Jot your own notes in the margin of this guide, when each discussion comes to its natural close.

6. Have a Bible and the *Secret of the Scribe* available for each lesson.

Look up all the Bible passages in the text. Those in the footnotes are optional. Just because students know a particular Bible story or passage of Scripture, do not shortchange your family's ability to see it in the larger context. This guide highlights major themes that are developed across multiple texts of Scripture. Bible stories are well known; Bible themes are not.

7. To begin:

There is no other teacher prep work required before each lesson. All lessons have been designed to be read aloud and discussed. There is, however, one lesson which you may need to modify according to the innocence of your child. Lesson 12, which looks at the consequences of idolatry, may be inappropriate for some children at the current time. Prayerfully consider how much *can* be covered, as it provides some of the clearest rationale for the goodness of biblical monotheism.

To begin these lessons with your students, have the children read the student introduction aloud, and familiarize them with the charts and the Jacob Journal. Make copies for additional Jacob Journal pages as needed. Remember to adapt the length of the lesson to the attention span of your children. For many families this course will take the entire school year.

Special Note: THERE ARE SEVERAL REASONS FOR THE HIGH DEGREE OF REPETITION IN THIS GUIDE. IT TEACHES SOME DEEP THEOLOGICAL CONCEPTS THAT MANY YOUNG PEOPLE WILL NOT READILY GRASP THE FIRST TIME AROUND. IT IS WRITTEN TO DEVELOP A BIG PICTURE PERSPECTIVE THAT FOR MANY REQUIRES REITERATION. THE GUIDE IS BUILDING AN AWARENESS OF BIBLICAL THEMES WHICH ARE DISCOVERED THROUGH REPETITION.

Student Introduction

For the next several months you and your teacher/parent will be discussing ideas that relate to the story of *Secret of the Scribe* and the story of the Old Testament. If it surprises you that this Christian Reader's Guide contains months worth of conversations, we have something in common. Before writing this guide, I wondered *"Just how much will there be to discuss from this engaging but simple story?"* I soon discovered that even though the story is undemanding, the task of comparing ancient polytheism to biblical monotheism is not. The comparison is challenging and deeply thought-provoking. Challenging and thought-provoking may not be words that excite you, but if you are between the ages of 10 to 13 or older it's time for you to start honing some thinking skills you will use for the rest of your life. Luckily, you should find the process enjoyable. The guide is filled with lots of fascinating stories, engaging discussion questions and a series of charts to record your learning.

So just what exactly are you supposed to learn from this study guide? Well, as we already noted, this guide compares ancient polytheism to biblical monotheism. Polytheism, the worship of many gods, is called *paganism* in the Bible. Biblical monotheism refers to the belief in one God that begins with the nation of Israel in the Old Testament and, after Christ's death and resurrection, continues with Christians of eventually every nation in the New Testament. One major reason why you are learning about the ideas of polytheism is because it will actually enable you to understand and appreciate your own faith better. After teaching many worldview classes, I've realized that most kids your age have some major gaps in their understanding about what Christianity actually is or why certain Biblical ideas really matter. It's time to fill in these holes. Without a more complete understanding of the truths of God's Word, you will not develop a truly Christian view of the world. This guide and the companions to the other Historical Novels for Engaging Thinkers have been designed to help you see where Christian ideas and the ideas of opposing worldviews lead.

This knowledge will be especially valuable when you enter a season of doubt. At some point in your growing up years, you will probably start to wonder whether what you have been told about God and the Bible is true. This is a normal and healthy process that most young people go through. Doubts that prompt deeper questions about your faith help you make what you've been taught your own. To guide you through this time, this guide and its companions offer a series of compare and contrast charts which you will use to record the difference between Christianity and other worldviews. The other tool is just some blank pages for a "Jacob Journal". While the charts are required, the journal is not. It's simply available for you to use now or in the future when, like Jacob, you need to wrestle with God.

The story of Jacob wrestling with God is recorded in Genesis 32. Jacob was returning to the land of his father in Canaan. That was a good thing, but the prospect of meeting up with his brother whom he cheated out of his birthright was not. Jacob was sure Esau was out for revenge, and Jacob thought his only hope of avoiding what he had coming to him was in buying his brother off with lots of valuable gifts. The gifts were sent on ahead of his caravan so they would meet Esau before Jacob, who spent the night alone. Perhaps he was going to spend some time contemplating what a schemer he had been, but out of nowhere a man appeared and an all-out wrestling match ensued. Somewhere into the match, which lasted the whole night through, Jacob realized his wrestling partner was God in a human form. That didn't deter Jacob in the least. He refused to let God go without being given a blessing. It was then that God changed Jacob's name to Israel because he had "struggled with God and with men and had overcome." This is a mysterious story, but one thing is certain: God came to Jacob, knowing he needed to wrestle. God could have showed up in the form of an eight-foot giant and pinned Jacob with a few easy moves. But the body God took on did not posses superior human strength. Jacob actually got the upper hand. Jacob knew that he needed something from God, and God wanted Jacob to ask. Out of this wrestling match, Jacob got a new name, a face to face confrontation with God, and a wounded hip that reminded him that God will always win.

By pondering this story, we get permission to do our own wrestling with God. Remember, God will take you on! In fact, I think He rather delights in the process. Your doubts may seem like an eight-foot giant, but if you are willing to struggle, God will eventually win, and you will be blessed with a faith that is far stronger than you have now.

You may not be struggling with questions that cause you to doubt your faith, but you may have some questions you haven't gotten satisfactory answers for. You should write them down. I've had questions that I walked around with for more years than you have been alive. When I finally got a satisfying answer, it was really something to treasure. I wish now that I had written more of my questions down. It would be rewarding to record answers so many years later. Beyond current or future questions and struggles, you can use this journal just to capture your private thoughts about God and your faith. Be prepared: this guide is going to challenge your thinking about what Christianity is all about. You may want to record your reactions in your Jacob Journal. Record as little or as much as you like. What you record is up to you.

Lastly, you are going to be rereading a lot of Bible stories you've heard many times. Resist the temptation to think that you already "know" that story. Yeah, you know the story, but this guide will help you see the story as it compares to similar pagan stories, or how this story fits into the larger story, the grand story of God's Word. The Bible is actually one big story, with a beginning, middle and end. There is a setting, main characters, plot, conflict, climax and themes. It has all the elements of any other great epic, but, unlike the rest, the Bible is God's story through which He reveals Himself to mankind. As such, it is more important than any epic ever written. This guide will help you understand the sweeping narrative of the Bible.

So keep your Bible, your notebook, charts, Jacob Journal, and your *Secret of the Scribe* book handy as you work through these lessons with your parent and/or teacher. You'll be doing a lot of reading aloud and discussion. Learning how to talk about the ideas like those covered in this guide is an essential skill for growing up. If you're doing this in a group, remember that people will have varying levels of ability when it comes to talking about ideas. Give each other lots of grace and courtesy. If you like to talk, you'll need to hold yourself back from time to time so others can share their ideas. If you don't like to talk, work on moving out of your comfort zone in order to start developing an ability you will use the rest of your life.

Before you begin, you might take a look at the comparison charts that are contained in your notebook.

ENJOY THE JOURNEY!

Parent/Teacher Introduction · 17

LESSON I:

A Comparison of the Gods, Their Creations, Their Creatures and the Beliefs They Birthed

The story of the *Secret of the Scribe* takes place in a culture dominated by a single worldview – that of polytheism, or what the Bible calls paganism. Pagans or polytheists worship many nature gods. While you'd be hard pressed to find someone today who believes that the forces of nature are actually gods and goddesses, this belief dominated the ancient world. From Sumer to Egypt to Greece to Briton, polytheism was the worldview practiced in the earliest recorded histories. It should not surprise us that when we compare polytheism to the beliefs of Christianity, we will spend a lot of time looking at the Old Testament. Indeed, *the major conflict of the Old Testament is the clash between polytheism and monotheism – the clash between worshipping idols and worshipping the living God.*

While the events of *Secret of the Scribe* take place before the Old Testament was written, the religion practiced by Tabni looked very much like the belief system of nations mentioned in the Bible, e.g. the Canaanites, Babylonians, Assyrians, Moabites and many other countries that surrounded Jewish people. The Jews, with their belief in one creator-God, were intended to be the stark contrast to cultures of the ancient world. Thus the focus of this comparative study will contrast the beliefs of the polytheistic world with those of monotheistic Israel.

* * *

Look up and re-read aloud the paragraphs from *Secret of the Scribe* listed below. Listen for ideas that help you understand what the Sumerians believed about the gods and goddesses, about their creation – man, and the world they lived in.

Read the paragraphs beginning with the following phrases:

PAGE 3 – "I no longer believe Father ..."

PAGE 15 – "Our lives are only dice, ..."

PAGE 38 – "In the open workshop ... face of a goddess into a chunk of rock."

PAGE 42 – "That I had lived to feel hunger astounded me...."

PAGE 49 – "Pulling the fish amulet ... settle in the silt.

PAGE 61 – "My brothers and I are careful ... since I had gotten it for free."

PAGE 71 – "I have seen you here often. ... along with all the other – happy!"

PAGE 78 – "In a somber voice, ... They don't seems to hear us."

PAGE 89 – "It's a well known fact ... "

PAGE 98 – "Are you trying to make fools of the gods, ... watch out for their fury!"

Discussion Questions:

1. From the quotes you read, how would you describe some of the character qualities of the gods and goddesses?

2. How might you describe Tabni's feelings about the gods and goddesses?

3. Come up with three adjectives summarizing the character of the Sumerian gods and goddesses.

4. Look up the word capricious in the dictionary or online. Write the definition or several synonyms:

_____

5. What examples from the excerpts above show that the word "capricious" is an appropriate description for Sumerian gods?

6. Can you think of an antonym for the word "capriciousness" that could describe the God of the Bible?

_____

7. Are there any stories in the Bible in which God shows this type of behavior?

8. Add the words to your chart that describe the characters of both the gods and goddesses and your antonym for the God of the Bible.

Open your notebook to chart **CC-1, The Nature and Works of the Gods**. You will see that it compares the Sumerian gods and goddesses to the God of the Bible. From the novel excerpts and the discussion questions, fill in some adjectives and/or short sentences under the column *Sumerian Gods and Goddesses* and the row labeled *Character Qualities of the Creator(s)*. Add your contrasting adjective to describe the character of God under the column *The God of the Bible*.

A Comparitive Study using *Secret of the Scribe* · **19**

The Creation Accounts and the Beliefs They Birthed

The Sumerian origin story does not appear in our novel; nonetheless, the presence of these beliefs are felt throughout this story. How was the world created, what are the gods like and what is man's purpose? The answers to these questions all find their source in the Sumerian stories about how the world was created. Sumerian origin myths went something like this:

IN THE BEGINNING, THE WATERS OF NAMMU, THE PRIMEVAL SEA, UNCOVERED THE MOUNTAIN OF HEAVEN AND EARTH.

THEY BROUGHT FORTH THE AIR, ENLIL, WHO DIVIDED THE MOUNTAIN AND DROVE HEAVEN (HIS FATHER AN), APART FROM HIS GODDESS MOTHER KI (THE EARTH). ENLIL TOOK THE GODDESS NINLIL AND SHE CONCEIVED AND BORE THE MOON, FATHER NANNA. THE MOON GOD, NANNA, MARRIED THE GODDESS NIGAL, AND UTA THE SUN WAS BORN. THEN ENLIL TOOK HIS MOTHER EARTH (KI), AND SHE CONCEIVED MANY GODS AND GODDESSES, WHO COMPRISE MOST OF THE ELEMENTS OF EARTH AND SKY. THE SEA GOD'S TIDES WASHED OVER KI THE EARTH, NANNA THE MOON AND UTA THE SUN SHONE NIGHT AND DAY, AND ENLIL THE AIR STOOD BETWEEN EARTH AND HEAVEN. THE OTHER ELEMENTS OF NATURE AND CIVILIZATION WERE MADE UP OF THE CHILDREN OF ENLIL AND KI. THE WHOLE

EARTH WAS COMPRISED OF MANY GODS AND GODDESSES. SOME GODS (LIKE ENLIL AND NANNA) WERE GREAT RULER GODS. THEY DEMANDED THAT THE LESS IMPORTANT GODS SERVE THEIR NEEDS. BUT FEEDING, HOUSING, AND CLOTHING THE RULER GODS BECOME VERY WEARISOME. THE LESS IMPORTANT GODS HERDED GOATS AND SHEEP AND INVENTED TOOLS THAT BROUGHT ABOUT FRUITFUL HARVESTS. THEY LABORED TO STORE THE GRAIN AND PREPARE GOOD FOOD. THEY CONSTRUCTED CHANNELS AND DAMS SO THE RIVER GOD WOULD NOT DESTROY THEIR FOOD SUPPLIES DURING ONE OF HIS RAGES. DAY IN AND DAY OUT, THEY SWEATED AND GROANED TO KEEP THE RULER GODS HAPPY. THOUGH THEY WERE GODS AND GODDESSES, THEY WERE VIRTUALLY SLAVES TO THOSE OF HIGHER RANK. "WE CANNOT DO ALL THAT THE RULER GODS REQUIRE!" THEY CRIED RESENTFULLY. AT LAST, MOTHER EARTH ACKNOWLEDGED THEIR COMPLAINTS.

AFRAID THAT THE LESSER GODS' REBELLION COULD START A WAR THAT WOULD DESTROY THE WORLD, SHE DECIDED TO CONSULT HER WISE SON ENLIL. "CANNOT YOU CREATE SOMETHING THAT COULD ALLOW ALL THE GODS AND GODDESSES TO LIVE IN EASE AND COMFORT?" SHE ASKED. ENLIL PONDERED. THEN HE TOOK A LUMP OF CLAY AND KNEADED IT INTO A BALL. "HERE," HE SAID TO THE OTHER GODDESSES. "SEE WHAT YOU CAN MAKE WITH THIS." THEY SET TO WORK, ADDING CLAY AND SHAPING SHOULDERS AND LIMBS. AFTER THEY HAD WORKED FOR MANY HOURS, ARMS AND LEGS BEGAN TO APPEAR. THEY PLACED A HEAD ON TOP AND POKED A HOLE FOR A MOUTH. BUT IT WAS NOT A LIVING THING. "I HAVE AN IDEA," SAID ONE GODDESS. "LET US PLACE THE CLAY INSIDE MY WOMB. WHEN IT IS BORN, IT WILL HAVE LIFE ... AND THE ABILITY TO PERFORM OUR LABOR." THE OTHER GODDESSES AGREED. AS THEY WAITED FOR THE CLAY TO BE BORN, THEY GLOATED AMONG EACH OTHER ON THEIR BRILLIANT SOLUTION

FOR HOW TO BRING FORTH LIFE WITHOUT THE HELP OF THE MALE GODS. FINALLY THE DAY CAME WHEN THE CLAY WAS BORN. THE GODDESSES CLOTHED HIM AND PUT THEIR TOOLS IN HIS HANDS. "HERE," THEY SAID, "GO OUT AND HERD THE FLOCKS. DIG THE FURROWS FOR THE SEEDS. WATER THEM AND WEED THEM AS THEY GROW INTO CROPS. WHEN THE CROPS ARE RIPE, HARVEST THEM. DIG WALLS AND CANALS TO KEEP THEM SAFE FROM THE RIVER GOD. BUILD BARNS IN WHICH TO STORE THEM. THEN COOK THEM AND BRING THEM TO US TO EAT." THEY MADE MANY SLAVES AND GAVE THEM THE NAME MAN, FOR MEN WOULD NOW TAKE OVER ALL THE TOIL DONE BY THE LESSER GODS. NOW ALL GODS – GREAT AND SMALL – LIVED IN PEACE, REJOICING THAT THEY COULD REST AND LIVE AT EASE.[3]

Discussion Questions:

1. What was the cause behind the creation of the world (according to polytheism)?
2. What was each newly birthed aspect of nature?
3. What was the difference between the greater gods and the lesser gods?
4. What was threatening the created order?
5. What would have happened to the world if some of the gods and goddesses rebelled?
6. What was Enlil's solution?
7. How was man created?

---

[3] This story is a paraphrase of the two myths "The Birth of Man" and "Cattle and Grain", as described at http://www.geocities.com/garyweb65/history.html, with creative license used for narrative details.

8. How was the creation of man unique compared to the way everything else was made?

9. What was the purpose of man's creation?

10. Who rested after the creation of people, and why?

From the Sumerian origin story, add to chart **CC-I** what you learned about the gods, the nature and origin of the world, and the creation and purpose of man. Fill in the rest of the rows under the column: *Sumerian Gods and Goddesses*.

Now let's contrast the Sumerian origin story with the biblical account.

Read Genesis 1 and 2 and discuss the following questions:

1. How did God make the creation?

2. Reread Genesis 1:2. In the Sumerian story, the primeval sea is what? (Primeval means the original state of the water.)

3. How is this different from the picture described in Genesis 1:2?

4. Is God a part of the deep, or separate and above it?

5. Is the "deep" animate (a living thing such as an animal or person) or inanimate (a non-living thing such as a rock)?

6. While both the Genesis and Sumerian stories start with a great body of water, according to the description of Genesis 1:2, 6, how are these stories different?

7. Is there any conflict happening in the Genesis story?

8. How is the creation of God described?

9. What do you learn about God's character from His actions of creation?

10. What is every aspect of nature except for man in the Sumerian story?

11. All aspects of nature in the Genesis story are what? Man is also a

    _____.

12. How and why was man created?

13. What makes man special and above the rest of God's creation?

A Comparitive Study using *Secret of the Scribe* · 23

14. What gives man His unique worth?

15. How does man reflect the image of God? (Hint: Take each of the following in brackets, fill in the blank and ask, "How does man ___reflect the image of God"?) {ruling, caring for the garden, filling the earth, as two made one flesh – or substitute "Why is it not good for man to be alone when he was meant to reflect the image of God?"}

In comparing these stories one can't help but notice the remarkable difference between man made to be a slave and man made to be God's representative. In the Biblical story of creation, God gives people unique value and purpose because they alone are uniquely *made in the image and likeness of God*. But this is not just an idea communicated in Genesis. This idea starts in the beginning and is woven into the entire story of God's Word. It is a major idea of the Bible and, like a sparkling gemstone, this truth has many facets. The more aspects we understand, the more light will shine upon our souls. For now, make sure that you have a firm grip on the idea that people are unique because their Maker alone gives them value and purpose.

Finish this lesson by **reading Psalm 8** and listening to the psalmist marvel at a God who would care so much for His creation, man. The psalmist was surely aware of his neighbor's view that men were slaves and nature was made up of various gods. As you read Psalm 8, listen for a word used to describe man that a pagan would never apply to all people. (note verse 6)

> Complete your **CC-1** chart, adding the important ideas you gleaned from the biblical creation story under the column *The God of the Bible*.

24 · Christian Theology & Ancient Polythesism

LESSON II:

All God's Creatures Great and Small, or All Gods Great and Small?

Tabni's culture was blinded by superstitions and fears of a world man could not control except through his efforts to keep the gods happy. The world itself was animate, a collection of many living beings, comprised of multiple personalities and various powers that controlled the fates of men. To live in fear of the gods was to live in fear of the world around them. Consider this as you read the following quotations:

> ...I gazed up through the swaying grass at a few scattered stars. Nanna [the moon god] was not even visible tonight. He had left the sky altogether, perhaps to spend the night in the shrine at the top of the ziggurat, where the priests kept a chamber in his honor. It was just as well. Should he look down on me and discover my irritation with him, he would surely unleash his fury. (p. 79)

> I worked as hard as ever, buying amulets and depositing them daily at Nanna's and Ningal's shrines, in hopes that this would cancel out my bitter thoughts toward all the gods. At least I'm doing what's required of me, I comforted myself, even if I cannot feel devotion. (p. 82)

> You'll never make it! a voice echoed in my ears. The gods will kill you today! (p. 104)

> His eyes dropped to the pouch. "It is only a scuffed and worn leather bag," he said. "Your cast-off possessions are not enough to reverse Nanna's anger." (p. 99)

> "Take them to the river, and toss them in with a prayer for forgiveness... Ask Enki [the water god] to persuade the gods to accept them as a substitute for the necklace.... So I have dutifully dropped them, one by one, into the canal.... I hope he will hear my prayer. I believe he will ... if he is not too tired or forgetful today, or in a bad mood.

In contrast to the beliefs of Mesopotamia, Israel was the first culture to believe in an inanimate universe. The universe was not the sum total of many supernatural beings; rather, the world was the grand natural creation of the One supernatural God.

A Comparitive Study using *Secret of the Scribe* · 25

Unlike the world of the unpredictable pagan gods, the world God made was purposeful. Neither people nor nature are gods; both are creations whose purpose is to reflect the Creator God. By reflecting the character and nature of God, the creation brings Him glory. Man's purpose was to be a unique mirror of God in many ways. Man reflects the Lordship of the Creator by ruling His creation as steward. Man does not own the world, but has been entrusted with its care. Man's rule should reflect the rule of God; he must value and care for the world as God's handiwork, without losing sight of the fact that the world was created to be man's source for God's provision. The land produced food to sustain man. As Provider, God gave man the world. As receiver, man must use this gift with wisdom and gratitude.

Read Genesis 1:11,29,30; 2:9,15,19,20-22 (Adam's action of naming was how the ancients expressed rule or lordship) **and Psalms 19:1-4; 24:1-2 and discuss the questions:**

1. How is the Genesis understanding of nature different from the Sumerian? How does the pagan worldview of nature affect man's relationship to the world around him?

2. By implication, according to the Sumerian view, which is more important: man or nature?

3. According to the above passages in Psalms and Genesis, what is the value and purpose of nature?

4. Sometimes it is easy to confuse purpose and value. To understand value or worth, imagine two old paintings, discovered after years of being hidden away in a museum basement. Both are equally beautiful, but one was painted by Michelangelo and the other by an unknown artist. Which painting would have greater value, and why? According to the Bible, what is the source of value for both the world and man?

5. Why was man given the job of ruling God's creation? What does this say about God, and what does this say about man?

6. Why is man's role as ruler of nature best described as a steward?

7. From the Bible, how would you demonstrate that man has a responsibility to care for creation, rather than just use the creation to feed his wants and greed?

8. Who is man accountable to for his use and care of creation? Why is he accountable?

9. To what verse(s) would you point to show that God intended His creation to provide for the needs of man?

10. Can you see the telling contrast between a God who uses the world to meet the needs of people, and the gods of Sumer who use people to meet their own needs? What do you think about this contrast?

Understanding the biblical view of nature in relation to man and man in relation to God lays one of the important foundational pieces of a Christian's view of God and the world. The verses you read from Genesis were selected to help you to see that from the beginning God planned to be man's provider; nature is one of God's provisions for man. Nature is both a source of provision and an inspiration, telling us of the glory of God.

The idea that God provides is a big idea of Scripture. This idea starts in Genesis 1 and develops through Abraham and his descendants in the Old Testament. It climaxes with the provision of Christ on the cross and continues through His providing the Holy Spirit to all who will believe. We cannot have eternal life – let alone fulfill our purposes for this life – without the gifts of Father, Son, and Spirit. Man utterly depends upon the God who provides. God, the Provider is a grand theme of Scripture.

Depending on your age, your study of literature may or may not have included learning about themes. The odds are pretty good that regardless of your age, you haven't spent much time studying themes of Scripture. It's time to change that. Since one of the goals of this course is to help you understand some of the most important ideas in the Bible, learning more about theme will be immensely helpful. Let's start with a definition:

> **Theme** (theem): a common thread or repeated idea that is incorporated throughout a literary work. A theme is a thought or idea the author presents to the reader that may be deep, difficult to understand, or [the basis of the narrative's messages about right and wrong]. Generally, a theme has to be extracted as the reader explores the passages of a work. The author utilizes the characters, plot, and other literary devices to assist the reader in this endeavor.... *In truly great works of literature, the author intertwines the theme throughout the work, and the full impact is slowly realized as the reader proceeds through the text. The ability to recognize a theme is important, because it allows the reader to understand part of the author's purpose in writing the book.*[4] (italics added)

---

4 Excerpted from the website: Glossary of Literary Terms located at http://www. uncp.edu/home/canada/work/allam/general/glossary.htm

A Comparitive Study using *Secret of the Scribe* · **27**

Since theme is an important characteristic of literature, it is essential that you understand that the Bible is a great work of literature. Indeed, it is the greatest story of all time, and the best part is: it's true. If you have spent much time in Sunday School and/or family devotions you have learned a lot of Bible stories. You've heard stories about Noah, Abraham, David, Jonah, Peter and Paul more times than you can count. Bible stories are filled with many different characters, but the Bible is truly one epic story with one main character – just one protagonist or hero. The hero is God. The Bible is His story. All those individual Bible stories help us see who God is through His work within the lives of people. God's story has a beginning, a climax and ending. It has a setting, plot and main characters. It has all the literary devices we find in any great work of literature, including theme.

In this guide we will highlight some of Scripture's great themes. Theme brings lots of different Bible stories together into one. Without the connection of a unifying theme, stories are like piles of unstrung popcorn and berries. Just as a needle and thread turns kernels and cranberries into a beautiful garland, themes link Bible stories into a single sweeping narrative. This guide will give you a needle and thread to help you string the stories together into one long garland. You are old enough to start asking, "What is the Bible all about, and why does this understanding matter so much?" Theme will help you find those answers.

In the lessons covered thus far, we've already taken a first look at two of the Bible's great themes. "God as Man's Provider" and "Man as God's Representative". Man made in His image, as His representative, filling the face of the earth is an idea developed across the pages of the Bible. In much the same way, so is the idea of God the Provider. Both are great themes of Scripture which we will discuss numerous times during this course.

For advanced 7th and 8th grade students and high school students working through this guide, we've provided some theme charts to help you track these and several other great ideas as they unfold. You should be aware that most of the Bible's great themes actually start in Genesis 1-3. So don't be surprised if your charts start from this point frequently.

Turn in your notebook to chart **CC-2, A View of Nature**. Record the important ideas you discussed about the differences between the Sumerian (Polytheism) view of nature and that which God gave to the Israelites (Monotheism). Ignore the two other columns on this chart for Naturalism and Pantheism. We will come back to these in subsequent reader's guides. After completing your **CC-2** comparison chart, older students will begin the **ST-1, God as Man's Provider** and **ST-2, Man as God's Representative** theme charts. Note several examples from Genesis 1 and 2 that show God's provision for man, and several ways that God uniquely created man to be His representative.

---

28 · Christian Theology & Ancient Polythesism

LESSON III:

Gilgamesh's Flood versus the Genesis Flood

Read the portion of the ancient story of *Gilgamesh* **as quoted in** *Secret of the Scribe* **on page 87.**

The excerpt you read came from an ancient story that would have been well known to the Sumerians living in Tabni's day. Gilgamesh was a great Sumerian king of the city-state Uruk, and lived about 700 years before the setting for *Secret of the Scribe*. Gilgamesh became legendary in his own time for the impressive walls he had built around his city. From there the story grew and intertwined with the Sumerian beliefs about the gods and goddesses. By the time it was handed down to the Babylonians, it was a larger-than-life epic about a half-man half-god whose exploits rival that of the legendary Greek hero, Odysseus.

Today's surviving tale was probably pressed into clay tablets by some Babylonian scribe around the time of King Hammurabi's reign (c. 1700 B.C.).[5] In the 1800s, these Cuneiform tablets were discovered in the ruins of the library of Ashurbanipal, king of Assyria (669-633 B.C.), at Nineveh by archeologist Sir Austen Henry Layard.[6] This was a fantastic archeological find, as *Gilgamesh* is the oldest surviving work of literature known to man. Yet what he found was still just a copy of a Mesopotamian story that had been told by bards and recorded by scribes for perhaps a thousand years.

Among the many tales told about Gilgamesh, there is a fascinating account of a great flood in which the gods destroyed the world. Everybody drowned except one man and his family who survived by building a big boat. Humm ... sound familiar? Below is a paraphrased version of the flood story told in *Gilgamesh*. Read it carefully, as we are going to compare it to the story of Noah's flood in the Bible.

---

[5] SCHOLARLY OPINION AS TO THE AGE OF THESE TABLETS WIDELY VARIES.
[6] ENCYCLOPEDIA BRITANNICA ONLINE

A Comparitive Study using *Secret of the Scribe* · **29**

GILGAMESH'S FLOOD

The city of Shurrupak, on the bank of the Euphrates River, grew large. As the number of people grew, the noise of the city increased, until it bothered the gods.

"The noise of the humans makes it impossible to sleep at night!" complained Enlil to the other gods. "Let us destroy them utterly." The other gods all agreed, but Ea sneaked away to the man Utnapishtim (oot-nah-pish-tim). He wanted to warn him.

"Listen! You must get rid of everything you own and rescue yourself. You must build a boat, with a beam as long as her length and a roof over her deck. Then you must put into the boat the seed of all living things."

"What will I tell the people in the city when they ask what I am doing?" said Utnapishtim.

"You must say that Enlil is very angry with you, so you must leave this city. Tell them, however, that Enlil will shower them with food and riches," replied Ea.

The very next day, just as the sun came up, Utnapishtim and his family and servants constructed the boat. Utnapishtim built the keel and the ribs and laid the planking. The entire floor of the boat was a square

– EACH SIDE WAS A HUNDRED AND TWENTY CUBITS IN LENGTH. IT WAS AN ACRE IN ALL, DIVIDED INTO SEVEN DECKS IN NINE SECTIONS. UTNAPISHTIM STOCKED THE BOAT WITH ALL HIS POSSESSIONS, FROM HIS FAMILY TO BOTH TAME AND WILD ANIMALS. THEN HE CLOSED THE BOAT.

THE VERY NEXT DAY, THE GODS SENT BLACK CLOUDS, THUNDER, LIGHTENING, AND HEAVY RAIN. THE STORM WAS SO TERRIBLE THAT THE GODS THEMSELVES WERE FRIGHTENED AND REGRETTED IT. THEY RAN AWAY AS FAR AS THEY COULD FROM THE SIGHT OF THEIR OWN DEVASTATION. ISHTAR WEPT, "WHY DID I WISH THIS EVIL ON MANKIND?" ALL THE GODS WAILED AND MOURNED.

THE TERRIBLE STORM LASTED SIX DAYS AND NIGHTS. WHEN, ON THE SEVENTH DAY, THE RAIN CEASED AND THE WINDS DIED DOWN, UTNAPISHTIM PEEKED OUT OF THE BOAT. ALL HE COULD SEE WAS WATER EVERYWHERE, EXCEPT A MOUNTAIN, ON WHICH THE BOAT WAS GROUNDED. AFTER SEVEN MORE DAYS, UTNAPISHTIM SENT OUT A DOVE, WHICH RETURNED BECAUSE SHE COULD NOT LAND ANYWHERE. THEN HE SENT A SWALLOW, WHICH LIKEWISE RETURNED. THEN HE SENT A RAVEN, WHICH DID NOT COME BACK. SHE MUST HAVE FOUND LAND. UTNAPISHTIM CELEBRATED BY MAKING A BIG SACRIFICE TO THE GODS. HOWEVER, ENLIL WAS ANGRY WHEN HE SAW THAT SOME HUMANS HAD SURVIVED THE INUNDATION. EA GENTLY REBUKED HIM. "WE MUST NOT CHASTISE MANKIND TOO HARSHLY. BETTER FOR HIM TO SUFFER FROM FAMINE OR WILD BEASTS THAN FROM A FLOOD!" SO THEN ENLIL BLESSED UTNAPISHTIM AND HIS WIFE AND MADE THEM IMMORTAL AND "SENT THEM TO LIVE IN THE DISTANCE, AT THE MOUTH OF THE WATERS".[7]

---

7 THIS STORY IS BASED ON A COMPILATION OF NUMEROUS PASSAGES FOUND IN *The Epic of Gilgamesh*

Discussion Questions:

1. Who was the god who decided to send the flood, and what was his role relative to man's creation in the Sumerian creation story from lesson 1?

2. Why did Enlil send the flood?

3. Does this story give you any clear understanding about why Ea decided to save Utnapishtim and his household?

4. What warning/instructions did they give him for saving himself and his household?

5. What is Utnapishtim supposed to do in terms of his city? Did he warn his countrymen?

6. What do you note about the size of the boat, the duration of the rain storm and the final destination of the boat?

7. What purpose did the birds serve?

8. What is Utnapishtim's response to surviving the flood?

9. How do the gods respond to his sacrifice?

10. What is Enlil's blessing of Utnapishtim?

Answer three questions on chart **CC-3, The Great Flood**, for the Gilgamesh Flood column, beginning with "Why was man wiped out?"

Now let's compare Gilgamesh's flood with the biblical account.

Read Genesis 6-9:17 and discuss the following questions:

1. Why did God send the flood?

2. Why did God choose to save Noah and his household?

3. What warning/instructions did God give him for saving himself and his household?

4. What do you note about the size of the boat, the duration of the rainstorm and the final destination of the boat?

5. What purpose did the birds serve?

32 · Christian Theology & Ancient Polythesism

6. What is Noah's response to being saved from the flood?

7. How does God respond to Noah's sacrifice?

8. How is God's blessing in Genesis 9:1-7 like Genesis 1:26-30? Do Noah and his offspring who live after the fall still have the same purpose as Adam and Eve? What else does God promise Noah and his descendants in verses 8-17?

9. Now compare the blessing God gave to Noah, with the blessing that Enlil gave to Utnapishtim. Stage a mock debate, picking sides about which god gave the better blessing. Each side should come up with reasons for why Enlil's or God's blessing was the best. Get creative, spend a few minutes and have some fun coming up with your best supporting arguments for each side.

10. It appears Utnapishtim was saved because he was favored by one of the gods, but there is little told us about his character and why he found favor. In contrast, we are told a good deal about the character of Noah. Why is Noah's character so important to this story?

11. Why is the lengthy description of the evil committed by the people God wipes out equally important to this story?

12. What is the consequence of sin?

13. What have you learned about the difference between the supernatural being(s) (God and Enlil) through comparing these two flood accounts?

> Go to chart **CC-3**, noting the similarities between the Gilgamesh flood and the story of Noah. Answer the first two questions under the Noah's Flood column.

THE BULK OF THE ACTUAL GILGAMESH FLOOD STORY CAN BE READ ONLINE. GOOGLE "GILGAMESH FLOOD TABLET XI". READING THIS ACCOUNT IS HIGHLY RECOMMENDED FOR OLDER STUDENTS. IN IT, GILGAMESH SEEKS UTNAPISHTIM, WHO HAD BEEN GIVEN THE GIFT OF IMMORTALITY. AS YOU READ, LOOK FOR PARALLELS IN GILGAMESH TO THE GARDEN OF EDEN AND MAN'S LOSS OF IMMORTALITY.

LESSON IV:

Diving Deeper – the Flood Continued

There are three gods in the Gilgamesh account of the flood which play a specific role: Enlil, the grumpy, irritable god who causes the destruction of mankind; Ea, the sneaky spoiler of Enlil's plans who saves one man and his family; and Ishtar, the weeping, benevolent goddess who grieves over the destruction of mankind. The three actions – destroying, saving and weeping – are done by three different supernatural beings with three different sets of motives. The Babylonian scribe who wrote this tale down could never imagine a single God who would destroy, grieve and save all in the same story. What motivation could explain all three actions of God?

The world was not destroyed by a flood because God was kept "awake by man's noise". The flood was not some capricious whim. God had to destroy humankind because they had chosen sin and death. From the beginning, people were made to reflect the likeness of God, but to fulfill their God-given purpose was dependent upon man's choice. People were given free-will. Man could choose to be like God through obedience, or man could choose to be a god unto himself – making his own rules – and disobeying and rebelling against the authority of God. While God gave man this freedom, He also provided the clearest of warnings – to choose disobedience would result in death. "In the day you eat of it, you shall surely die."[8] In the Garden, Adam and Eve chose death by eating of the Tree of the Knowledge of Good and Evil. By the time of Noah, rebellion against God was so great that everyone except Noah was deserving of death. Therefore, the creatures made to be the very representatives of the all-good God had to be destroyed, because they had become utterly evil.

Now let's stop a minute. If people had become utterly evil through exercising their ability to disobey God, why did an all knowing God give human beings free-will to begin with? God could have pre-programmed people to make decisions by instinct, like the rest of the creatures. On the other hand, God could have just stopped with the creation of animals. Think about it; without free-will God would have been a zoo keeper. There would have been no sin, no evil, no suffering – just a lot of beautiful creatures living in God's beautiful world. But without free-will and the possibility for sin, man would never have known real love. At least not the highest form of love – love based on choice. Without the ability to disobey, man would not have had the genuine ability to obey God. Man expresses his love to God through his obedience. God expresses His love to man through His provision. God's provision is ultimately an invitation to participate in His very life. This life is a life of love, for God is love. Man was given the freedom to receive God's gifts of love and to share in His life, or he could reject both His life and love. Most of humanity said no to God. This freedom to choose led to the destruction of the flood, but this same freedom also made it possible for Noah to walk with God.

---

[8] Genesis 2:16,17

Discussion Questions:

1. Why did God destroy the world?

2. What did God give man that made sin possible?

3. Why did God give people free-will?

4. What's the difference between the love we have with our pet and the love we have with our parents? What is your parents' love for you based on? What is their love for each other is based upon? How is the love of adoptive parents different from those who give birth to their children? (These questions point out that there is a difference both in the quality of love and in the basis of love. When a man and woman marry, they are choosing to love each other for a lifetime. When parents adopt a child, they are choosing to love a person they did not give birth to.) Why is choice an essential part of our love relationship with God?

5. How or why is our obedience to God an expression of our love for Him?

Some might still be wondering: why all this discussion about love and free-will? God punishes wicked people and saves righteous people ... it's that simple. Is it? Is God just sitting in His heaven looking for people to reward or punish? Is He like some cosmic Santa Claus who periodically passes out presents or lumps of coal? The answer to all of these questions is no. While Scripture clearly teaches that God judges mankind and blesses or punishes the deeds of the righteous and the unrighteous, He is not indifferent to the impact of His judgments. God is transcendent, high above and separate from His creation, yet He is also present in His creation and affected by His dealings with mankind. **Again, read aloud Genesis 6:5-8.**

Think about what you just read. God grieved. He suffered pain both because of mankind's evil and the destruction He caused. It was Ishtar who grieved in the Babylonian account of the flood. She was tenderhearted while Enlil was ruthless ... that's easy to understand. But try to wrap your heads around the idea of an all-knowing, all-powerful God who both justly sentences people to death while He willingly suffers because of their damnation.

The idea of God giving man free will just got more complicated. Why would God make a free willed creature, knowing man's choices would cause Himself pain and suffering? Again, why would God suffer? He is God. While we're asking questions, how is it that our sin and suffering can affect God when He is so big and all-powerful and is enthroned above the earth? How could what happens here affect Him way up there?

36 · Christian Theology & Ancient Polythesism

Let's start with the second question first. How can our sins affect God? To clarify, there is one way that our sin does not affect God even while our suffering does. God is incorruptible. He cannot be corrupted by our sin. When I was young someone taught me a very bad analogy about God. They said God is like a big white sheet, and if He were to have a relationship with a sinner like me, it would be like throwing a mud clod on the sheet. God would no longer be pure. That bad analogy leads to a faulty understanding about God because it implies, among other things, that the way God stays holy is by keeping His distance from things that are not. If that were the case, then after Adam and Eve sinned, God should have had no more contact with the human race until Christ came and covered people's unrighteousness. After Genesis 1 and 2, there goes the whole Old Testament, in which God is said to have been friends with people who were real sinners. God can befriend sinners because man's sin does not stain God.

The truth which the Scriptures teach is that God is holy. He is so holy, nothing can taint His purity. God is holy whether He is in heaven, on earth or in the depths of hell. He cannot be corrupted by your (or anyone else's) sin. He is God. Thus His Spirit can live inside the hearts of people like you and me who still struggle with sin, but we do not sully Him.

God is incorruptible, but God is not untouchable. God is compassionate, tenderhearted and long suffering. My sin and suffering affects God in much the same way that people are affected by the suffering of a close relative or friend who is dying of cancer. We didn't cause their cancer, nor can we catch their cancer, but we are greatly grieved by our loved one's pain. Grieving over the suffering of another is a characteristic of being a person. Our personhood was given to us by our Maker, in whose image and likeness we were created. God is a Person who grieves over us because He loves us.

Now let's go back to the first question. God knew the pain He would endure because of our sin and suffering before He made the world. So why did He make people, knowing the suffering they would cause Him? Now it might be tempting to jump to the wrong conclusion: "God must have needed someone to love pretty badly if He was willing to suffer like that." This idea could not be further from the truth. God does not need anyone to love. Remember God is one God who is

A Comparitive Study using *Secret of the Scribe* · 37

three Persons called the Trinity. The Father, Son and Spirit have been sharing a communion of love since before the world began.[9] Out of the overflow of this Trinitarian love, God chose to create man, knowing the tremendous price He would pay. He bore the pain of mankind because to share with us the life and love of the Father, Son and Spirit was worth more than all the suffering of God and humanity combined.

Thus, for the same reason that God made the world, God saved the world through Noah. God's first great act of salvation was demonstrated through the ark. It was God, not some angel sneaking behind His back, who warned and provided the means by which Noah and his family could be saved. God loved Noah and Noah loved God. Noah sought to obey God. He was God's representative in a dark and corrupt world. When the Bible says, "Noah walked with God" it means that Noah was truly experiencing life with God. This was the life man was created for and this was the life God saved and carried through the flood in an ark.

God chooses to suffer and to save because God is love. It is impacting to ponder the idea that God has been choosing to suffer down through the ages of time.

When God wiped out His creation with the flood, he suffered. When God saved Noah he willingly took on more suffering because He knew that his descendants would not walk with Him as Noah did. The Old Testament goes on to recount many instances in which God would be given reason to grieve and suffer again. Across the pages of human history, His sufferings climaxed on the cross. Nailed to a torturous tree, God would not only suffer for man, He would die. Why would God suffer and die? The answer lies deep in the love of God.

We cannot fully understand this because we cannot comprehend the depth, width and breadth of His love. Christ, knowing the love of the Father, endured the inestimable suffering and shame of the cross for the joy set before Him. Suffering is limited to the scope of time. In eternity it will be no more, while the love of God will endure forever. Precisely because of His enduring love, God

---

9 JOHN 17:23,24

chose to make the world, knowing that for the span of human history He would suffer.

Discussion Question:

1. In Gilgamesh's flood Enlil destroys, Ea saves, and Ishtar grieves. Why is it difficult for people to comprehend a God who would do all three things?

2. Enlil destroys people because he was put out by their noise. Ea saves Utnapishtim for some unexplained reason. Ishtar grieves because her beloved people are being destroyed. What character quality of God explains all three actions?

3. Can God be a God of love while still condemning some people to destruction? How do we know that God still loved people even though He caused the destruction of the flood? Why did He destroy so many people with a flood?

4. What does God's choice to save Noah and grieve over those He did not save teach you about God?

5. How did Noah's choice to obey and walk with God result in life – his own and ours as well?

6. If people never died and continued to live in a sin-filled world, could they eternally bear the ages and ages of human suffering? When God limited man's lifespan, by stopping his access to the Tree of Life, was this a gift of mercy?

7. In addition to the immensity of God's love, what does the fact that God bears all this suffering say about the strength of God?

8. When we are tender-hearted and compassionate towards someone who is suffering, even someone who is suffering because of their own bad choices, who are we being like?

In this lesson, we have come face to face with the love of God. This love of God is the greatest theme of Scripture. To attempt to contain this theme on some paper chart would be impossible, so we will content ourselves with a series of smaller themes, which when taken all together will reflect our humble recounting of the everlasting love of God. If you are keeping a Jacob Journal it would be good to reflect there about the love of a suffering God. This might be helpful to you now or in the years ahead when you will face suffering. We will come back to the topic

A Comparitive Study using *Secret of the Scribe* · 39

of pain and suffering and how it affects people towards the end of these lessons where you will find other discussion questions that will help you to delve into this topic further.

Consider ending this lesson in prayer, as it calls us to ponder the love of our suffering Creator and Savior.

> All students should go to the chart **CC-3** and fill in the final question under the *Noah's Flood* column.
>
> Older students should add the account of God saving Noah from Genesis 6 – 8 to the theme chart **TC-1** and the re-establishment of man's purpose after the flood from Genesis 9 to chart **ST-2**. In this lesson, we introduced the importance of man's free will. Man's free will is his decision to either obey or disobey God. That decision is ultimately the choice between life and death. Man's choice introduces another major theme of Scripture. Older students should go to (**Choose Life or Choose Death**), chart **ST-3** and answer the question regarding free will. Note man's first choice to disobey from Genesis 2. From Genesis 6 note the condition of man's heart in Noah's day and the consequences man receives for his evil choices. Finally, turn to the last theme chart **ST-4** on **Suffering**. Note the suffering of God and man from Genesis 6 – 8. See the parent charts for further clarification.

LESSON V:

Worship: Seven Days of Idolatry or Imitation

Down through the years of human history, religion has played a key role in shaping great cultures. What people believe about the world around them is based upon whether they believe in God, in several gods, or in no gods at all. Beliefs about the supernatural directly determine the value and purpose people give to the physical world and to themselves. What they make reflects what they believe. Culture is what people make out of the "stuff" in the physical world. People build practical things like cities and homes and artistic things like sculptures and paintings from natural materials obtained from the earth. Culture also includes how a group of people go about establishing what is right and wrong and the laws that result from this understanding. A culture's laws reflect its beliefs about the supernatural, as these beliefs generally determine how people should be treated. As the histories of virtually all civilizations include a strong belief in some form of the supernatural, each culture has places and practices for worship. The study of various cultures always includes their religious beliefs, as these are at the heart of culture.

Calendar stories are a wonderful reflection of what a culture values, as they commemorate religious events, holidays and festivals. In comparing the cultures of Sumer and Israel, we need to look at their calendars. They have a number of things in common, the most significant being the fact that both cultures practice a seven-day week. The practice of a seven-day week, which has no astrological basis, was a direct result of their beliefs in God or the gods. Nevertheless, the purposes behind the practice were vastly different. The Sumerian seven-day week revolved around the worship of a different force of nature each day, such as the sun, rain, and fertility. By keeping all these gods happy, the Sumerians hoped to persuade them to provide for the needs of their "slaves". Sumerians made images of their nature gods, called idols. With idols they worshipped a different powerful nature god each day of the week. In contrast to a calendar that tracked idol worship, Israel's seven-day week was an expression of her role as God's image bearer. Like God, she worked six days, creating what was good, and rested on the seventh. Representing God through imitating His creation week was her act of worship.

The ultimate contrast between these two practices of a seven-day week was the difference between man worshipping idols (the man-made representatives of the nature gods) and man worshipping the one true creator God through being His representative.

Tabni lived in a world where not only the seven great gods and goddesses were worshipped, but also hundreds of lesser gods of varying importance, including those as menial as the pot god. Everywhere, every seemingly inanimate thing was an

A Comparitive Study using *Secret of the Scribe* · **41**

expression of a god or goddess who must receive his or her due. It was, as Tabni's life illustrates, an endless and thankless task. As you read the following quotes from *Secret of the Scribe*, take mental note of the various names of the gods and goddesses, if given, and the force of nature they represented..

While keeping all the gods happy was essential to the religion of Sumer, worshipping idols – and the forces of nature they represented – was strictly prohibited in Israel. God's commands against idol worship set Israel apart from all her neighbors. Israel was called to depend upon God and to worship the Maker of heaven and earth alone.

Consider with Tabni the impossibility of keeping all these gods happy, in these following quotes from *Secret of the Scribe*:

> "Would I have enough strength and time left over to devote to pleasing the hundreds upon hundreds of gods who ruled this world? Only a priest could keep straight the seven-day cycle of worship, in which each sky god had his day of honor. And yet I was expected to play a part in keeping these gods – along with all the others – happy!" (p. 71)

> "I chased the goat's tail as the ashipu stalked him from the front, muttering a prayer to Shakan, god of goats." (p. 6)

> "A good wind blows today. It means Enlil blesses our journey. We have waited a long time for Enlil's blessing, haven't we, Naram-Sin?" (p. 24)

> "Those of us who still lived had our own gods to serve. Entering the temple compound, we approached an outdoor shrine attended by a priest and priestess. The worst thing I could do would be to arrive in the city of Father Nanna and offend him straightaway … Such a powerful god required the best I had to give … From a high pedestal, a statue of the god gazed down on us, with flowing beard and four horns on his head. The young priestess played a tambourine while a priest with shaved head chanted hymns and prayers." (p. 37)

42 · Christian Theology & Ancient Polythesism

Even if the underworld goddess, Ereshkigal, chose to forgive my mother's brazen act of disobedience, that did not mean Utu, Ninisinna or Nanna would forgive. As if to tempt them to strike me, here I stood before the altar of the greatest god, father of them all – Nanna. (p. 38)

"Amata glanced over his head to a small house-hold shrine. It held tiny clay figurines of Nanna and Ningal. Beside them stood another figure of glazed clay, the goddess Inanna, Queen of Heaven. A small bowl containing a serving of spiced mutton sat before the mute trio, surrounded by brightly painted miniature pots and a stack of shell and lapis lazuli bracelets." (p. 79)

Discussion Questions:

1. Ancient peoples all around the world believed in nature gods. Why do you think this belief was so dominant in the ancient world?

2. How did Sumer (and later, Canaan, Babylon and Assyria) use their seven-day week to worship their gods?

3. Besides worshipping their gods and goddesses, what else were polytheists doing every day of the week?[10]

4. How would you describe a person participating in idolatry? If you drew a picture of an idol worshipper, what would you draw?

5. If you grew up in one of these cultures, what things would matter most to you?

6. The Old Testament mentions many cultures that Israel interacts with. How many can you name? (Think about the culture Abraham was called out of, or the land where Israel was enslaved, the cities which the Children of Israel defeated under Joshua, the nation that Goliath was from, the birthplace of Ruth, or the great civilizations that would eventually conquer and take Israel into captivity.) Were these cultures monotheists, worshipping one God, or polytheists, worshipping many gods? What name does the Bible give to the beliefs of these cultures?[11]

7. In Sumer, what was the most important thing that each city-state built?

8. In Israel's culture, what was the most important thing she built?

---

10 ANSWER: WORKING
11 ANSWER: PAGAN

A Comparitive Study using *Secret of the Scribe* · 43

9. What did these significant buildings in Sumer and Israel share in common?

10. Historically, why do you think places of worship are essential and valuable to most cultures?

> Go to chart **CC-4, Worship: Seven Days a Week** and answer the first three questions for the *Ancient Polytheist* column.

Read Exodus 20:8-11; 31:12-17 and Ezekiel 20:12 and discuss the following questions:

1. How was Israel's seven-day week an expression of her worship of God?

2. How many days of the week was she worshipping God?

3. God gave Israel the great Ten Commandments to obey and many great feasts to celebrate. Why do you think God established the Sabbath laws as the way His chosen people were to express their special relationship with Him?

4. Think about what idols were for. How is their purpose like the purpose of Israel's seven-day week?

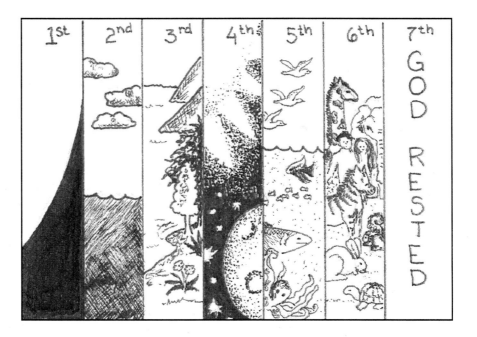

5. What did the Sabbath represent?

6. At this point in this lesson, how would you define the word *idolatry*?

> Return to chart **CC-4** and answer the first three questions under the column *O.T. Monotheism*.

Have you ever thought about how idolatry got started? The Bible actually reveals very little about the origins of idolatry – the sin that leads to the central conflict of the Old Testament. However, if we take what is known from Scripture and archeology and use some deductive reasoning, we can piece together an approximate early history. Let's do a little time travel deep into the ancient world in search of the roots and development of idolatry.

A History of Idolatry:

Our journey begins in a garden – a special home God had provided for a man and a woman, who were made to be God's representatives. They were to rule and care for God's creation as His stewards. They were to have many children and spread the likeness of God across the whole earth. The life that was created from their marriage union reflected the life-giving Trinity. The unique roles the man and woman played in their marriage also represented the communion of the Triune God. Man and woman were God's special creation because they were uniquely equipped to reflect the character and personhood of the Triune God.

Then a thief entered the garden in the form of a serpent. He tempted the woman with a lie: she didn't have to be just a representative of God; she could be a god herself. Both the woman and her husband swallowed Satan's deception. They lost their access to eternal life that day, and their offspring became slaves to sin, shame and death.

Once the idea grew that a creation of God could be a god unto itself, a whole host of evils jumped out of "Pandora's box". People eventually lost sight of their creator God – the provider of all man's needs. Now man looked at the rest of creation and saw how dependent he really was. Man had many needs that the forces of nature had the potential to provide or the potential to withhold ... food, children, animals, shelter, clothing and more. So it was the goodness and mercy of Nature that man believed he needed.

More lies were birthed about these forces of nature being gods themselves. These "gods" had needs too, which man must meet through sacrifices, rituals and ceremonies. So people swallowed these lies and lived in fear of the nature gods and the power they held over life and death. Fear replaced what had once been trust. Would harvest fail? Did they do enough to keep the gods happy? They hired craftsmen to fashion stone and wooden images of the nature gods, reminding them to worship the gods on which they depended. *People became slaves to the creation they had once been given the job to rule over.*

†††

"For although they knew God, they neither glorified him as God nor gave thanks to him, but their thinking became futile and their foolish hearts were darkened. Although they claimed to be wise, they became fools and exchanged the glory of the immortal God for images made to look like mortal man and birds and animals and reptiles. They exchanged the truth of God for a lie, and worshipped and served created things rather than the Creator – who is forever praised. Amen." (ASV) Romans 1:21-23, 25

†††

Discussion Questions:

1. Let's pause our story and reflect on what has just been read. Why would people "exchange the glory of the immortal God for images made to look like mortal man and birds and animals and reptiles ..."?

2. What lies did people have to believe in order to become slaves to the creation they had been given to rule over?

3. Where do you think the "lies" about nature gods came from?

4. If they came from Satan or his demons what did they stand to gain from circulating these lies? Why would Satan want people to believe these lies? (Think about the reasons why Satan fell from heaven and the being he became after his fall. Think also about what these lies did to the people who believed them. Why would this result please Satan?)

5. Read I Corinthians 10:20. What light does this verse shed on the subject?

LESSON VI:

The Sacrifices of Sumerian and Israelite Worship

A History of Idolatry: *continued*

In the fullness of time, Truth would conquer lies. When God called Abraham out of Sumer, He put into motion His sovereign plan to restore the truth and crush the lies of Satan. The first major step was re-establishing a people to be God's representatives, a people through whom He would bring the Light of the world.

God's special relationship with Abraham was based on a covenant, or promises. Covenants generally boiled down to God's good provision and man's faithful obedience. God promised to give a good land to Abraham's descendants. Yet Abraham's offspring (called "the Israelites") ended up a long ways from the land of promise as slaves in Egypt. As it turned out, Egypt was a classroom in which

God taught Israel to hate slavery. Through a lamb, she was taught that God delivers from death. She also witnessed the contrast between the power of her God and the gods of Egypt. God had not forgotten His covenant with Abraham. Israel was set free so she could learn to worship the one true God, who provides deliverance for His people in bondage.

Israel's second classroom was the Sinai desert. In her very first wilderness lesson, she was taught to abhor idols. *"You shall have no other gods before me. You shall not make for yourself an idol in any form of anything in heaven above or on earth beneath or in the waters below. You shall not bow down to worship them; for I, the Lord your God, am a jealous God ... "* Israel miserably failed. Making and bowing down to a golden cow, she forsook the God who had brought her through the Red Sea. In consequence, the Levites were commanded to take swords through the camp, where they killed 3,000 people for Israel's idolatry. She had a lot to learn.

For forty years, God schooled Israel. He is the Creator God, the one Who provides. In the desert, God taught Israel to practice a seven-day week through His daily provisions of food and the requirement that she gather twice as much on Friday so she could rest on Saturday. In doing so, Israel imitated her creator God, and she expressed her faith in His provision, rather than the forces of nature. With manna from heaven, quail from the sky, and water from the rock, God taught Israel to depend on Him for everything. For forty years, God never failed.

Israel's third classroom was the Promised Land. Here she was given two missions: to bring God's judgment upon the idol worshippers in the land and to practice the Sabbath rest. Beyond her weekly Sabbath, in every seventh *year* land and worker would see a Sabbath rest. No tilling, no planting, no harvesting. How would Israel be sustained in the seventh year? God would provide. In the sixth year the land would offer such an abundance that it would sustain her until it could be planted and harvested again. While the Canaanites worked ceaselessly, Israel rested. Every seventh day, she would cease from her labors, as did her one true creator God. Unfortunately, in this Promised Land classroom, Israel would fall short again. She failed to administer God's judgment and to rest and rely on God by giving rest to the land.

Had she kept the Sabbath rests, Israel would have presented to the world around her a powerful argument for the existence, goodness and strength of the one true God. Through resting in God's provision, rather than relying on human strength or idolatrous nature gods, she would reflect the image of the true Creator to a lost world. But as the Bible sadly reveals, Israel would continually disobey God's Sabbath laws. Like Adam and Eve, Israel too gave way to temptation. So like her first parents, Israel would eventually be driven from the home God had provided.

Yet despite her failures, God would still fulfill His promise to provide through Israel the means by which all the world would be blessed – so that one day we would find rest for our souls.[12]

---

12 Luke 6:5; Matthew 11:28-30

Read Exodus 20:1-6; 23:10-13; 31:15, Leviticus 25:1-23, Deuteronomy 4:25-27; 8:19-20 and Isaiah 42:8 and discuss the following questions:

1. What are the first two commandments about?

2. Why was idolatry so abhorrent to God?

3. What was the consequence for idol worship?

4. Knowing this consequence, why do you think Israel was tempted to bow down to idols?

5. What was the consequence for not keeping the Sabbath?

6. Why do you think this penalty was so severe?

7. How did God teach Israel to practice the Sabbath?

8. In this ancient society where food production depended on the labors of man and the weather conditions, why would it have been difficult to keep the Sabbath laws?

9. How was Israel's weekly and seven year rest for people and the land an expression or demonstration of her faith in God's provision?

10. How was Israel's practice of resting every seventh day, and allowing the land to rest every seven years, the antithesis of idolatry? ("Antithesis" means "opposing position".)

11. You have probably heard the expression, "imitation is the highest form of flattery." We imitate what we esteem or admire. Admiration is a form of worship. Was Israel's imitation of God through her work and her rest a tangible expression of worship? If so, name some of the ways we can imitate God today.

Through this account of the history of idolatry, we have seen again the significance of the idea that God is the provider and man was made to reflect His image. Idolatry opposes both the Person of God and the purpose of man. When God's image bearers bow down to a piece of wood or stone made to represent created things on which man relies, man degrades himself and robs his Maker. Idolatry incurs God's righteous anger. An account of Israel's first terrible idolatry is recorded in Psalm 106:19-23 "At Horeb,

A Comparitive Study using *Secret of the Scribe* · 49

they made a calf and worshipped an idol cast from metal. They exchanged their Glory for an image of a bull, which eats grass. They forgot the God who saved them, who had done great things in Egypt ... and awesome deeds by the Red Sea. So he said he would destroy them – had not Moses, *his chosen one*, stood in the breach before him to keep his wrath from destroying them." This paraphrase of events that took place at the foot of Mt. Sinai captures the essence of the central conflict of the Old Testament – will people choose to worship and rely on God or worship what God has made – true worship or idolatry? The first choice leads to life, the second leads to destruction.

The story of the New Testament flows from the life of another Chosen One – Jesus Christ the God/man, who would bear God's wrath and save man from destruction. Christ is both the ultimate provision of God and the perfect reflection of the image of the Father. Christ also is the One who will say, "Come unto me, all you who are weary and heavy laden and I will give you rest."

> Turn to chart **CC-4** and add the definitions for idolatry and rest provided below to the columns for *Ancient Polytheism* and *O.T. Monotheism*. Answer the last question for both columns.

Rest: Rest represents God ceasing from His labor simply because He has provided everything man needs. In obedience to this reality, man imitates God's rest and thereby expresses his trust in His provision. (If you studied the idea of rest through the Scripture you would see that it is a metaphor for God's salvation. By the way, the meaning of Noah's name is "rest".)

Idolatry: Idolatry is trusting in and depending on the provision of something other than God. Idolatry is placing our hopes, affections and desires in something other than God. Idolatry is giving the worship due God to something God has made.

> For older students, the ideas associated with the Sabbath laws provide more material for theme charts 1 & 2. On **ST-1** chart note the significance of God's rest as representing the completion of His provision for man. Starting with the seven days of creation, God was teaching man about Himself and about us. In Genesis, God modeled rest for His people. In Exodus, God's people practiced the seven-day week both as a means to reflect God and as an expression of their dependence on God. Creation is God's first revelation of Himself. God's people Israel were called to imitate God's seven-day week as their representation of Him to the world. Note the importance of God's provision on **ST-1** and the importance of Israel imitating God through the Sabbath Rest on chart **ST-2** for the verses corresponding with lesson 6.

---

50 · Christian Theology & Ancient Polythesism

LESSON VII:

Pagan Sacrifices and the Eight Great Sacrifices of the Bible

> **Note to Parent/Instructor:** This is a lengthy lesson. As the end of each sacrifice example provides a natural lesson break, insert lesson breaks as often as needed. At whatever point you decide to close this lesson, have your students go to chart **CC-5: Worship through Sacrifice**. At your first lesson break, note the reasons for the sacrifices of ancient polytheists and those of the eight biblical sacrifices covered thus far. Once you start noting the purpose for sacrifice from the New Testament, have your students record their answers under the Biblical Monotheist. Refer to the parent comparison chart **CC-5** for an example.

As we have seen, the cultures of Israel and Sumer shared a seven-day week in which they expressed their worship of their God or gods. The Canaanites, Israel's nearest neighbor, also practiced a seven-day week worshipping idols of nature gods. While idol worship was prohibited in Israel, Israel and her neighbors alike offered sacrifices. However, as with the seven-day week, the meaning and purpose for the sacrificial system varied between polytheistic and monotheistic cultures.

In Sumer, sacrifices were said to please the gods. As sacrifices were offered to many different nature gods, they were another form of idolatrous worship. So why did the Sumerians and other polytheistic cultures offer sacrifices? On page 71 of *Secret of the Scribe*, a priest of Ur said to Tabni, *"I have seen you here often. That's good. Keep sacrificing to Father Nanna, and perhaps he will be pleased with you. It is obvious that the gods were angry with you in the past, causing you to suffer. Your offering may persuade them to change their minds."*

How is it that sacrifices could change the minds of the gods? To understand the answer to this question, let's start with an example from the world in which you live. Have you ever tried to change your mother's mind about something? What methods of persuasion did you use? Did you try offering a good attitude and no procrastination with your school work for a whole week, some peace and quiet for the entire afternoon, doing your chores without being told, doing extra chores or even making dinner? Sometimes one or more of those offerings may actually work. Why is it that sometimes you can persuade your mother? You can offer things your mother *needs*. Sumerian gods were not unlike your mother. They too had needs, even though they were more powerful super-human beings. According to Sumerian origin stories, the purpose of man's sacrifice was actually to meet the gods' needs. Through sacrifices gods were nourished and their strength was increased. *Gods who have needs can be manipulated.*

Pagan gods had needs because, among other things, they were not all-powerful. Ultimately, the slave – man – was made to ensure the strength and stability of the gods through both his work and through offering sacrifices. The slave was highly motivated to do this because the survival of his culture depended on the strength of his gods. This idea becomes more clearly developed in later origin stories of the Babylonians.

Sumerians also recognized their complete dependence upon the will and whims of the gods. For personal needs such as illness or other calamities, they offered sacrifices in hopes of making amends for their offenses or to entice the help of the gods.

> "AND HE (GOD) IS NOT SERVED BY HUMAN HANDS, AS IF HE NEEDED ANYTHING, BECAUSE HE HIMSELF GIVES ALL MEN LIFE AND BREATH AND EVERYTHING ELSE."
> ACTS 17:25

Discussion Questions:

1. What do you think about the analogy of your mother and Sumerian gods?

2. Can you think of other needs your mother has which you have the potential to meet?

3. Name some ways she is not like the Sumerian gods and goddesses.

4. Why were sacrifices given to Sumerian gods, and what could the one who offered the sacrifice hope to gain by it?

Now let's think about Israel's sacrifices. Their sacrifices pleased God too. Yet, in sharp contrast to gods and goddesses, the God of the Bible has no needs. God did not need Israel's sacrifices. God is all-powerful and completely sufficient within His Trinitarian nature. Why, then, do you think He instituted Israel's sacrificial system? (Discuss your responses.)

52 · Christian Theology & Ancient Polythesism

The Old Testament establishes a number of reasons why God's people should offer sacrifices. But rather than give you a list here, it's more important to gain an overall perspective of the Bible's teaching on offerings to God and the role they play in worship. To gain this biblical understanding, we will look at *eight* examples of sacrifice from the Old and New Testament. In addition, there are two stories from the lives of the first two kings of Israel that teach us about the meaning of sacrifice. You will discover that sacrifices are not only necessary to understand the worship of Israel's culture, but *grasping these ideas is foundational to thinking Christianly.*

Read the following passages and discuss the questions relating to the eight key sacrifices:

Sacrifice 1 – God covers man's shame: Read Genesis 3:7, 21

1. Why do Adam and Eve sew fig leaves together?

2. What does God provide in place of the fig leaves?

3. What had to die to cover Adam and Eve's shame?

4. Who was guilty: the one who was sacrificed or the one who was covered?

Sacrifice 2 – Sacrifice on God's Terms: Read Genesis 4:2-6

1. Man's offer of sacrifices to God must be on _____ terms.

2. Why do you think Abel's sacrifices were pleasing to God and Cain's were not? (Try to answer the question on the basis of the sacrifices alone, rather than on the reaction of Cain towards Abel.)

3. What type of sacrifice did God require?

A Comparitive Study using *Secret of the Scribe* · 53

Sacrifice 3 – Salvation and Sacrifice: Read Genesis 8:15-21

1. Why did Noah offer God a sacrifice immediately after leaving the ark?

2. What is man's correct response to God's salvation?

3. How did God respond to Noah's sacrifice?

Sacrifice 4 – God Will Provide: Read Genesis 22:1-19

1. What does God ask Abraham to do?

2. Was child sacrifice uncommon in that era of history?

3. What is the text's stated purpose for God's asking Abraham to sacrifice his son?

4. What was God testing?

5. Why is God called "The Lord Will Provide" (future tense) even after God provided the ram?

6. This story is a picture of God's ultimate provision. How will God provide for man?

7. What did God promise Abraham because of his obedience?

Sacrifice 5 – The Lamb that Saved His People: Read Exodus 12:1-14, 21-32

1. The blood of the Passover lamb applied to the doorposts of each man's home saved the Israelites from _____ and freed them from _____ .

2. Why do you think this story is called the Old Testament's great story of redemption? Look up the meaning of the word redemption if you do not have a clear understanding of the word.

3. What were the Israelites sent free to the desert to do?

54 · Christian Theology & Ancient Polythesism

4. In what ways is this story a direct parallel to the New Testament's great story of redemption?

Sacrifice 6 – The O.T. Sacrificial System: Read Leviticus 1-4, 7:11-18; 23 *(note the instructions below before you read.)*

Instructions: As this section includes almost six chapters of reading, the fastest reader should read. Read the questions below before reading the texts above. Interrupt reading to discuss answers as they are provided from the text.

1. Keep a running list of the purposes for which people offered sacrifices.

2. Note the times when sacrifices were given, or the feasts they were associated with.

3. What kind of sacrifices could people bring?

4. What does God say about where the sacrifices should take place?

5. What kind of special preparation does God require for the sacrifice?

6. Note some of the special requirements given about the blood of the sacrifice.

7. What did the priest who offered the sacrifice receive?

8. What did the people receive?

9. What did the burnt offerings send up to God?

10. What were fellowship offerings, and how did they differ from other sacrifices?

11. How did sacrifices express gratefulness and/or dependence upon God?

12. How was the sacrificial system an expression of Israel's worship of God?

Read Leviticus 17:8-12

What were the Israelites taught about the blood of all living creatures? Why were they forbidden from drinking blood? Do you remember where you read this idea before? (Genesis 9:4, 5)

A Comparitive Study using *Secret of the Scribe* · 55

Sacrifice 7 – God's sacrifice for man's greatest needs: Read John 1: 28, 29

John's gospel does not begin with the birth of Christ, but with the declaration that Christ was with God from the beginning and that Christ was both the Creator and Light of the world. One cannot miss John's message – Christ is God. His gospel's first introduction of God in the flesh is through John the Baptist, proclaiming that Christ is the sacrifice for the whole world. Christ's sacrifice is the pinnacle of the entire sacrificial system and the turning point for the entire Bible.

1. What was John the Baptist doing at the Jordan River?

2. What did he say when he looked up and saw Christ coming?

3. Of the sacrifices we have looked at thus far, what picture(s) would this metaphor of Christ create in the mind of a Jewish person?

Christ – the sacrifice of God, what did that mean? The idea that a man could be the "Lamb of God" would have been repugnant to a godly Jew. Let's try to image how this news would have sounded to the people who heard John utter those very words. The man who would become the apostle Andrew was one of those people.

One of John the Baptist's disciples was a man named Andrew. He had repented of his sins and been baptized by John in the Jordan River. Believing that John had been called of God to announce the arrival of the Messiah, he must have waited expectantly day after day. When that day finally came, it was a rather ordinary-looking man who came walking towards the river. John looked up and cried, "Behold, the Lamb of God who takes away the sins of the world!" John went on to make it clear; this was the Holy One they were waiting for. But Andrew must have had many questions. Why was he called the "Lamb of God? Lambs were sacrificed for man's sin. How could a man be a sacrificial lamb? Perhaps Andrew remembered the only incident in Jewish history in which God called for human sacrifice - Abraham and his son Isaac. "But that was only to test Abraham's faith," thought Andrew. Or was it? Was that the only reason Abraham had been asked to sacrifice his son? Had not John also called this man the Son of God? Could this be how "God Will Provide"? Andrew had to find out. He would follow this Jesus that John had

56 · Christian Theology & Ancient Polythesism

heralded as the Messiah[13]. He found himself one of twelve disciples, who were the first of hundreds and then thousands of people who followed and proclaimed Jesus as the Messiah. Yet his miracles were even more persuasive than the crowds.

Jesus had been teaching an enormous crowd from a mountainside overlooking the lake of Galilee. The day wore on. Children were whimpering with hunger to their mothers. With no food on the mountainside, the disciples wanted Jesus to send them all away so they could go and buy some bread. But Jesus said to feed them. How could they do that? Andrew brought to Jesus a young lad who had a few loaves and fishes.[14] Christ blessed the bread and, before Andrew knew it, he was passing out basket after basket of bread and fish. That small lunch fed more than 5,000 people. The next day, the people were back in larger numbers. Some were no doubt seeking another free lunch, while others were demanding greater proof that Jesus was the Messiah. They hinted that if Jesus actually rained down bread from heaven, they would believe. Instead Jesus said that He was the Bread from heaven who would bring life to the world. God's manna in the wilderness had been life for the Israelites. Now Christ was claiming to be God's source of eternal life for man.

The crowd was visibly disquieted by what Jesus was saying. Some were scowling, others were shaking their heads, and a few were standing up ready to leave. But Jesus seemed unconcerned by their response to His shocking words, for His words grew more alarming by the minute. People began to leave in droves.

As the Bread from Heaven, He told His stunned listeners that His flesh was food and that drinking His blood was the source of this eternal life.[15] Andrew was horrified. Every good Jew knew that life was in the blood; a Jew would never drink the blood of an animal, let alone a man. Andrew staggered, trying to make sense of what Jesus had said. Animal sacrifices covered sins, but their blood could never give life. Could it be that only the shed blood of the Lamb of God might give man real life – life eternal?

Could he believe that and resolve the dissonance he felt in the command,

---

13 JOHN 1:32-42
14 JOHN 6:8,9
15 JOHN 6:47-59

A Comparitive Study using *Secret of the Scribe* · 57

*"Eat my flesh, drink my blood, or you will have no life in you."?
Ultimately belief or unbelief comes down to a decision of the will.
Abraham reasoned that God was a good God who kept His promises; he
decided to trust God, even to the point of sacrificing him who was most
dear.[16] Perhaps with lingering uneasiness, this was the moment Andrew
chose to believe and follow Jesus no matter where He would lead.*

*Little more than a year later, Andrew would face his greatest horror
at the foot of a cross. His Savior was bleeding and dying – shedding
His blood on the day of Passover. Looking up through weeping eyes, he
would behold the Lamb of God, taking away the sin of the world.[17] Was
John's prophecy being fulfilled, when just last night they were sharing the
Passover meal together?[18] Then Andrew vividly remembered. Jesus had
broken bread and said, "Take, eat, this is my Body." Then He had taken a
cup of wine and said, "This is my blood of the covenant, which is poured
out for many." Before Andrew now hung the broken bleeding body of His
Savior.*

*As Andrew left that day, he may have been overcome by the realization
that the cross was once a tree. The fruit of Christ's broken body and shed
blood was being offered up for all who by faith would take and eat and
receive eternal life. The cross had become the Tree of Life.[19]*

Discussion Questions:

1. What feast were the Jews celebrating when Christ died on the cross?

2. What did the Jews' annual Passover commemorate? What two things did God redeem His people from?

3. How is Christ like the Passover lamb?

4. Christ could have died on the Day of Atonement, the annual sacrifice that cleansed the people and priests from their sins. Why was the Passover an even more appropriate day for Christ's sacrifice?

5. How are we saved from death and freed from slavery (to sin) through Christ's death and resurrection? (Talk about the symbolism of what each Israelite family had to do in order to be saved from the angel of death.)

---

16 Genesis 22:10, Hebrews 11:19
17 Scripture makes no mention of Andrew being at Christ's crucifixion. It was added here for story telling purposes.
18 I Corinthians 5:7b, Matthew 26:1-2, Mark 14:1, Luke 22:1-2
19 Genesis 3:22

6. A Jewish day begins at sundown and continues through the next day. Passover began the night before Christ died. This was the meal He was sharing with His disciples when He instituted the Lord's Supper. Communion, or the Eucharist, is the central practice or sacrament of Christian belief. Why is this act so important? What does it commemorate or celebrate?

7. Do you think the timing of Christ's death was just a "coincidence", or do you think this was a "God-incident" planned from before the world began?

8. How is Christ's Body and Blood like the fruit of the Tree of Life, from which God barred Adam and Eve in Genesis 3:22-24? What was the difference between "living forever" and the eternal life provided by Christ?

We have looked at Scripture's seven great sacrifices culminating in Christ's death on the cross. Christ's sacrifice put an end to the continual sacrifice of lambs and goats. Not only did His sacrifice cover our sins once and for all, but His shed blood did what the blood of animal sacrifice could never do – it restored to man God's gift of eternal life.

With the climactic sacrifice of Christ, surely the need for all other sacrifices is over. You have forgotten there are actually eight great sacrifices in Scripture. Which one did we forget, you may ask. There are lots of other sacrifices in the Old Testament, but most of these fall under the sacrificial system established through the Law. Our eighth sacrifice actually comes from the New Testament. Any guesses? This sacrifice is offered daily, and it produces a sweet aroma unto God. Get ready to hop onto the altar, because the answer is *you*.

Sacrifice 8 – The Christian's Sacrifice: Read Romans 12:1

1. What kind of sacrifice are Christians called to make?

2. Just like the Old Testament sacrifices, this sacrifice is an act of what?

Read Ephesians 5:1

1. The Israelites were called to imitate God's act of creation; what action of God are Christians called to imitate?

2. Christ's sacrifice was the supreme example of God's

   _____.

3. What kind of life are we called to live?

A Comparitive Study using *Secret of the Scribe* · 59

Read I Corinthian 6:19c, 20

1. What did Christ purchase with His blood?

2. What demonstrates that someone has been purchased or redeemed by God?

Read Romans 6:13-18

1. What are the two masters that people can serve?

2. A person who has been brought back to life should feel what towards the one who saved them?

3. Does God's forgiveness because of Christ's sacrifice give us the right to sin?

4. What does slavery to sin lead to?

5. What does obedience lead to?

6. Christ has set us free from slavery to sin; in exchange for life we are slaves to what?

This passage goes on to say that slavery to righteousness leads to holiness. "But now that you have been set free from sin, become slaves to God. The benefit you reap is holiness, and the result is eternal life. For the wages of sin is death, but the gift of God is eternal life in Christ Jesus our Lord." Romans 6:22, 23

Christ purchased your life with His precious blood. "You are not your own, you have been bought with a price."[20] Christians live an exchanged life. We exchanged our life of sin and death for one of holiness and eternal life. A Christian daily sacrifices the desires of the sinful nature unto God. Instead of sinning, we strive to be like Christ. This is not easy. Indeed, the genuine Christian life can be described as a struggle against sin,[21] a struggle to obey God and deny ourselves.[22] This is our sacrifice, which produces a sweet aroma unto God.

"Put off the old self, which is being corrupted by its evil desires ... and put on the new self, created to be like God in true righteousness and holiness." (Ephesians 4:22-24)

In the Old Testament, God's people were called to represent Him by imitating God's act of creation through the practice of a seven-day week. Their worship was seen both in their work and in their rest – their dependence upon God. In the New Testament, our worship, an imitation of Christ's life and death, is seen both in our rest (our dependence on the work of His sacrifice) and in our work to strive

---

20 I Corinthians 6:20
21 Hebrews 12:4
22 Ephesians 4:22-24

to be like Him. Our striving to obey God is our sacrifice unto Him, which, like Noah's, is promoted by our grateful response to God's salvation.

In summary, sacrifice is man's response to the God on Whom *we* depend to meet all our needs. God is not needy; we are. We humbly acknowledge our need for forgiveness and by faith accept His sacrifice. Then the sacrifices of our wants and our desires are the *reflection* of His good work in us – His new creation.

On the chart **CC-5**, record the purposes of the eight great sacrifices under the columns of O.T. and biblical monotheist. For older students, on the **ST-1** chart note those sacrifices that demonstrate the provision of God. On the **ST-2** chart note how people as God's representatives reflect the image of Christ through the 8th sacrifice.

LESSON VIII:

To Obey is Better than Sacrifice

In our last lesson, we learned that even in the Old Testament God provided a means by which His Chosen People could be saved from sin. The vehicle of God's forgiveness was the sacrificial system, but this system did not eliminate Israel's responsibilities before God. She was called to keep her covenantal promises – promises to obey God's Laws. When she failed, God's mercy comforted the repentant and His judgment condemned the proud. The lives of Israel's first two kings teach us that while sacrifice is the means of forgiveness it is sometimes used as an excuse for sin, and sacrifice means nothing if it is not coupled with true repentance. As you read the stories below, think about whether or not they have relevance for someone living after the sacrifice of Christ.

The first account about King Saul is one of the saddest stories in the Old Testament. Much can be learned about the necessity of obedience from I Samuel 15. Ponder the passage and discuss the following questions that spring from this text:

Read I Samuel 15 and discuss the following questions:

1. What was God's command to Saul?

2. What were Saul and his men unwilling to destroy?

3. How did Saul greet Samuel?

4. What were Saul's reasons for disobeying God?

5. What did Samuel think about Saul's desire to offer sacrifices to God?

6. What is better than sacrifice, and why?

7. Find examples from the text that show Saul's rebellion and arrogance.

8. Saul acknowledged that he had sinned several times. Is there evidence from the text that suggests that he was not truly repentant?

9. What was the consequence of Saul's disobedience?

10. Based on this story and what was covered about Christian sacrifice in the last lesson, why do you think obedience is essential to God? (Hint: Think

about your answer in light of God's purpose for people, free-will and the consequence of Adam and Eve's disobedience.)

While there are powerful lessons to be learned from Saul's life, Saul was not the only King over Israel who grossly sinned. In I Samuel 15:28, the "neighbor" Samuel referred to was a shepherd boy who would receive Saul's kingdom. Leaving his sheep behind, David became a commanding king, a powerful warrior, and (like Saul) a serious sinner. Nevertheless, David is best remembered for the title given him by God – "a man after God's own heart".[23] The psalms David wrote give us a glimpse into the heart of this man.

Psalm 51 was probably written shortly after David was confronted by the prophet of his day, a man named Nathan. In II Samuel 12, David is convicted of stealing another man's wife and killing her husband by assigning him to the front line of battle. After Nathan's confrontation, David's immediate response was, "I have

---

23 ACTS 13:22

sinned against the Lord." While these words are very much like the words that Saul eventually said to Samuel, each king's response to his own sin was radically different. To Samuel, Saul excused himself and blamed others; to Nathan, David offered no excuses. By his own acknowledgement he deserved death. Yet hoping in God's mercy and compassion, he humbled himself and asked for God's forgiveness.

Read Psalm 51 – David's Psalm of Repentance. Discuss questions below:

1. What statements demonstrate the differences between the hearts of David and Saul?

2. What were David's desires?

3. What did he ask from God?

4. Note the references to worship in this psalm.

5. Sacrifices should only come after what?

6. What is a "righteous" sacrifice?

Saul wanted to be forgiven so his honor could be preserved.[24] David wanted to be forgiven so that he could sing of the righteousness of God. Saul desired His own glory; David sought glory given to God. To purposely sin assuming the sacrifice will cover wrongdoing mocks God's provision. God will not be mocked. God's response to Saul was just; his response to David was merciful. While David suffered grievous consequences for his sin, his relationship with God was restored. Saul, on the other hand, slowly dissolved into madness.

A repentant and humble heart is the antecedent of forgiveness. A heart that agrees with God and grieves with God over the wretchedness of our sin and a mind that purposes to live differently – this pleases a gracious God.

The story of King Saul is a powerful reminder to purpose afresh in our hearts to obey God. The example of King David should challenge us to wholehearted repentance, understanding that no forgiveness of sin – and no true worship of God – can happen without it. This is why God took the kingdom from one king and promised the other that his descendant would rein on his throne forever.

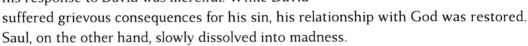

25 I Samuel 15:30

> Note on your chart **CC-5** under *O. T. Monotheism* the necessity of repentance and obedience in the life of an Israelite wanting God's forgiveness for sin.

Saul, David and the believer after Christ: We can see from the Old Testament and from the writings of Paul that you read in a previous lesson, that repentance and obedience are essential for the Christian life.

Discussion Questions:

1. Christians today are called to obey God – to live a life dead to sin, but what do we do when we have sinned? Is David's prayer in Psalm 51 still a helpful guide for dealing with issues of sin in the Christian's life?

2. What is helping you cultivate a heart of repentance like David?

3. As Christ died for all our sins, past, present, and future, why don't we have the freedom to sin, knowing we are forgiven?

4. What is nurturing your desire to obey God?

While the need for obedience and repentance does not change between Old and New Testament believers, Christ's sacrifice is far superior to the Old Testament sacrificial system. Not only does it grant forgiveness once and for all and is the only provision for life eternal, but Christ gives those who place their faith in Him many gifts that help in the battle against temptation.

We have been given the power and the person of the Holy Spirit.[25] In Psalm 51, David asked God not to take his Holy Spirit from him. In the Old Testament, the Holy Spirit was given to selected people for selected times to enable them to accomplish some great work for God. In the New Testament, the Holy Spirit has been given to all believers to enable us to do God's will and to demonstrate the fruits of Christ's character – this includes self-control.[26] Not only does the Spirit of God live within us, He joins us to the Body of Christ.[27] From the beginning, it was "not good" for man to be alone, so God made a marriage, which is ultimately a picture of Christ and the Church. The Church is called to shepherd and care for its members, helping us grow up into Christ. And we are called to exercise the gifts that we have been given to build up the Church. What else has God given us to equip us for this battle against sin?

---

26 II Corinthians 3:18; Galatians 5:22-24; Matthew 28:18-20
27 Galatians 5:22
28 Ephesians 4:11-13

A Comparitive Study using *Secret of the Scribe* · **65**

Read Ephesians 6:10-18 and discuss the questions:

1. Name every resource listed here that equips or empowers the believer to battle against the temptations of Satan.

2. How does continual prayer help us not to sin?

3. How do the other resources displayed in this passage help the Christian not to sin?

We have been immensely blessed, not only because Christ's sacrifice was and is perfect, but because He has thoroughly equipped us with every good gift to become perfect – holy like Christ. This is what we are aiming for, while knowing this is only possible in Him and through Him and to Him. To Him be the glory forever! Amen.[28]

In summary: biblical sacrifice, the sacrifice of saying no to our sinful desires, is a person's grateful response to God for meeting her needs. Pagan sacrifices were man's attempts to meet the needs of the gods, so they in turn would meet man's need. (Man initiates, the gods respond.) Invert the last sentence, to get the biblical maxim. (_____ initiates, _____ responds.) God initiated the ultimate sacrifice, offering forgiveness and eternal life to all. We respond with humble repentance, faith in Christ's sacrifice, and obedience by daily saying no to our will and yes to God's. This is what it looks like when a person walks with God.

Note the importance of obedience and repentance under the *New Testament Monotheists* on chart **CC-5**. Summarize the reason for monotheist sacrifice in the last block.

---

29 ROMANS 11:36, II TIMOTHY 3:16,17

66 · Christian Theology & Ancient Polythesism

LESSON IX:

Prayer – The Names have Changed to Deceive Worshippers

Prayer is the subject of our final comparison between polytheistic and monotheistic worship. Our lessons on sacrifice included a prayer – a beautiful prayer of repentance – a model as powerful for the ancient Israelites as it is for us today. Do you think the Sumerians, Babylonians or Canaanites ever offered such prayers? Ancient polytheists did pray. Archeologists have uncovered hundreds of ancient prayers recorded on temples and prayer tablets, some the size people could hold in their hand and carry with them. Prayer was a part of these cultures. Why did ancient polytheists pray? Ancient polytheists understood rightly that all of life depended on the supernatural. Their error was not their dependence; it was their false ideas about the nature of the ones they prayed to. Let's examine some examples of the types of prayers pagans offered, before comparing them to the prayers of Israel. Pagan prayers and Hebrew prayers were central to each culture's worship practices.

Let's start with prayers of petition. A person who had a need would ask the gods or goddesses for help. Can you think of reasons why a god or goddess might help their slave?

Below is an actual Mesopotamian prayer to the goddess Ishtar, who was the tenderhearted goddess in the Babylonian account of the flood. During Tabni's day she was known as Inanna, Queen of Heaven, the goddess of fertility. She was one of the most powerful gods in the pagan pantheon. As you read this abbreviated prayer, which in its entirety is four times as long, note the requests of the person who is praying. What things does he want relief from?

A Comparitive Study using *Secret of the Scribe* · **67**

TO ISHTAR,
HE RAISES TO YOU A WAIL.[29]

1. HE RAISES TO YOU A WAIL;

HE RAISES TO YOU A WAIL

ON ACCOUNT OF HIS FACE WHICH FOR TEARS IS NOT RAISED,

HE RAISES TO YOU A WAIL;

ON ACCOUNT OF HIS FEET ON WHICH FETTERS ARE LAID,

HE RAISES TO YOU A WAIL;

5. ON ACCOUNT OF HIS HAND,

WHICH IS POWERLESS THROUGH OPPRESSION,

HE RAISES TO YOU A WAIL;

ON ACCOUNT OF HIS BREAST, WHICH WHEEZES LIKE A BELLOWS, HE

RAISES TO YOU A WAIL;

O LADY, IN SADNESS OF HEART I RAISE TO YOU MY PITEOUS CRY,

"HOW LONG?"

O LADY, TO YOUR SERVANT – SPEAK PARDON TO HIM,

LET YOUR HEART BE APPEASED!

TO YOUR SERVANT WHO SUFFERS PAIN – FAVOR GRANT HIM!

15. THROUGH A LONG LIFE LET ME WALK BEFORE YOU!

MY GOD BRINGS BEFORE YOU A LAMENTATION,

LET YOUR HEART BE APPEASED!

MY GODDESS UTTERS TO YOU A PRAYER,

LET YOUR ANGER BE QUIETED!

---

29 ANCIENT HISTORY SOURCEBOOK, A COLLECTION OF ANCIENT BABYLONIAN PRAYERS, C.1600
HTTP://WWW.FORDHAM.EDU/HALSALL/ANCIENT/1600BABYLONIANPRAYERS.HTML

Discussion Questions:

1. What kind of prayer would you call this?

2. Who was the polytheist praying too?

3. What does he believe about the goddess he is praying to?

We can see that ancient peoples asked their gods and goddess for help, but did they confess their sins and offer the type of prayers of repentance that David did? The answer is yes. Read this next prayer and note what the person is asking forgiveness for. Do you find similarities with David's prayer of Psalm 51? Are there differences that you also see?

PRAYER OF LAMENTATION TO ISHTAR[30]

SEE ME O MY LADY, ACCEPT MY PRAYERS.

PROMISE MY FORGIVENESS AND LET THY SPIRIT BE APPEASED.

I AM BEATEN DOWN, AND SO I WEEP BITTERLY.

WHILE SICKNESS, HEADACHE, LOSS, AND DESTRUCTION ARE
PROVIDED FOR ME;

ANGER, CHOLER, AND INDIGNATION OF GODS AND MEN.

TO THEE HAVE I PRAYED; FORGIVE MY DEBT.

FORGIVE MY SIN, MY INIQUITY, MY SHAMEFUL DEEDS,
AND MY OFFENCE.

LOOSEN MY FETTERS; SECURE MY DELIVERANCE;

ACCEPT THE ABASEMENT OF MY COUNTENANCE;

HEAR MY PRAYERS.

HOW LONG, O MY LADY, WILT THOU BE ANGERED SO THAT THY
FACE IS TURNED AWAY?

SUBDUE MY HATERS AND CAUSE THEM
TO CROUCH DOWN UNDER ME.

---

30 ANCIENT HISTORY SOURCEBOOK, A COLLECTION OF ANCIENT BABYLONIAN PRAYERS, C.1600
HTTP://WWW.FORDHAM.EDU/HALSALL/ANCIENT/1600BABYLONIANPRAYERS.HTML

A Comparitive Study using *Secret of the Scribe* · **69**

> LET MY PRAYERS AND MY SUPPLICATIONS COME TO THEE.
> LET THY GREAT MERCY BE UPON ME.
> AS FOR ME, LET ME GLORIFY THY DIVINITY AND THY MIGHT
> BEFORE THE BLACK-HEADED (PEOPLE), [SAYING,]
> ISHTAR INDEED IS EXALTED; THE LADY INDEED IS QUEEN.

Discussion Questions:

1. What similarities do you see between this prayer and the prayer of David in Psalm 51?

2. Who was the polytheist praying to?

3. Name some ways polytheists could offend their gods.

4. Would they receive forgiveness of their sins?

As the prayers above demonstrate, there are similarities found between these pagan prayers and some of the prayers recorded in the Bible. However, biblical prayers and psalms were also used to exalt the name of God, to tell of His glory. Will you be surprised that the Sumerians and other Mesopotamian people did this too? Below is a short prayer to Nanna, the moon god, and a longer one to Bel, the Babylonian name for "god of land" called Baal in the Old Testament. As you read you might highlight or note in the margins the things that these gods are extolled for.

SINCE SUMERIANS AND BABYLONIANS WERE CONSTANTLY BUSY WORKING FOR THEIR GODS, HOW COULD THEY FIND TIME TO PRAY TO THEM ALL? THEY SOLVED THE PROBLEM BY MAKING STATUES OF THEMSELVES, AS THEY MADE STATUES OF THEIR GODS, WITH HANDS FOLDED IN PRAYER AND LARGE EYES FOCUSED ON THE WORLD OF THE GODS. SUMERIAN PRAYER STATUES REASSURED THE PEOPLE THAT THEIR PRAYERS WERE BEING OFFERED EVEN WHILE THEY SLAVED AWAY FOR THE GODS.

TO NANNA, LORD OF THE MOON[31]

5. O LORD, NANNA, FIRSTBORN SON OF BEL,
YOU STAND, YOU STAND
BEFORE YOUR FATHER BEL.
YOU ARE RULER, FATHER NANNA;
YOU ARE RULER, YOU ARE GUIDE.
O BARQUE, WHEN STANDING IN THE MIDST OF HEAVEN,
YOU ARE RULER.

15. FATHER NANNA, THE HERD YOU RESTORE.
WHEN YOUR FATHER LOOKS ON YOU WITH JOY,
HE COMMANDS YOUR WAXING;
THEN WITH THE GLORY OF A KING BRILLIANTLY YOU RISE.
BEL A SCEPTER FOR DISTANT DAYS
FOR YOUR HANDS HAVE COMPLETED.
IN UR AS THE BRILLIANT BARQUE YOU RIDE,

TO BEL, LORD OF WISDOM[32]

1. O LORD OF WISDOM RULER ... IN YOUR OWN RIGHT,
O BEL, LORD OF WISDOM ... RULER IN YOUR OWN RIGHT,
O FATHER BEL, LORD OF THE LANDS,
O FATHER BEL, LORD OF TRUTHFUL SPEECH,

15. FROM THE LAND OF THE RISING

---

31 GEORGE A. BARTON, ARCHAEOLOGY AND THE BIBLE, 3RD ED., (PHILADELPHIA: AMERICAN SUNDAY SCHOOL, 1920), PP. 398-401
32 ANCIENT HISTORY SOURCEBOOK, A COLLECTION OF ANCIENT BABYLONIAN PRAYERS, C.1600
HTTP://WWW.FORDHAM.EDU/HALSALL/ANCIENT/1600BABYLONIANPRAYERS.HTML

TO THE LAND OF THE SETTING SUN.

O MOUNTAIN, LORD OF LIFE, YOU ARE INDEED LORD!

O BEL OF THE LANDS,

LORD OF LIFE YOU YOURSELF ARE LORD OF LIFE.

O MIGHTY ONE, TERRIBLE ONE OF HEAVEN,

YOU ARE GUARDIAN INDEED!

O BEL, YOU ARE LORD OF THE GODS INDEED!

20. YOU ARE FATHER, BEL, WHO CAUSE THE PLANTS OF THE

GARDENS TO GROW!

O BEL, YOUR GREAT GLORY MAY THEY FEAR!

THE BIRDS OF HEAVEN AND THE FISH OF THE DEEP ARE FILLED

WITH FEAR OF YOU.

O FATHER BEL, IN GREAT STRENGTH YOU GO, PRINCE OF

LIFE, SHEPHERD OF THE STARS!

O LORD, THE SECRET OF PRODUCTION YOU OPEN, THE FEAST

OF FATNESS ESTABLISH, TO WORK YOU CALL!

25. FATHER BEL, FAITHFUL PRINCE, MIGHTY PRINCE, YOU

CREATE THE STRENGTH OF LIFE!

Discussion Questions:

1. Who was the polytheist praying to?

2. What did they extol or praise their gods for?

3. Which of these praises really belong to God?

4. Look at your definition for idolatry on SC-4. As prayer is an expression of dependence and worship, were these prayers idolatrous?

Let's wrap up this look at ancient prayers with another prayer of David. Many people, who don't believe the Bible is the Word of God, say that the Hebrews just copied their stories and prayers from the polytheistic prayers all around them, while changing the reference to many gods into a reference to one God. There is a lesson in the appendix that deals with this type of charge at length, but for now read Psalm 8 again. It is similar to the prayer to Bel, as it also extols the name of God. What Bel is praised for, God could be praised for. But what things are included in David's praise of the one true God that no polytheist could ever utter to his god?

Read Psalm 8

1. What parts of God's creation does David praise God for?

2. What position does man have in God's created order?

3. What did God do with His creation, relative to man?

4. When God gave man the job to rule over His creation, what does this say about God and about man?

5. Would a polytheist ever praise his god or goddess for an act such as this? Why not?

6. Name some of the various types of prayers that have been covered in this lesson. Are all these forms of prayer – even those that ask for God to meet some kind of need – a form of worship? Why?

The peoples of Mesopotamia would never praise gods who elevated people over the creation. The gods were creation, people were slaves. Despite believing these lies, these polytheist nations still retained some kernels of truth. They knew (like Israel) that prayer was a vital form of worship – through prayer they communicated with their personal gods or God. Sumerians believed that the gods were the source of their provision. Israel understood that God was the source of her provision and help. Both extolled the greatness of their gods/God as more powerful than themselves, and they recognized that displeasing their gods/God was sin requiring repentance. With all these similarities, are the differences *that* important?

Both Israel and her neighbors believed in the necessity of prayer, but only Israel prayed to the one true all-powerful God. The Sumerians, Babylonians and Canaanites were praying to idols who ultimately represented demons.[33] Rather than worshipping the creator God, they were worshipping and praising *demons*; they were asking *demons* for help ... asking *demons* to forgive them. Their prayers were another form of worship unto *demons*. Their minds had been completely twisted by Satan's lies, which had perverted the truth of God.[34] Words belonging only to God were being uttered to the "god of this world". *Polytheism is not just*

---

33 DEUTERONOMY 32:17-18
34 II CORINTHIANS 4:4

A Comparitive Study using *Secret of the Scribe* · **73**

another religion; it is a gross perversion of God's truth that enslaves people and robs God of the glory due His name.

Discussion Questions:

1. Sumerians and other ancient polytheists had retained some of God's truth. What did they know about prayer that was true?

2. What is the purpose of prayer?

3. What was wrong with the prayers of polytheists?

4. After reading these pagan prayers, can you state another reason why God hated idolatry?

Thou shalt not make ... any graven image, or any likeness of any thing that is in heaven above, or that is in the earth beneath, or that is in the water under the earth. Thou shalt not bow down ... to them, nor serve them: for I the LORD thy God am a jealous God, visiting the iniquity of the fathers upon the children unto the third and fourth generation of them that hate me; And showing mercy unto thousands of them that love me, and keep my commandments. Exodus 20:4-6 (KJV)

God justly punishes idolatry. However, the extent of God's punishment is a fraction of the extent of His love and mercy. God hates idolatry but still loves the person caught up in this terrible sin. To bow down and serve that which is not God is to deny God. To reject God is to choose death, because God – and God alone – is the Source of Life. Satan, the Father of lies, for all his powerful deceptions, can never author life or death. God grants both and determines a person's eternal destiny based upon the person's choice as expressed by their actions and sourced by their faith.

Add what you have learned about the power of biblical prayer to chart **CC-6**. Make sure you note that prayer is another expression of worship through which man offers his praise and adoration to God. When people pray, they humbly acknowledge that they are dependent upon God for His provision. We repent and confess to God when we fail to live according to His purposes for us. Ongoing obedience and repentance in the life of the believer prompt the display of God's power. Fill in the answers to the last two questions.

---

74 · Christian Theology & Ancient Polythesism

LESSON X:

Prayer as Power or the Power of Prayer

As already noted, the prayers of polytheists raised to the forces of nature were prayers to demons. This thought should make us shudder. Another surprising difference, beyond to whom these ancient cultures prayed, is what they believed about the words of the prayers themselves. Sumerians, like other ancient peoples, believed that the *words* of certain types of prayers actually contained power in themselves.

Some prayers held magical powers; the power of the words themselves could bring about or sustain reality. Prayers were the containers for the power of the words. These powerful words were called incantations. This was especially true of prayers associated with the annual ritual of retelling and reenacting the creation of the world. Through man's ritual of reenacting the creation story and the magical words of the recited prayers, the gods renewed their power, ensuring the stability of the created order for another year. It was not only the labors of the people that sustained the gods; it was also the very words the Sumerians and Babylonians spoke that had life-giving power. Hmm ...

Just for fun, you can read a Babylonian prayer or incantation whose words were believed to curse and drive out the worm that caused a toothache. Yes, you read that right. Haven't you heard that toothaches, a common ailment in ancient societies, were caused by worms? Read on:

A Comparative Study using *Secret of the Scribe* · 75

The Worm and the Toothache

After Anu [had created heaven],
Heaven had created [the earth],
The rivers had created the canals,
The canals had created the marsh,
(And) the marsh had created the worm—
The worm went weeping before Shamash,
His tears flowing before Ea:
"What wilt thou give me for my food?
What wilt thou give me for my sucking?"
"I give thee the ripe fig,
(And) the apricot."
"Of what use are they to me, the ripe fig and the apricot?
Lift me up among the teeth
And in the gums cause me to dwell!
The blood of the tooth will I suck,
And of the gum I will gnaw its roots!

Fix the pin and seize its foot.[35]
Because thou hast said this, O worm,
May Ea smite thee with the might of his hand!

---
[35] The ancient method of extracting "worms" from ones teeth

76 · Christian Theology & Ancient Polythesism

Babylonians believed that some ungrateful disgusting little worm whined enough to a weak-willed, thoughtless god. Ea, our "hero" of the flood story, permitted people's mouths to be invaded by the little wretch made for the marsh. Now it was up to people who, through their belief in incantations, would see the little leach extracted.... well, maybe. Ancient polytheists believed that words alone had power – both as curses and as sources of renewing life.

Discussion Questions:

1. What did polytheists believe about the power of the words of certain prayers?

2. What are these prayers called?

3. In the Bible, incantations are associated with practices that are strictly prohibited to the people of God. What are these practices called?[36]

> Fill in the third row on chart **CC-6** for the Ancient Polytheist, recording what they believed about the power source of prayer. Make sure you use the word "incantation".

The Israelites also believed in the power of prayer, but in sharp contrast, the power to effect prayer resided in the One to whom the prayers are raised. The deeper question, then, must be what prompts God to act on behalf of the prayers of His creation?

The same God who hung the sun and moon in the heavens, and separated the dry land from the seas, established prayer as the way His people would communicate with Him. As the Author of prayer, He is the Source of its power, and the One to whom all prayers are raised. The God who hears these prayers also gave His people a clear understanding about the conditions under which their prayers would be most effectively heard by Him. That which makes a prayer powerful is not the words being said, but the life being lived.

The story of the dedication of the Temple which David's son, King Solomon, built for God records Solomon's prayer and God's answer. This story has much to teach us about the conditions under which God acts on behalf of His people. Below is a recap from the Bible of this dedication service, which includes Solomon's prayer. Then you will read God's response from the Bible.

---

36 ANSWER: WITCHCRAFT OR SORCERY

A Comparitive Study using *Secret of the Scribe* · **77**

Based on
I Kings 8 and II Chronicles 5, 6:

*I*T WAS GOING TO BE A BIG CELEBRATION. *All the people of Israel were going to be there. The temple King David had longed for had now been built by his son, King Solomon. The Ark of the Covenant containing the Ten Commandments was being moved to a beautiful new temple dedicated to Israel's great and awesome God. When the day dawned, the priests lifted the Ark, carried it into the temple, and set it in the Most Holy Place. Angels spread their wings over the Ark. The presence of the Lord filled the temple in a cloud that was so thick the priests could not perform their jobs!*

King Solomon stood up in front of all the gathered families of Israel and said, "Praise be to the Lord, the God of Israel. See! God has kept the promises he made to my Father David. He chose Jerusalem in which to build a temple for his Name. He enabled me to build it and place within it the Ark of the Lord. The Lord also promised that David would never lack a descendant to rule over Israel, and I sit upon my father's throne."

Then King Solomon went into the new temple in front of all the watching people. Kneeling before the altar, he held out his arms and prayed:

> *"Lord God, no one in heaven or earth is like you – you keep your covenant of love with your servants who continue wholeheartedly in your way. May you keep your promises to my father David always. How can this temple built for your Name contain you when the highest heavens cannot? Nevertheless, may this temple always be a place in which you incline your ear to hear the prayers of your people. Hear our prayers, oh Lord, and forgive us our sins. When one man hurts another, condemn the guilty man and prove the innocent man. When your people Israel are defeated by their enemies because they sinned against you, forgive them when they repent, and restore them. When there is a drought because your people sin against you, and they repent, forgive them and restore them. When there is a famine or a disaster, and your people Israel pray to you, deal with them according to their hearts, so that they will fear you. When your people prepare to fight their enemies and they pray to you toward this temple, hear them and make them strong. When they sin against you and confess and repent, forgive them.*

May you come to your resting place, O Lord God, and may your priests be clothed with salvation. May your saints rejoice because you are good. Oh Lord, do not reject me as king over Israel, remembering always your love to your servant David."

When the king was finished praying, he stood up, turned around so that he was looking at all the people, and shouted, "Praise God for his faithfulness to us! May he always make us obedient to him. May he remember my words to him and help us, his people. Make sure that you always do what he says and live obediently."

Discussion Questions:

1. In the above condensed version of Solomon's prayer of dedication, what things did he praise God for?

2. If you know other stories from Solomon's history, then you will recall that he had a track record of asking God wisely. What did he repeatedly ask God for in this prayer?

3. Solomon's request for God's forgiveness of the people was tied to what?

4. What do you think Solomon meant when he prayed "deal with them according to their hearts, so that they will fear you." How would this help people fear God? In what way is it good to fear God? **Read** God's response to Solomon's prayer in II Chronicles 7:12-22

5. Which of Solomon's prayers or requests did God answer?

6. To what did God tie His forgiveness and supernatural relief of the people's hardships? Was this consistent with what Solomon had already prayed?

7. Verse 14 outlines four specific things sinful people must do. What are they?

8. What did God say would happen to Solomon's descendants and the people of Israel if they did not continue to follow after God?

9. Just as He did for Adam and Eve, God gave to Israel a clear understanding of the consequence of her disobedience. How would you describe the choice that will lead to life and the choice that will lead to destruction?

A Comparitive Study using *Secret of the Scribe* · 79

This story about prayer and earlier lessons about sacrifice share a common idea. Answered prayer is like effectual sacrifice – the obedience and repentance of the one who prays and the one who sacrifices matters to God. This idea about obedience and repentance shows up again in the New Testament where the apostle James talks about effective prayers. James 5:16 says. "Therefore confess your sins to each other and pray for each other so that you may be healed. The prayer of a righteous man is powerful and effective." For both Israel and the Christian today, the power of prayer lies with the One who hears, and God inclines His ear to those who walk with Him.

Discussion Questions:

1. What word(s) could be used to describe a righteous person?

2. Why are these characteristics important in the person who prays to God?

3. While there are few people who can be described as righteous, God also answers the prayers of those who are repentant. How is repentance demonstrated in the first half of James 5:16? How can confessing our sins to others help us live a more obedient life?

4. When the Hebrews prayed, what did they believe about the power of the God they prayed to?

5. What did they believe about the prayer words themselves? Did words contain or release pent up power?

6. Is there power in prayer?

   a. Where is that power located?

   b. According to the Old Testament story about the dedication of the temple, what is it about the person or people praying that makes some prayers more effective than others?

> Add what you have learned about biblical prayer to chart **CC-6**. Make sure you have noted that prayer is another expression of worship through which man offers his praise and adoration to God. Through prayer people present their needs to God in humble acknowledgement that He is our provider. Repentance and confession are offered to God when we fail to live according to His purposes for us. Ongoing obedience and repentance in the life of the believer prompts the display of God's power. Fill in the answers to the last two questions.

80 · Christian Theology & Ancient Polythesism

LESSON XI

Modern Worship in Modern Culture

Choosing between true worship and idolatry still matters today. The lessons ahead reveal that what a person worships determines who he is, where he is going, and what this life is all about. Sumerian culture was shaped by the worship of the forces of nature. To our modern scientific world, the worship of nature gods seems quite ridiculous. However, our culture has more in common with Sumerian idolatry than we know.

In Tabni's world the production of food depended on the labors of people and the cooperation of the forces of nature. In our twenty-first century culture, the vast majority of people don't physically labor for their food and we rarely give any thought to how the behavior of nature will affect our food supply. To the mind of a typical young person, food comes from the supermarket, or perhaps simply from money, as the food we get from grocery stores, restaurants or even vending machines all comes to us by way of money. But money and grocery stores are *not* the source of food. All foods – meat, apples, bread, eggs – come from the earth or the animals upon it, and all are dependent upon rain and sunshine and the labors of people. If you lived in a world without supermarkets, let alone vending machines, a world in which your food was dependent upon the farming and herding success of your family, how might your view of the world be affected? If the sun or rain was irregular, or disease suddenly swept through your livestock, what impact could such events have upon your life?

As food is just one of the many commodities that money buys, people in our world are very preoccupied with how to get more money. People labor long and hard to get money and go to incredible lengths to get more. Money not only buys the things we need, but it also gives protection from harm. While throwing away a valuable amulet seems crazy to us, the pagans' plea for their gods to hold back flood waters was not much different from spending money today on flood insurance. It seems that in our world, many have just exchanged the gods of Nature for the god of Money.

The pursuit of money is not the only thing that occupies the attention of people – so does the pursuit of pleasure. Last summer while on vacation with my family, we thought we'd give the Disney channel a try. With every commercial, the Disney spokes-kids popped up, repeating the words, "It's all about you, it's all about you, it's all about you!" While we didn't make it through the program, throughout the day we bantered about, "It's all about you!" So if it really is "all about you," as Disney would like you to believe, what is the purpose of everything around you?

Shouldn't it exist for your pleasure, to keep you happy? The notion that the world exists to give pleasure is not a new idea. Indeed, it comes right out of the Bible; the only problem is that the reference is talking about God, not you! The truth is, "It's all about God, it's all about God, it's all about God!"

People were put on this earth for God's pleasure, but when God is taken out of man's view of reality, then the earth is here for man's happiness. As the top of the evolutionary chain, people become God. Hmm, that's sounding an awful lot like Satan's temptation of Eve, "You will be like God ...". Again, Satan did not mean *like God in character*, he meant *like God in position and privilege*. In a culture that by and large believes it's all about you, Disney is only *one* of the many voices propagating the lie that everything exists for *your* good pleasure, for *your* glory, for *your* praise.

In large part, our world does not worship the God of the Bible; instead, our culture worships money, self, pleasure and fame. This worship is idolatry. Some may scoff at the idea that they are practicing idolatry. They certainly aren't bowing down to wooden statues. But remember the first commandment says, "You shall have no other gods before me." *To worship, or to give ardent love, desire or attention to things that are not God is idolatry.* So in a culture that has largely abandoned its belief in the supernatural, we still worship idolatrous things.

Discussion Questions:

1. Give some examples of how people live for pleasure, glory, or fame in our culture. (Also think about our cultural expressions like music, art and other forms of entertainment.)

2. How do these things tempt people into breaking the first commandment?

3. What are some things in your life that can tempt you to break the first commandment?

As Christians we live in a world much like Israel's. She was surrounded by and tempted by the idolatrous worship of her neighbors, and so are we. The nation of Israel ended up yielding to the temptation of idolatry, but a small number of Jewish people were faithful to the worship of the one true God. The Bible calls these faithful few the "remnant". It is a sad truth that today, many more Christian young people abandon their faith in their young adult years than those who hold on to it. In a recent poll 7 out of 10 Christian high school students had left the church by age 23.[37] Placing the love of self and pleasure above our love for God is undoubtedly at the root of many people's choice to leave the faith. Despite this

---

37 USA Today: YOUNG PEOPLE AREN'T STICKING WITH CHURCH BY CATHY LYNN GROSSMAN

sobering reality, we have hope because Christ has given us everything we need to stand firm in Him. But we must choose, day-in and day-out, to stand.

Much of the New Testament is about what Christ has given to help us remain in Him. There are many biblical passages and plenty of entire books that encourage the believer in his or her walk of faith. Colossians 3 is one of these passages. In it, Paul uses a metaphor about clothing. Certain types of behaviors such as rage and bitterness are like dressing in rags, while compassion and forgiveness are fine apparel. Paul's metaphor is aptly illustrated by Mark Twain's story, *The Prince and the Pauper*. The story is a case of mistaken identity, simply based on how two boys dressed – one like the son of a king, the other in the rags of a pauper. Our dress displays who we are. In the same way that every morning a person picks out the clothes he wears, dressing in the character of Christ is a choice we must make every day. A reminder about the "clothes" we wear is just one of the helpful ideas from Colossians 3 for those who desire a faith that will last.

"The special clothing of Israel's high priest set him apart as God's representative, just as we are set apart when we put on Christ to represent Him."

Read Colossians 3:1-17 and discuss the following questions:

1. What does Paul tell the believer to set his or her affections and thoughts on? (v. 1,2) Why is this instruction about our thought life helpful for a believer who wants to remain strong in the Lord?

2. At what point did you die? (vs. 3) Is dying a onetime event or an ongoing activity for the believer? If it is the latter, what is being continually put to death? Why? (v. 5-9)

3. Why are the things listed in verse 5 called idolatry?

4. What we put to death is to be replaced by what? (vs. 10,11)

5. What's another description for God's chosen people? (vs. 12)

6. Who is the source of all the character qualities listed in verses 12-14?

7. In Rom. 13:14 Paul says, "Put on Christ …" or in another translation, "Cloth yourself with Christ …". What are we taking off and putting on in order to dress like a Christian?

8. What is the opposite of peace and thankfulness? (vs. 15)

9. Why are peace and thankfulness characteristic of God's image bearers? Thankfulness, or gratitude, gets mentioned three times in verse 15-17. How does cultivating this character quality help someone remain true to their faith?

10. In what areas of our speech should the words of Christ most clearly influence what comes out of our mouths?

This passage goes on to talk about obedience, hard work and prayer. The Christian life isn't for slackers. We have a purpose for living, given to us by our heavenly Father, and a glorious eternity awaiting us. This life is a life of sacrifice, a life in which we must continually chose Christ's life over our own. But let us not think that the Christian life is one of drudgery. When we strive to live like God, there is "joy in the journey … and freedom for those who obey."[38] Christ's salvation accomplished two great works: it freed us from having to live a life of slavery to the sinful demands of our flesh and gave us life now and for eternity. Compare the person wearing the "articles of clothing" listed in verses 5-9 to those listed in 12-14. Whose shoes would you want to walk in? Ultimately, what we sacrifice now in order to put on Christ is "lightweight suffering" when compared to the "heavyweight glory" we will bask in for all eternity.[39]

"Be imitators of God, therefore, as dearly loved children and live a life of love, just as Christ loved us and gave Himself up for us as a fragrant offering and sacrifice to God."[40]

> You are strongly encouraged to close this lesson time by spending some personal time writing in your **Jacob Journal**. You might write about things you learned from this lesson or ideas you have prompted from the following questions. These questions are meant to be answered between you and God. *Do I, as commanded in Ephesians 5:1, strive to imitate God? Why is it difficult to live a life of love? Do I live to please God or to please myself? Anything given a higher importance or greater affection than God is idolatry. If I am convicted of the sin of idolatry, what do I need to do?* Go back to Psalms 51, if you need a model to follow.

---

38 Lyrics from Michael Card's song Joy in the Journey
39 II Corinthians 4:17, parallel wording from Joan Law
40 Ephesians 5:1,2

LESSON XII

The Consequences of Idolatry

> **Note to parent/instructor:** This lesson contains material that will not be appropriate for some children. Please review in advance of reading aloud.

The ideas associated with all worldviews have consequences. The ideas we believe guide us down certain paths, towards certain destinations. In short, ideas take us places. Evaluating worldviews requires looking at where ideas lead – what are their "implications" for good or for ill. All ideas have implications. Many ideas sound great at first, but when judged in light of where they lead, they're not so wonderful after all. Everything we discuss in this lesson has to do with the implications of polytheism.

We must ask: where do the ideas of polytheism – the ideas that the world is comprised of nature gods and goddesses – lead? We have already seen that paganism leads away from worship of the one true God into worshipping created things. This is robbery of the worst kind, because it steals what belongs only to God. The crime is called idolatry and its penalty is ultimately death.[41] Worshipping things that are not God will ultimately destroy the worshipper, even if God does not directly punish him or her. Idolatry lures people away from God into three destructive sins: sexual immorality, child sacrifice and witchcraft. These sins are the eventual outworking of idolatry in any culture.

The first sin evident in polytheistic cultures involves gross sexual immorality. Prostitution was a central practice in pagan temple worship. In *Secret of the Scribe* Tabni transformed herself into a scribe to survive. She had few options. Many young girls orphaned at Tabni's age had to become temple prostitutes if there were no relatives to care for them. Tabni's plan gave her a means to escape what she was likely destined for.

Across many differing cultures, wherever there were temples and religious festivals honoring the nature gods and goddesses, there was prostitution and other forms

---
41 Leviticus 26:1,14-16

of sexual immorality. Unlike the God of the Bible "who *said*, Let there be light" and caused brilliance to burst forth from darkness, the nature gods *birthed* each form of creation. Some came through marriage unions, some through rape, some through incest – with every act some new god or goddess was born, some new aspect of nature was created. Each offspring added to the created order, the order on which man must depend. Temple prostitution was thus a religious reenactment of the "creation" performed by gods and goddesses. Sumerians, Babylonians, and Canaanites believed they were imitating their gods and inciting them to continue to renew the sources of life. Within pagan society, what God designed for marriage was abused, perverted, and justified by the immorality of the gods and goddesses. Thus, human beings behaved like those they worshipped.

ASHEROTH

In Canaan, the chief god was Baal, typically represented as a bull. His consort was Asherah, the fertility goddess, whose symbols were carved wooden poles and spreading trees. The sexually perverted worship of Asherah went on throughout the lands of Canaan, whether in temples or under sacred trees or next to Asherah poles. The Canaanites prostituted themselves before their gods. As Israel did not drive out the Canaanites, the sexual nature of their worship proved a grave snare to Israel, and she fell into all her neighbor's sins. I Kings 14:22-24 says,

BAAL

"Judah did evil in the eyes of the LORD. By the sins they committed they stirred up his jealous anger more than their fathers had done. They also set up for themselves high places, sacred stones and Asherah poles on every high hill and under every spreading tree. There were even male shrine-prostitutes in the land; the people engaged in all the detestable practices of the nations the LORD had driven out before the Israelites."

The Bible teaches that the Triune God brought forth the creation through the *power of His spoken word*. God made the sacred act of procreation exclusively for the marriage union, because marriage is a material picture of the immaterial Trinity. When a couple through their love relationship produces new life, they are imitating the spiritual reality of the life-giving God of love. Polytheism degrades procreation to the level of animal behavior. Monotheism elevated procreation as a symbolic picture of God's divine life. Out of love, the Trinity created man and wife. Out of love, man and wife procreate children.

> On chart **CC-7, Consequences of Idolatry**, provide a response to the question regarding "Human Sexuality." Note the *reason* how and why the ideas associated with idolatry lead to sexual immorality and why monotheistic ideas lead to morality.

The Canaanites' second destructive sin is linked to their sexual immorality. When the act of procreation is not considered sacred, the life that it produces is also devalued. Unbelievably, polytheists justified the sacrifice of infants and children unto their gods. Why? People were made to be slaves. Thus, to the pagan, the value of human life was measured according to its usefulness. As the gods created men to serve their own needs, it was natural for the Canaanites to use each other, even their children, to serve their own needs. When the gods were angry, their rage was unleashed through wars, famine, disease or other natural disasters. Any terrible calamity was attributed to the displeasure of the gods – the people had failed to please their gods and must atone for the sins they had committed. Only the most precious sacrifice could appease the wrath of the gods. It was unto Molech, the Canaanite's fire god, that so many innocent children were burned to death.

This horrific sin was slowly introduced into Israel through her kings who married the pagan princesses of other nations. Nations which Israel had been commanded to wipe out infected and destroyed God's people from within. Psalm 106:34-38 says,

> *"They did not destroy the peoples as the LORD had commanded them, but they mingled with the nations and adopted their customs. They worshipped their idols, which became a snare to them. They sacrificed their sons and their daughters to demons. They shed innocent blood, the blood of their sons and daughters, whom they sacrificed to the idols of Canaan, and the land was desecrated by their blood."*

When Israel embraced the twisted thinking of her neighbors, she abandoned the value that God gives to human life. Human life was *never* created because it was useful in relation to meeting some need of God. God has no needs. Human life is valuable not for what it *does* but for what it *is* – a reflection of a relational, loving God. A helpless baby girl is a wondrous creation of God, the daughter of her mother and father, and the sister of her older brother. She is a grandchild, a niece, a cousin and someday a friend. From her conception in her mother's womb, God formed this child with loving tenderness.[42] Before she was held in her mother's arms, this babe was known to her Father in heaven. She is His workmanship, created to be like Christ Jesus. Human life is infinitely valuable, both as a creation and as a relational expression of God. Human life is priceless, both because of Who made us and Whom we were made to be like. The worth of a life is derived from its Maker.

> On chart **CC-7**, note how and why the ideas associated with polytheistic and monotheistic thinking impact the "Value of Human Life". (second question)

With no thought of a loving relational Creator, polytheists were driven to child sacrifice and into the darkness of witchcraft. Before the nation of Israel entered the land of Canaan to overthrow the people living there, God warned them in Deuteronomy 18:10:

> *"Let no one be found among you who sacrifices his son or daughter in the fire, who practices divination or sorcery, interprets omens, engages in witchcraft, or casts spells, or who is a medium or spiritist or who consults the dead. Anyone who does these things is detestable to the LORD, and because of these detestable practices the LORD your God will drive out those nations before you. You must be blameless before the LORD your God. The nations you will dispossess listen to those who practice sorcery or divination."*

Secret of the Scribe opens with the scene in the queen's bedroom in which a witch doctor attempts to cure the queen by sending the demon out of her body with various potions and magic. The queen dies anyway, and her last few hours of life were certainly even less pleasant because of the goings-on of the witch doctor. While this made for a rather comical read, it is only a small indicator of how sorcery pervaded this pagan culture.

Witchcraft, or sorcery, is the effort of a human being to connect with the supernatural powers of the underworld. It is the belief that through the power of words called spells or incantations, the supernatural power of demons can be called upon to influence natural life. The pursuit of power flows naturally from polytheism, in which the gods

---

42 PSALM 139

were not all-powerful. Thus achieving and maintaining power was their central occupation. This quest was imitated by man, who sought to snatch some piece of supernatural power for himself. In addition to spells and incantations, there were other rituals believed to attract dark forces. Foretelling the future, conjuring up the dead, or interpreting the signs in the stars were some of the sorcerer's methods. To have access to supernatural power without having to depend on a supernatural all-powerful God or abide by His high moral standards can be a real temptation.

Witchcraft is grave evil; it seeks the power of demons rather than depending on the power of God. Only God knows the future, only God heals or brings death; the fate of others is clearly in God's dominion, not ours. The Bible tells us that supernatural powers of darkness are real.[43] Yet rather than figuring out how to harness demonic powers for human purposes, Christians are to fight against them through God's strength. The Christian does seek supernatural power, but this power comes from the Holy Spirit, and its purpose is to produce godly character and to transform us into the likeness of Christ.

> On chart **CC-7**, note how and why the ideas associated with polytheistic and monotheistic thinking impact the "View of Demonic Powers".

Not surprisingly, idolatrous cultures eventually became saturated with demonic oppression, sexual perversion and the habitual murder of innocent children. Why? Because we become like what we worship. If we worship a God of love and truth, we strive for those things in ourselves. If we worship gods of self-ambition, darkness and lies, we look like them in turn. The ideas of polytheism – the detestable practice of idolatry – lead down the road to destruction, ending in death. God ordered death and destruction to the Canaanites as just payment for their horrifying sin. Rather than a flood or fire and brimstone, Israel would be the tool God planned to use to wipe the evil of the Canaanites from the face of the earth. Read and discuss the following passages:

Read Deuteronomy 9:1-6

1. Knowing that God loves the righteous man, did God wipe out the Canaanites because of Israel's goodness?

2. How did God describe Israel?

3. What was the reason for the destruction of the Canaanites?

4. Who alone can judge and sentence both external and internal wickedness?

LIKE A GOOD PARENT, GOD GIVES HIS CHILDREN EVERY POSSIBLE WARNING ABOUT THE PITFALLS THAT LIE AHEAD AND WHAT REALITY WILL LOOK LIKE FOR THOSE WHO FALL. DESPITE THE TERRIBLE CONSEQUENCES THIS SONG DESCRIBES, ISRAEL IS TO FIND HOPE IN GOD HER SAVIOR. PEOPLE FALL, BUT GOD HAS GREAT MERCY. HIS NEVER-FAILING LOVE REACHES TO THE REPENTANT FALLEN AND PULLS THEM OUT OF THE MIRY CLAY. GOD WILL ATONE FOR HIS CREATION. THIS IS THE STORY OF GOD AS REVEALED THROUGH ISRAEL.

---

43 EPHESIANS 6:12

Read Deuteronomy 18:9-13; 20:17, 18

1. What sins caused the Canaanites to lose their land?

2. Who was bringing this judgment against her?

3. Why was Israel told to completely destroy the people living in the land?

God was in effect wiping out a terrible cancer, which, if not destroyed, would ravage everything it came into contact with. Israel did not obey God; they did not wipe out the inhabitants of the land; they intermarried with the Canaanites, and the infectious sin of idolatry almost completely destroyed God's chosen people.

> "THOSE WHO MAKE THEM [IDOLS] BECOME LIKE THEM; SO DO ALL WHO TRUST IN THEM."
> —PSALM 115:8

Even though the ideas of ancient polytheists seem remote and far away, we face this same choice today. We live in an idolatrous culture. While there are no statues of gods or goddesses, most people live to please themselves. Disney's commercial jingle "It's all about you!" could be our national motto. While our culture's worship of self did not arise from the ideas of polytheism,[44] nonetheless, our culture's idolatry produces the same effect. We live in a society which practices gross immorality, abortion on-demand and witchcraft as a primary source of popular entertainment in novels, movies, and television shows. While behind the scenes, the practice of the occult is steadily growing in our country. This is the natural result of worshipping that which is not God. We can choose to worship God, worship self, worship nature or worship demons; only one choice leads to life. Think about the implications of the ideas you chose to live your life by. Ideas have consequences. May you choose life!

As we close this series of lessons comparing the worship practices of ancient and modern idolatry to biblical monotheism, we pray that you have learned how destructive and pervasive idolatry is and also how the worship of God should pervade every aspect of our lives. Worshipping God is a seven-days-a-week activity. It involves daily sacrifice as we imitate a God who provided everything we need to experience His life and love. Worshipping God calls us to a life of prayer in which we daily express our dependence on Him and our praise for our great God and Savior.

> **People were made to worship God.**
> **People were created to be like God.**
> **Man becomes like what he worships.**
> **Who or what is worshiped determines the man.**

On chart **CC-7**, fill in the column under *Modern Idolatry*. For older students, add to your charts 2 and 3 by answering the questions for lesson 12.

---

44 WORSHIP OF SELF IS A BY-PRODUCT OF THE IDEAS OF MODERNITY. THESE IDEAS WILL BE EXPLORED IN THE READER'S GUIDE WHICH, LORD WILLING, WILL ACCOMPANY *BENEATH THE CAT'S CLAW*.

LESSON XIII

The Men and the Purposes Behind Babylonian and Hebrew Law

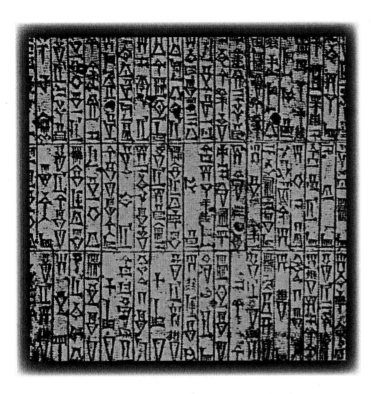

Throughout this guide we have compared pieces of ancient literature to their counterparts in the Bible. This lesson begins with a comparison between Hammurabi's Code – the most famous work of Mesopotamian and Mosaic Law – the heart of the Old Testament. Students as young as third or fourth grade can tell you about the great Babylonian King, who wrote down the 282 laws he received from his gods. These laws ruled Mesopotamia for several hundred years. They also influenced later empires that developed between the Tigris and Euphrates rivers for some 1500 years. Hammurabi's Code was inscribed on a seven-foot black stone (stele) with a picture carved at the top. The picture shows the king receiving his laws from Shamash, the sun god of wisdom. As a monument, the stone both informed the people of Babylonian law and reminded them of the greatness of the king who issued its decrees.

For many years, Hammurabi's Code was believed to be the earliest record of human laws. It predates the Law of Moses by 300 to 500 years. Therefore, many skeptics of the Bible claim that Moses copied Hammurabi. As it turns out, Hammurabi probably copied earlier laws of Sumerian kings that predate his own code by as much as a thousand years. It seems that as long as there have been city-states, people have recognized the need for written laws which define right and wrong, justice and injustice. Most ancient cultures believed that laws which defined standards applying to the whole city or country had to come from the gods who were higher and wiser than mere human beings. Having defined what is good, right, and just, laws were a reflection of the very character and nature of

A Comparitive Study using *Secret of the Scribe* · 91

the gods, or at least what people believed about the character and nature of the gods. People were expected to live up to the gods' standards. To fail to obey the law of the gods could bring about punishment administered either by the law or directly from heaven.

Hammurabi's Code can be divided into three parts: the prologue, the laws, and the epilogue. A good portion of the prologue and the laws are provided in this guide, but older students may wish to read the whole thing on-line.[45] If a student is reading the entire Code, he should read only one section at a time.

The first section of Hammurabi's Code could be called the Preamble. While the word simply means "introduction" it sounds important – Hammurabi would have probably preferred this title. From a simple reading of his Code, you will see that King Hammurabi was pretty impressed with himself, and he wanted his readers to share his opinion. In the preamble, Hammurabi recognizes the gods for giving him his law and its purpose (first paragraph). Then he memorializes his many achievements (second and third paragraphs). While the first paragraph below comes straight from Hammurabi's Code, the second paragraph has been shortened by about half. In its entirety, the second paragraph includes many more successes of the king. It could have been shortened even more, but it is important for the student to notice how much of this ancient law is devoted to praising Hammurabi. The odd names used in the text usually refer to city-states, many of which Hammurabi conquered as he united the first great Babylonian empire. There are also many gods/goddesses mentioned who are well pleased with the beloved Hammurabi. For help in reading this text, [cs] has been added after the mention of a city-state and [g] after the name of a god or goddess.[46] All the verbs in the second paragraph with few exceptions refer to Hammurabi along with most of the descriptive nouns.

---

45 HTTP://EAWC.EVANSVILLE.EDU/ANTHOLOGY/HAMMURABI.HTM
46 DEFINITIONS OF ALL THE UNFAMILIAR WORDS IN HAMMURABI'S CODE ARE AVAILABLE AT: HTTP://AVALON.LAW.YALE.EDU/ANCIENT/CODEIND1.ASP

Hammurabi's Code of Laws[47]

WHEN ANU[G] THE SUBLIME, KING OF THE ANUNAKI[G], AND
BEL[G], THE LORD OF HEAVEN AND EARTH, WHO DECREED
THE FATE OF THE LAND, ASSIGNED TO MARDUK[CHIEF GOD OF
BABYLON], THE OVER-RULING SON OF EA, GOD OF RIGHTEOUSNESS,
DOMINION OVER EARTHLY MAN, AND MADE HIM GREAT AMONG
THE IGIGI[G], THEY CALLED BABYLON BY HIS ILLUSTRIOUS NAME,
MADE IT GREAT ON EARTH, AND FOUNDED AN EVERLASTING
KINGDOM IN IT, WHOSE FOUNDATIONS ARE LAID SO SOLIDLY AS
THOSE OF HEAVEN AND EARTH; THEN ANU[G] AND BEL[G] CALLED
... ME, HAMMURABI, THE EXALTED PRINCE, WHO FEARED GOD,
TO BRING ABOUT THE RULE OF RIGHTEOUSNESS IN THE LAND, TO
DESTROY THE WICKED AND THE EVIL-DOERS; SO THAT THE STRONG
SHOULD NOT HARM THE WEAK; SO THAT I SHOULD RULE OVER THE
BLACK-HEADED PEOPLE LIKE SHAMASH[G], AND ENLIGHTEN THE
LAND, TO FURTHER THE WELL-BEING OF MANKIND.

HAMMURABI, THE PRINCE, CALLED OF BEL[G] AM I, MAKING
RICHES AND INCREASE, ... WHO CONQUERED THE FOUR QUARTERS
OF THE WORLD, MADE GREAT THE NAME OF BABYLON[CS],
REJOICED THE HEART OF MARDUK[G], HIS LORD WHO DAILY
PAYS HIS DEVOTIONS IN SAGGIL[G]; ... WHO ENRICHED UR[CS]; THE
HUMBLE, THE REVERENT, WHO BRINGS WEALTH TO GISH-SHIR-
GAL[TEMPLE IN UR]; THE WHITE KING, HEARD OF SHAMASH[G],
THE MIGHTY, WHO AGAIN LAID THE FOUNDATIONS OF
SIPPARA[CS]; ... THE LORD WHO GRANTED NEW LIFE TO URUK[CS],
WHO BROUGHT PLENTEOUS WATER TO ITS INHABITANTS, ... SHIELD
OF THE LAND, WHO REUNITED THE SCATTERED INHABITANTS OF
ISIN[CS]; ... THE PROTECTING KING OF THE CITY, ... WHO FIRMLY

---

47 TRANSLATED BY L. W. KING AND TAKEN FROM THE SITE HTTP://EAWC.EVANSVILLE.EDU/
ANTHOLOGY/HAMMURABI.HTM

FOUNDED THE FARMS OF KISH[CS], ... REDOUBLED THE GREAT HOLY TREASURES OF NANA[G], ... THE DIVINE KING OF THE CITY; THE WHITE, THE WISE; ... THE MIGHTY, THE LORD TO WHOM COME SCEPTER AND CROWN, WITH WHICH HE CLOTHES HIMSELF; ... THE PROVIDENT, SOLICITOUS, WHO PROVIDED FOOD AND DRINK FOR LAGASH[CS] AND GIRSU[CS], WHO PROVIDED LARGE SACRIFICIAL OFFERINGS FOR THE TEMPLE OF NINGIRSU[G]; WHO CAPTURED THE ENEMY, ... THE PURE PRINCE, WHOSE PRAYER IS ACCEPTED BY ADAD[G]; WHO SATISFIED THE HEART OF ADAD[G], THE WARRIOR, THE KING WHO GRANTED LIFE TO THE CITY OF ADAB[CS]; ... THE PRINCELY KING OF THE CITY, THE IRRESISTIBLE WARRIOR, WHO GRANTED LIFE TO THE INHABITANTS OF MASHKANSHABRI, ... THE WHITE, POTENT, WHO PENETRATED THE SECRET CAVE OF THE BANDITS, SAVED THE INHABITANTS OF MALKA FROM MISFORTUNE, AND FIXED THEIR HOME FAST IN WEALTH; WHO ESTABLISHED PURE SACRIFICIAL GIFTS FOR EA[G] AND DAM-GAL-NUN-NA[G], WHO MADE HIS KINGDOM EVERLASTINGLY GREAT; THE PRINCELY KING OF THE CITY, ... WHO PRESENTS HOLY MEALS TO THE DIVINITY OF NIN-A-ZU[G], WHO CARED FOR ITS INHABITANTS IN THEIR NEED, PROVIDED A PORTION FOR THEM IN BABYLON IN PEACE; THE SHEPHERD OF THE OPPRESSED AND OF THE SLAVES; WHOSE DEEDS FIND FAVOR BEFORE ANUNIT[G], ... WHO RECOGNIZES THE RIGHT, WHO RULES BY LAW; ... THE SUBLIME, WHO HUMBLES HIMSELF BEFORE THE GREAT GODS; ... THE SUN OF BABYLON, WHOSE RAYS SHED LIGHT OVER THE LAND OF SUMER[SOUTHERN MESOPOTAMIA] AND AKKAD[NORTHERN MESOPOTAMIA]; THE KING, OBEYED BY THE FOUR QUARTERS OF THE WORLD; BELOVED OF NINNI[G], AM I.

WHEN MARDUK[G] SENT ME TO RULE OVER MEN, TO GIVE THE PROTECTION OF RIGHT TO THE LAND, I DID RIGHT ..., AND BROUGHT ABOUT THE WELL-BEING OF THE OPPRESSED.

Discussion Questions:

1. From the first paragraph, what was the purpose of Hammurabi's Code? Is this purpose good?

2. Hammurabi acknowledges many gods and goddesses, but who gets the most praise in this introduction?

3. What types of achievements does Hammurabi have recorded in stone?

4. What word would describe Hammurabi's opinion of himself?

The record of Hammurabi's triumphs recorded in stone was typical in the ancient world. Beyond written records, there were "arches of triumphs" and other monuments that had been raised to memorialize the achievements of the great leader. Hammurabi was indeed the greatest king of the first Babylonian Empire, with many achievements to his credit over the course of his lifetime. How the significant achievements of great leaders are treated is where we shall begin our comparison between Hammurabi's Code and Mosaic Law. In comparison to Hammurabi, Moses too was a great leader and the greatest of all of Israel's prophets. However, you'll find that there is nothing so grand about Moses written in the first five books of the Old Testament (the Torah). Why not?

Discussion Question:

1. Off the top of your head, name some things Moses did that could be used to create an impressive list of achievements.

The lack of a significant biblical narrative listing and praising Moses' achievements was not due to a wont of material: Moses had a royal upbringing. He confronted and defeated the most powerful ruler in the land – the pharaoh of Egypt. With the pointing of his staff, the Red Sea parted and the people escaped through the sea walking on dry ground. Moses destroyed Pharaoh's army with a point of the same rod. Throughout his entire tenure as Israel's leader, he performed many astounding miracles. He gave his people a set of laws that, unlike Hammurabi's Code, are still quoted today. Moses spent so much time with God that his face actually glowed. He successively fed and led the nation of Israel through the desert to the Promise Land. The list goes on, but there are no grand passages recorded in the first five books of the Bible to the glories of Moses, and there were never any monuments erected to honor him. The glories that Moses records are always credited and directed to God. The achievements recorded by the Babylonian king, save the law itself, were credited to Hammurabi. When comparing these two law-

A Comparitive Study using *Secret of the Scribe* · 95

givers, both were great men, but the pride of one and the humility of the other is a dramatic contrast between them.

Discussion Question:

1. Again, off the top of your head, can you think of any examples that show that Moses was a humble man?

Perhaps you recalled that after his flight from the Egypt, Moses became a shepherd – a job that was not highly esteemed. Frankly, shepherds were viewed as lowly people. Moses could have easily omitted this job from his account of his life. When God called Moses out of the burning bush, he genuinely believed that he was not qualified to lead God's people, let alone confront the mighty Pharaoh. This story of the reluctant leader was recorded by Moses in less than flattering tone, and reveals that, if he was once a proud and self-confident young man in the courts of Pharaoh, his time in the desert had changed all of that.

Perhaps you recalled the story of Moses coming down from Mt. Sinai with God's signature on tablets of stone, only to discover the people engaged in worshipping an idol of a calf. Moses was furious and broke the tablets. God was furious and said He would destroy all the people and start over again making Moses the father of His chosen people. Rather than seizing this opportunity to make himself great, Moses fell on his face fasting for forty days and pleading with God to spare these sinful people for the honor of His name.[48] Moses sought the glory of God rather than his own glory.

But Moses was not a perfect man. In his accounting of Israel's history and Israel's sins, he included sins of his own; his rash murder of an Egyptian, his stalling when God called him, his failure to circumcise his son, and his disobedience to God by striking the rock in his anger – a disobedience so serious it cost him his entry into the Promise Land.[49] Though Moses is clearly the author of the first five books of the Bible through divine inspiration, there are a few examples of passages that God wrote through other men. One is the account of the death of Moses, which concludes the book of Deuteronomy. The unknown

---

48 Exodus 32:11-14; Deuteronomy 9:7-29
49 Number 20:2-13

author (perhaps Joshua) called Moses, "the servant of the Lord", noting that there was never a prophet in Israel like Moses whom God knew "face to face".[50] This was Moses' greatest claim to fame – his personal knowledge of the Holy One.

Now let's return to Hammurabi. Can you imagine Hammurabi including his short-comings among his extensive list of accomplishments? How might his introduction read differently, if the majority of the text was spent praising his gods and goddesses rather than his own deeds? Earlier in this guide, we noted a "list of Moses' accomplishments" for comparison to Hammurabi; however, Moses never described them as *his* achievements. He grew up in the pharaoh's palace because God saved him in the basket of bulrushes woven by his faithful mother. The defeat of Egypt's mighty king was accomplished by the miraculous plagues God sent to punish the Egyptians for enslaving His people and worshiping nature gods. The power of God delivered the people from Pharaoh's mighty army. Midway through the Red Sea, the terrified Egyptian soldiers realized that God was fighting against them. But it was too late to escape; they all drowned.[51] Though God worked in and through Moses, Moses' chronicle of these events never gave his readers the illusion that he took credit for any of them. Moses knew that without God he was nothing but a rash young man, or a hesitant middle-aged shepherd. It was God who made Moses great, and that knowledge made Moses humble.

Numbers 12 tells an interesting story of a challenge Moses' siblings, Miriam and Aaron, posed to his authority. Believing they should be recognized as God's spokespersons and thus considered equal to Moses, they spread their own opinions throughout the Israelite camp. It was not Moses who confronted them. It was God who called Miriam and Aaron to account and defended Moses' unique position as His special servant. Speaking out of the pillar of cloud, God said to them,

> *"Hear now my words: if there be a prophet among you,*
> *I Jehovah will make myself known unto him in a vision,*
> *I will speak with him in a dream.*
> *My servant Moses is not so; he is faithful in all my house:*
> *with him will I speak mouth to mouth, even manifestly,*
> *and not in dark speeches;*
> *and the form of Jehovah shall he behold: wherefore then were ye not afraid*
> *to speak against my servant, against Moses?*[52]

Miriam, who must have been the instigator, was struck with leprosy as punishment, but immediately Moses pled with God to be merciful and restore his sister. Only a humble man could resist the temptation to be glad Miriam got

---

50 DEUTERONOMY 34:5-12
51 EXODUS 14:13-31
52 NUMBERS 12:6-8 (ASV)

A Comparitive Study using *Secret of the Scribe* · 97

what she deserved. Moses returned good for evil. This chapter points out, in what appears to be a later scribal note, that Moses was the most humble man who lived on earth.[53] God accomplished the recording of Israelite law and sacred history through a man of great humility.

Moses knew God, and that knowledge enabled him to see himself clearly. Moses was bold enough to plead with God on behalf of his people, yet humble enough to accept his own punishment not to set foot in the Promise Land. Moses never insisted that his faithfulness should entitle him to special treatment. Moses could have used his position with God to bolster his own reputation as Hammurabi did. The Code closes with "Beloved of Ninni[g], am I. When Marduk[g] sent me to rule over men, to give the protection of right to the land, I did right ..., and brought about the well-being of the oppressed." While Moses was indeed loved by God, Moses was concerned with the glory of God's name rather than his own. After the miraculous escape from Egypt and victory over Pharaoh's army, Moses led the people in this praise unto God:

> "I will sing unto the Lord, for he is highly exalted. The horse and rider he had hurled into the seas. The Lord is my strength and my song; he has become my salvation. ... Your right hand, O Lord, shattered the enemy. In the greatness of your majesty, you threw down those who opposed you. ... Who among the gods is like you, O Lord? Who is like you – majestic in holiness, awesome in glory, working wonders? The Lord will reign for ever and ever."[54]

The contrast between the writings of these two men clearly reveals both their perspectives about themselves and their gods/God.

Discussion Questions:

1. In the epitaph written after Moses' death, he was called, "Moses, the servant of the Lord ..."[55] Why do you think he was remembered as the servant of God?

2. What character quality is essential in any great man or woman, who would lead others as a servant of God?

3. When Moses wrote down God's Law, who did he want people to see?

4. When Hammurabi wrote down his god's law, who did he want people to see?

---

53 Numbers 12:3 See NIV study note
54 Exodus 15:1,2,6,11,18
55 Deuteronomy 34:5

98 · Christian Theology & Ancient Polythesism

5. Do you think it is common for people with great achievements to struggle with pride? Why or why not?

6. In the early church, pride became known as one of the seven deadly sins. Can you think of some verses or stories from the Bible that illustrate how God views pride in man?

7. Why do you think God so strongly detests this sin?

8. Even though Hammurabi's gods were false, how did his pride affect his perspective on his achievements and the honor he gave his gods?

> Go the comparison chart **CC-8, Hammurabi's Code and Mosaic Law** and answer the first question.

We've compared the men behind the laws; now let's turn to our second comparison and examine the purpose of Babylonian and Hebrew *law*. Earlier you read the purpose of Hammurabi's Code from his introduction: *"Hammurabi, the exalted prince, who feared God, [received these laws] to bring about the rule of righteousness in the land, to destroy the wicked and the evil-doers; so that the strong should not harm the weak; so that I [Hammurabi] should rule over the black-headed people [the Babylonians] like Shamash, and enlighten the land, to further the well-being of mankind."*

We can summarize the purposes of Babylonian law like this:

1. "to bring about the rule of righteousness in the land," *(to provide justice)*

2. "to destroy the wicked and the evil-doers; so that the strong should not harm the weak;" *(to eliminate evil doers, protect the weak)*

3. "so that I should rule over the black-headed people like Shamash[g], and enlighten the land," *(to further the rule of Hammurabi)*

4. "to further the well-being of mankind." *(to promote the good of humanity)*

Justice for all, eliminate evil persons, protect weak persons, advance the rule of the king and bring good to all people – these are noble aims. Overall, wanting a just, orderly, prosperous society is a decent aim for any culture.

Unlike summarizing Hammurabi's Code, which has a concise statement of purpose, the student of Mosaic Law has to work a little harder to unearth its purpose. Additionally, there is a great deal more material in the Torah than what is contained in Hammurabi's 282 laws. No less than four of the five books of the

Bible contain specific laws written by Moses. So since God through Moses did not record for us a statement beginning, "This is the purpose of the whole Law:" etc., the Bible student has to do some careful reading and observation. He must look for repetition of ideas in much the same way we discover an author's theme in a great piece of literature. This might sound reasonable in theory, but Exodus, Leviticus, Numbers and Deuteronomy are pretty big books. For the level of work we are doing in this course, you will not be required to read all of these books. However, you may want to consider reading Deuteronomy.

The historical setting of Deuteronomy takes place during the last months of Moses' life. The forty years of wandering in the desert have come to an end, and Moses is preparing his successor Joshua to take over the leadership of Israel. The Promised Land waits just beyond the Jordan. However, the people Joshua will lead into the Promised Land are not the same ones Moses led out of Egypt. When the Law on Mt. Sinai was given forty years earlier, most of the people who would eventually enter the Promised Land were either too young to understand the significance of the event, or not yet born. Thus the book of Deuteronomy is a retelling of God giving His people the Law, through which he established his special relationship with them. This relationship was based on a series of promises called a covenant, something like a legal agreement between two parties. As a retelling of the Law to the next generation, Deuteronomy highlights or summarizes much of the content of Exodus, Leviticus and Numbers. Thus, Deuteronomy is a good place to start looking for the purpose of the Law. Below are a series of passages from Deuteronomy in which you will find several repeated phrases that point to the purposes of Mosaic Law. Make a list of these phrases as you look for God's purpose in giving His people His Law.

Take turns reading and discussing the following passages: Deuteronomy 4:9-10,20, 35,39; 6:3-7; 8:6-9; 7:6; 10:12; 11:1,8,9,13,22; 13:6-11; 14:2; 17:12,`13; 19:9,19,20, 21; 28:1-6, 9; 30:16; 32:46-47

1. What were some of the repeated ideas that you found in these passages?

2. Did any of these ideas associated with the Mosaic Law surprise you?

100 · Christian Theology & Ancient Polythesism

If we tried to summarize the repeated ideas from Deuteronomy in the fashion of Hammurabi's Code, the purpose of Mosaic Law might look something like this:

1. To reveal and remember the one true God

2. To love, obey and fear God

3. To keep Israel from sinning and forsaking God

4. To give the Hebrews a long life, good land, and much prosperity

5. To make a holy people, a royal priesthood, God's treasured possession

In paragraph form we might put the purpose of the Law this way: The Law is a written testimony revealing the one true God. Do not forget the Lord your God, and teach your children not to forget Him. Love, obey and fear God – this will keep you from sinning. Obedience will bring you blessing and prosperity and enable you to fulfill your purpose – to be a holy people, a royal priesthood unto the Lord, God's treasured possession.

Discussion Questions:

1. From the verses above, the summary provided here, and the list of purposes for Hammurabi's Code are there any similar ideas?

2. Which of Hammurabi's purposes bears the least resemblance to the intentions of Mosaic Law?

3. Hammurabi's Code established his own kingly rule. Whose rule does the Law of Moses establish?

4. Which purpose(s) in the Law of Moses seem least like anything you see in Hammurabi's Code?

Go to chart **CC-8** and answer the second question comparing the purposes of Hammurabi's Code to Mosaic Law.

A Comparitive Study using *Secret of the Scribe* · 101

LESSON XIV

The Code of Hammurabi and the Laws of Moses

In this lesson, you will read some actual laws from Hammurabi's Code and then compare them to laws in Exodus. As you read the sampling of Babylonian law below try to find laws that instruct the people about how they should relate to their gods. You'll be hard pressed to find any. In fact, in Babylonian law, there is nothing like the Ten Commandments that defines the nature of their gods or people's relationship to them. Hammurabi's Code lacks both a concise framework upon which all laws are built and a basis for that law in the character and nature of the gods. Instead, it is based upon the power of the king, who is the only representative of the gods. Thus, much time is devoted in the beginning and again at the end of Hammurabi's Code to ensure the power and prestige of the human law giver is understood. In contrast Israel's laws are based upon the character of God as expressed in the Ten Commandments. The first four Commandments focus exclusively on who God is and how Israel is to relate to Him. While there are comparisons in Babylonian law to the second half of the Ten Commandments dealing with the treatment of one's neighbor, in general you will find a much lower standard in Hammurabi's Code for human relationships than in Mosaic Law.

With this understanding in mind, read the sampling of about 60 laws from Hammurabi's Code below. As you read, make a list of the type of laws and punishments prescribed for breaking Babylonian law. (To guide you in your observations, you may wish to skip ahead a few pages first and skim the upcoming discussion questions.)

Hammurabi's Code of Laws[56]

2. IF ANYONE BRING AN ACCUSATION AGAINST A MAN, AND THE ACCUSED GO TO THE RIVER AND LEAP INTO THE RIVER, IF HE SINK IN THE RIVER HIS ACCUSER SHALL TAKE POSSESSION OF HIS HOUSE. BUT IF THE RIVER PROVE THAT THE ACCUSED IS NOT GUILTY, AND HE ESCAPE UNHURT, THEN HE WHO HAD BROUGHT THE ACCUSATION SHALL BE PUT TO DEATH, WHILE HE WHO LEAPED INTO THE RIVER SHALL TAKE POSSESSION OF THE HOUSE THAT HAD BELONGED TO HIS ACCUSER.

---

56 Translated by L. W. King http://eawc.evansville.edu/anthology/hammurabi.htm

3. IF ANYONE BRING AN ACCUSATION OF ANY CRIME BEFORE THE ELDERS, AND DOES NOT PROVE WHAT HE HAS CHARGED, HE SHALL, IF IT BE A CAPITAL OFFENSE CHARGED, BE PUT TO DEATH.

8. IF ANYONE STEAL CATTLE OR SHEEP, OR AN ASS, OR A PIG OR A GOAT, IF IT BELONG TO A GOD OR TO THE COURT, THE THIEF SHALL PAY THIRTYFOLD THEREFORE; IF THEY BELONGED TO A FREED MAN OF THE KING HE SHALL PAY TENFOLD; IF THE THIEF HAS NOTHING WITH WHICH TO PAY HE SHALL BE PUT TO DEATH.

9. IF ANYONE LOSE AN ARTICLE, AND FIND IT IN THE POSSESSION OF ANOTHER: IF THE PERSON IN WHOSE POSSESSION THE THING IS FOUND SAY "A MERCHANT SOLD IT TO ME, I PAID FOR IT BEFORE WITNESSES," AND IF THE OWNER OF THE THING SAY, "I WILL BRING WITNESSES WHO KNOW MY PROPERTY," THEN SHALL THE PURCHASER BRING THE MERCHANT WHO SOLD IT TO HIM, AND THE WITNESSES BEFORE WHOM HE BOUGHT IT, AND THE OWNER SHALL BRING WITNESSES WHO CAN IDENTIFY HIS PROPERTY. THE JUDGE SHALL EXAMINE THEIR TESTIMONY -- BOTH OF THE WITNESSES BEFORE WHOM THE PRICE WAS PAID, AND OF THE WITNESSES WHO IDENTIFY THE LOST ARTICLE ON OATH. THE MERCHANT IS THEN PROVED TO BE A THIEF AND SHALL BE PUT TO DEATH. THE OWNER OF THE LOST ARTICLE RECEIVES HIS PROPERTY, AND HE WHO BOUGHT IT RECEIVES THE MONEY HE PAID FROM THE ESTATE OF THE MERCHANT.

10. IF THE PURCHASER DOES NOT BRING THE MERCHANT AND THE WITNESSES BEFORE WHOM HE BOUGHT THE ARTICLE, BUT ITS OWNER BRING WITNESSES WHO IDENTIFY IT, THEN THE BUYER IS THE THIEF AND SHALL BE PUT TO DEATH, AND THE OWNER RECEIVES THE LOST ARTICLE.

11. IF THE OWNER DOES NOT BRING WITNESSES TO IDENTIFY THE LOST ARTICLE, HE IS AN EVIL-DOER, HE HAS TRADUCED, AND SHALL BE PUT TO DEATH.

14. IF ANYONE STEAL THE MINOR SON OF ANOTHER, HE SHALL BE PUT TO DEATH.

A Comparitive Study using *Secret of the Scribe* · 103

15. IF ANYONE TAKE A MALE OR FEMALE SLAVE OF THE COURT, OR A MALE OR FEMALE SLAVE OF A FREED MAN, OUTSIDE THE CITY GATES, HE SHALL BE PUT TO DEATH.

19. IF HE HOLDS THE SLAVES IN HIS HOUSE, AND THEY ARE CAUGHT THERE, HE SHALL BE PUT TO DEATH.

21. IF ANYONE BREAK A HOLE INTO A HOUSE (BREAK IN TO STEAL), HE SHALL BE PUT TO DEATH BEFORE THAT HOLE AND BE BURIED.

22. IF ANYONE IS COMMITTING A ROBBERY AND IS CAUGHT, THEN HE SHALL BE PUT TO DEATH.

53. IF ANYONE BE TOO LAZY TO KEEP HIS DAM IN PROPER CONDITION, AND DOES NOT SO KEEP IT; IF THEN THE DAM BREAK AND ALL THE FIELDS BE FLOODED, THEN SHALL HE IN WHOSE DAM THE BREAK OCCURRED BE SOLD FOR MONEY, AND THE MONEY SHALL REPLACE THE CORN WHICH HE HAS CAUSED TO BE RUINED.

54. IF HE BE NOT ABLE TO REPLACE THE CORN, THEN HE AND HIS POSSESSIONS SHALL BE DIVIDED AMONG THE FARMERS WHOSE CORN HE HAS FLOODED.

55. IF ANYONE OPEN HIS DITCHES TO WATER HIS CROP, BUT IS CARELESS, AND THE WATER FLOOD THE FIELD OF HIS NEIGHBOR, THEN HE SHALL PAY HIS NEIGHBOR CORN FOR HIS LOSS.

64. IF ANY ONE HAND OVER HIS GARDEN TO A GARDENER TO WORK, THE GARDENER SHALL PAY TO ITS OWNER TWO-THIRDS OF THE PRODUCE OF THE GARDEN, FOR SO LONG AS HE HAS IT IN POSSESSION, AND THE OTHER THIRD SHALL HE KEEP.

117. IF ANYONE FAIL TO MEET A CLAIM FOR DEBT, AND SELL HIMSELF, HIS WIFE, HIS SON, AND DAUGHTER FOR MONEY OR GIVE THEM AWAY TO FORCED LABOR: THEY SHALL WORK FOR THREE YEARS IN THE HOUSE OF THE MAN WHO BOUGHT THEM, OR THE PROPRIETOR, AND IN THE FOURTH YEAR THEY SHALL BE SET FREE.

120. IF ANY ONE STORE CORN FOR SAFE KEEPING IN ANOTHER PERSON'S HOUSE, AND ANY HARM HAPPEN TO THE CORN

IN STORAGE, OR IF THE OWNER OF THE HOUSE OPEN THE GRANARY AND TAKE SOME OF THE CORN, OR IF ESPECIALLY HE DENY THAT THE CORN WAS STORED IN HIS HOUSE: THEN THE OWNER OF THE CORN SHALL CLAIM HIS CORN BEFORE GOD (ON OATH), AND THE OWNER OF THE HOUSE SHALL PAY ITS OWNER FOR ALL OF THE CORN THAT HE TOOK.

121. IF ANY ONE STORE CORN IN ANOTHER MAN'S HOUSE HE SHALL PAY HIM STORAGE AT THE RATE OF ONE GUR FOR EVERY FIVE KA OF CORN PER YEAR.

129. IF A MAN'S WIFE BE SURPRISED (IN FLAGRANTE DELICTO) WITH ANOTHER MAN, BOTH SHALL BE TIED AND THROWN INTO THE WATER, BUT THE HUSBAND MAY PARDON HIS WIFE AND THE KING HIS SLAVES.

130. IF A MAN VIOLATE THE WIFE (BETROTHED OR CHILD-WIFE) OF ANOTHER MAN, WHO HAS NEVER KNOWN A MAN, AND STILL LIVES IN HER FATHER'S HOUSE, AND SLEEP WITH HER AND BE SURPRISED, THIS MAN SHALL BE PUT TO DEATH, BUT THE WIFE IS BLAMELESS.

132. IF THE "FINGER IS POINTED" AT A MAN'S WIFE ABOUT ANOTHER MAN, BUT SHE IS NOT CAUGHT SLEEPING WITH THE OTHER MAN, SHE SHALL JUMP INTO THE RIVER FOR HER HUSBAND.

136. IF ANYONE LEAVE HIS HOUSE, RUN AWAY, AND THEN HIS WIFE GO TO ANOTHER HOUSE, IF THEN HE RETURN, AND WISHES TO TAKE HIS WIFE BACK: BECAUSE HE FLED FROM HIS HOME AND RAN AWAY, THE WIFE OF THIS RUNAWAY SHALL NOT RETURN TO HER HUSBAND.

137. IF A MAN WISHES TO SEPARATE FROM A WOMAN WHO HAS BORNE HIM CHILDREN, OR FROM HIS WIFE WHO HAS BORNE HIM CHILDREN: THEN HE SHALL GIVE THAT WIFE HER DOWRY, AND A PART OF THE USUFRUCT OF FIELD, GARDEN, AND PROPERTY, SO THAT SHE CAN REAR HER CHILDREN. WHEN SHE HAS BROUGHT UP HER CHILDREN, A PORTION OF ALL THAT IS GIVEN TO THE CHILDREN, EQUAL AS THAT OF ONE SON, SHALL BE GIVEN TO HER. SHE MAY THEN MARRY THE MAN OF HER HEART.

144. IF A MAN TAKE A WIFE AND THIS WOMAN GIVE HER HUSBAND A MAID-SERVANT, AND SHE BEAR HIM CHILDREN, BUT THIS MAN WISHES TO TAKE ANOTHER WIFE, THIS SHALL NOT BE PERMITTED TO HIM; HE SHALL NOT TAKE A SECOND WIFE.

145. IF A MAN TAKE A WIFE, AND SHE BEAR HIM NO CHILDREN, AND HE INTEND TO TAKE ANOTHER WIFE: IF HE TAKE THIS SECOND WIFE, AND BRING HER INTO THE HOUSE, THIS SECOND WIFE SHALL NOT BE ALLOWED EQUALITY WITH HIS WIFE.

146. IF A MAN TAKE A WIFE AND SHE GIVE THIS MAN A MAID-SERVANT AS WIFE AND SHE BEAR HIM CHILDREN, AND THEN THIS MAID ASSUME EQUALITY WITH THE WIFE: BECAUSE SHE HAS BORNE HIM CHILDREN HER MASTER SHALL NOT SELL HER FOR MONEY, BUT HE MAY KEEP HER AS A SLAVE, RECKONING HER AMONG THE MAID-SERVANTS.

175. IF A STATE SLAVE OR THE SLAVE OF A FREED MAN MARRY THE DAUGHTER OF A FREE MAN, AND CHILDREN ARE BORN, THE MASTER OF THE SLAVE SHALL HAVE NO RIGHT TO ENSLAVE THE CHILDREN OF THE FREE.

181. IF A FATHER DEVOTE A TEMPLE-MAID OR TEMPLE-VIRGIN TO GOD AND GIVE HER NO PRESENT: IF THEN THE FATHER DIE, SHE SHALL RECEIVE THE THIRD OF A CHILD'S PORTION FROM THE INHERITANCE OF HER FATHER'S HOUSE, AND ENJOY ITS USUFRUCT SO LONG AS SHE LIVES. HER ESTATE BELONGS TO HER BROTHERS.

192. IF A SON OF A PARAMOUR OR A PROSTITUTE SAY TO HIS ADOPTIVE FATHER OR MOTHER: "YOU ARE NOT MY FATHER, OR MY MOTHER," HIS TONGUE SHALL BE CUT OFF.

195. IF A SON STRIKES HIS FATHER, HIS HANDS SHALL BE HEWN OFF.

196. IF A MAN PUT OUT THE EYE OF ANOTHER MAN, HIS EYE SHALL BE PUT OUT.

197. IF HE BREAKS ANOTHER MAN'S BONE, HIS BONE SHALL BE BROKEN.

198. IF HE PUT OUT THE EYE OF A FREED MAN, OR BREAK THE BONE OF A FREED MAN, HE SHALL PAY ONE GOLD MINA.

199. IF HE PUT OUT THE EYE OF A MAN'S SLAVE, OR BREAK THE BONE OF A MAN'S SLAVE, HE SHALL PAY ONE-HALF OF ITS VALUE.

200. IF A MAN KNOCK OUT THE TEETH OF HIS EQUAL, HIS TEETH SHALL BE KNOCKED OUT.

201. IF HE KNOCK OUT THE TEETH OF A FREED MAN, HE SHALL PAY ONE-THIRD OF A GOLD MINA.

202. IF ANY ONE STRIKE THE BODY OF A MAN HIGHER IN RANK THAN HE, HE SHALL RECEIVE SIXTY BLOWS WITH AN OX-WHIP IN PUBLIC.

203. IF A FREE-BORN MAN STRIKE THE BODY OF ANOTHER FREE-BORN MAN OR EQUAL RANK, HE SHALL PAY ONE GOLD MINA.

205. IF THE SLAVE OF A FREED MAN STRIKE THE BODY OF A FREED MAN, HIS EAR SHALL BE CUT OFF.

206. IF DURING A QUARREL ONE MAN STRIKE ANOTHER AND WOUND HIM, THEN HE SHALL SWEAR, "I DID NOT INJURE HIM WITTINGLY," AND PAY THE PHYSICIANS.

207. IF THE MAN DIE OF HIS WOUND, HE SHALL SWEAR SIMILARLY, AND IF HE (THE DECEASED) WAS A FREE-BORN MAN, HE SHALL PAY HALF A MINA IN MONEY.

209. IF A MAN STRIKE A FREE-BORN WOMAN SO THAT SHE LOSE HER UNBORN CHILD, HE SHALL PAY TEN SHEKELS FOR HER LOSS.

210. IF THE WOMAN DIE, HIS DAUGHTER SHALL BE PUT TO DEATH.

213. IF HE STRIKE THE MAID-SERVANT OF A MAN, AND SHE LOSE HER CHILD, HE SHALL PAY TWO SHEKELS IN MONEY.

214. IF THIS MAID-SERVANT DIE, HE SHALL PAY ONE-THIRD OF A MINA.

A Comparitive Study using *Secret of the Scribe* · 107

215. IF A PHYSICIAN MAKE A LARGE INCISION WITH AN OPERATING KNIFE AND CURE IT, OR IF HE OPEN A TUMOR (OVER THE EYE) WITH AN OPERATING KNIFE, AND SAVES THE EYE, HE SHALL RECEIVE TEN SHEKELS IN MONEY.

216. IF THE PATIENT BE A FREED MAN, HE RECEIVES FIVE SHEKELS.

217. IF HE BE THE SLAVE OF SOMEONE, HIS OWNER SHALL GIVE THE PHYSICIAN TWO SHEKELS.

218. IF A PHYSICIAN MAKE A LARGE INCISION WITH THE OPERATING KNIFE, AND KILL HIM, OR OPEN A TUMOR WITH THE OPERATING KNIFE, AND CUT OUT THE EYE, HIS HANDS SHALL BE CUT OFF.

219. IF A PHYSICIAN MAKE A LARGE INCISION IN THE SLAVE OF A FREED MAN, AND KILL HIM, HE SHALL REPLACE THE SLAVE WITH ANOTHER SLAVE.

220. IF HE HAD OPENED A TUMOR WITH THE OPERATING KNIFE, AND PUT OUT HIS EYE, HE SHALL PAY HALF HIS VALUE.

221. IF A PHYSICIAN HEAL THE BROKEN BONE OR DISEASED SOFT PART OF A MAN, THE PATIENT SHALL PAY THE PHYSICIAN FIVE SHEKELS IN MONEY.

222. IF HE WERE A FREED MAN HE SHALL PAY THREE SHEKELS.

223. IF HE WERE A SLAVE HIS OWNER SHALL PAY THE PHYSICIAN TWO SHEKELS.

228. IF A BUILDER BUILD A HOUSE FOR SOMEONE AND COMPLETE IT, HE SHALL GIVE HIM A FEE OF TWO SHEKELS IN MONEY FOR EACH SAR OF SURFACE.

229 IF A BUILDER BUILD A HOUSE FOR SOMEONE, AND DOES NOT CONSTRUCT IT PROPERLY, AND THE HOUSE WHICH HE BUILT FALL IN AND KILL ITS OWNER, THEN THAT BUILDER SHALL BE PUT TO DEATH.

230. IF IT KILL THE SON OF THE OWNER THE SON OF THAT BUILDER SHALL BE PUT TO DEATH.

231. IF IT KILL A SLAVE OF THE OWNER, THEN HE SHALL PAY SLAVE FOR SLAVE TO THE OWNER OF THE HOUSE.

Just about all of the remaining 50 laws (232-282) established government sanctioned prices Babylonians paid for various services. This included everything from hiring farming animals to having goods shipped up the Euphrates. These laws also included the type of fines levied on merchants or the local "Rent an ox for a day" company if the renter was dissatisfied with the services received.

Discussion Questions:

1. What types of laws did you find contained in this sampling of Hammurabi's Code?

2. What were some common punishments?

3. What laws or punishments surprised you?

4. What were the consequences for a thief?

5. How do you think some of the punishments that were given to doctors who performed an unsuccessful surgery or to a builder who had poor workmanship would affect the medical or building industry? What good could come from such stringent laws? What harm could such laws produce?

6. How were slaves and free men treated under Hammurabi's Code? Was the "well-being" of slaves ever considered?

7. Were slaves ever personally compensated for injuries they incurred? Based on what you know about pagan societies, give a reason for why slaves would not be personally compensated while their masters would be?

8. According to the purposes for Hammurabi's Code covered earlier in this lesson, what kind of evil-doers were "eliminated"?

9. How would having the payment/cost of work set by law affect the worker? In what ways might these laws be good or bad for society?

10. Hammurabi's Code claims to protect the weak. Note some examples where this was done.

11. What laws were given regarding prostitution and witchcraft?

A Comparitive Study using *Secret of the Scribe* · 109

12. Review the list of purposes for Hammurabi's Code. Do you think these laws would have supported these purposes well? Why or why not?

The closest biblical comparisons to Hammurabi's Code are three chapters written by Moses that immediately follow the Ten Commandments. These chapters contain laws like, "if you do this, such and such will be done to you." These laws reflect the practices of the Hebrew justice system, in the same way that the laws of Hammurabi were a reflection of how justice was doled out in Babylonian society. Don't be surprised to find some similarities between these sets of two laws as both were issued to cultures that shared similar concerns ... such as out-of-control farm animals and what to do with valuables without banks and safe deposit boxes. Both cultures were theocracies, meaning they were run by gods/God through human representative(s), typically priests or kings. However, when the culture changed (such as no longer being a society based on farming) or the form of government changed, many of these laws and their consequences were no longer useful to later societies. As a result, Hammurabi's laws were cast aside thousands of years ago and his famous monument is now housed in a museum – a relic from the past. In contrast, the Ten Commandments are still displayed on and in the United States Supreme Court building, a building completed in the 1930s. The Ten Commandments are not external legal rulings; they are laws established by God intended to shape the hearts and minds of all people for all time. These are the laws by which all people were meant to govern themselves. The Ten Commandments framed an Israelite's entire understanding of the purpose and nature of law. They defined man's moral responsibilities in light of his relationship with God and his neighbor. Therefore, in the reading of Mosaic Law outlined below, we must start with the basis of Hebrew life and judicial law – the Ten Commandments and their preamble.

Read aloud Exodus 19:1-6; 20:1-17; and chapters 21- 23:13, and discuss the following questions: (As with Hammurabi's Code, read the questions below before you read the text.)

ISRAEL'S LAW BEGINS WITH THE KNOWLEDGE OF THE HOLY ONE, THE GOD WHO LOVES AND CARES FOR HIS PEOPLE, HIS "TREASURED POSSESSION." IN BEING LIKE HIM AS A HOLY PEOPLE, ISRAEL REPRESENTED HIS LOVE, GOODNESS, JUSTICE AND TRUTH TO ONE ANOTHER AND TO THE WORLD, AND AS SUCH THEY WERE HIS ROYAL PRIESTHOOD.

> **Parent note:** If you have younger students, you may wish to read the scripture passages and omit Exodus 22:19; however, Exodus 22:18-20 prohibit practices that were common features of Canaanite paganism.

110 · Christian Theology & Ancient Polythesism

Discussion Questions:

1. What examples of mercy do you find in Mosaic Law?

2. How are thieves punished?

3. How is sorcery and prostitution treated?

4. Can you note examples of caring for those in need?

5. What reasons did the Israelite have to be compassionate?

6. Give some examples of laws between God and man.

7. Give some examples of laws between people and their neighbors.

8. Give some examples of laws between the people and the land. What ideas do these laws illustrate?

9. Were slaves ever personally compensated for wrongs done against them?

10. In general, what laws caught your attention and why?

11. What were some specific laws that were similar or dealt with the same issues as Hammurabi's law?

12. What differences did you notice between these two sets of laws?

Answer the third question on chart **CC-8**.

Family: One of the similarities that you probably noted was that both the laws of Hammurabi and Moses protected and elevated the family relationship. In Babylon and in Israel the family was the basis of society. As such, it required protection under the law. Those things that harmed the family, such as adultery, deserved punishment under the law. In both sets of laws, adultery was punishable by death, along with other immoral relationships that wounded the family. There is more "family law" in Hammurabi's Code than almost any other type of law. Even pagans who were far from God's truth still retained the knowledge of the importance of the husband and wife relationship – truth established by God in the Garden of Eden. So while many of the Babylonian stories involving their gods and goddesses included gross immorality, the requirement for faithfulness between husband and wife was chiseled into stone and erected in the temple courtyard of their pagan gods.

A Comparitive Study using *Secret of the Scribe* · **111**

Murderers and Thieves: In both sets of laws you probably noticed that if one person murders another person, the penalty is death. We might ask why murder is such a bad thing from the perspective of both a pagan and a biblical worldview. From a pagan worldview, the murderer has killed a slave of the gods and has consequently robbed the gods of their property. Under Hammurabi's Code, slaves were viewed as nothing more than property. From a biblical worldview, murder is a crime that justifies death because the criminal has destroyed an image bearer of God, one who was made to represent and relate to God.

Now think about the punishments prescribed for theft. Under Hammurabi's Code, thieves were put to death. Under Mosaic Law, those who stole property were required to make restitution, repaying stolen goods in excess of their value. Why the difference in these punishments? Under Hammurabi, the belief was that thieves committed no lesser crime than murderers because both crimes deprived the "owner" (be they gods or men) of his or her property. Without a higher value placed on human life, the law had virtually nothing more important to deal with than property. Thus in Hammurabi's Code even the prices one paid to acquire, improve, or store property were all tightly controlled and priced by the government. Property is the overarching concern of Babylonian law. Under Mosaic Law property always has less value than people, and thus theft is viewed as a lesser crime than murder. People, both free and slave, have a far greater value because their value to God is not based on the service they render Him (God needs nothing from people).[57] Human value is based on man's unique relationship to God.

Mosaic Law has nothing like the government price controls for goods and services that regulated Babylonian society. The purpose of Mosaic Law was not to control things; it was given to enable people to control themselves – to enable them to act in a way that was consistent with their Maker. This was one of the central purposes of the Ten Commandments. Thus, we should not be surprised that there is nothing similar to the Ten Commandments in Hammurabi's Code.

---

57 Acts 17:25

In general, when a society lacks both a high view of God and a high view of man, laws governing proper human behavior and relationships become less important, and the laws governing property and services become more important.[58] Israel had both a high view of God and man; Babylon had neither.

Discussion Questions:

1. In every culture there remains some knowledge of the truth. Christian scholars call this "common grace". What evidence in Babylonian culture showed that they still retained some knowledge of the truth? It is also possible for a culture to disregard the truth they have been given. What examples could be sited from our culture showing that we operate by less of the truth, when it comes to marriage, than the Babylonians did?

2. In your own words, explain why under a biblical worldview a thief should be punished differently than a murderer.

3. In Mosaic Law, provisions were made for "cities of refuge." What was the purpose of these cities and who was to flee there? What does this provision say even about the value of the life of a murderer and the wisdom in Mosaic Law about the importance of intentions behind a crime?

4. What gives human relationships and behavior value or importance? Put simply, why does it matter how I behave or how I treat others? What determines the standards for human behavior and relationships?

5. There is a common saying, "people are more important than things". What is behind this statement or why is it true?

6. What have governments forgotten when legislating "goods and services" becomes more important than laws about human behavior and relationships?

---

58 PARENT NOTE: MANY PAGES COULD BE WRITTEN FROM THIS OBSERVATION, BUT AS THIS IS NOT A COURSE ON GOVERNMENT, I HAVE RESISTED THE TEMPTATION TO EXPOUND HERE. HOWEVER, THIS DIFFERENCE BETWEEN HAMMURABI'S CODE AND MOSAIC LAW IS AN IMPORTANT POINT TO ADD IN YOUR REGULAR CONVERSATIONS ABOUT GOVERNMENT PROMPTED BY THE NEWS OF THE DAY, AND IN HIGH SCHOOL COURSES YOUR CHILD WILL TAKE ON THE SUBJECT.

> Answer the fourth question on chart **CC-8** dealing with a comparison of marriage, murderers and thieves.

Justice and Slavery: One of the most common points of comparison between Hammurabi's Code and Mosaic Law is the legal expression "an eye for an eye and a tooth for a tooth". While it may sound harsh to our ears, this standard established a norm whereby the punishment fit the crime. The existence of this standard actually demonstrated the sophistication of the justice systems of both cultures. "An eye for an eye" required that justice be worked out through the courts rather than through family feuds or personal revenge (which escalated violence). However, the remarkable contrast between the courts of Babylon and Israel was that in Israel this standard was applied to all people living in the land whether free or slave, native born or foreigner. In Israel, all people before God were created equal and were entitled to justice from the courts. Deuteronomy 1:16-17 says:

> *"And I charged your judges at that time, saying, Hear the cases between your brethren, and judge righteously between every man and his brother, and the stranger that is with him. Ye shall not respect persons in judgment;nbut ye shall hear the small as well as the great; ye shall not be afraid of the face of man; for the judgment is God's."*

"Not to respect persons in judgment" conveys the same idea as "all people are equal before the law". The principle behind "an eye for an eye" applied in the courts of Israel no matter who stood before the judges. In Babylon, the "punishment fit the crime" only when the conflict was between people who were viewed as equals. Babylonian society was divided into several different classes. There were upper and lower classes of people who were free-born, there were former slaves who had purchased their freedom or paid off their debt, and there were slaves. Re-reading a few of Hammurabi's laws will enable you to see this important distinction in Babylonian society: "If a man knocks out the teeth *of his equal*, his teeth shall be knocked out" (law 200). "If he knocked out the teeth of a freed man (former slave), he shall pay one-third a gold mina" (law 201). "If he put out the eye of a man's slave, or break the bone of a man's slave, he shall pay one-half its value." To whom? The slave's owner (law 199). For more examples of these distinctions, you may want to re-read laws 195-214. In Babylon, a criminal was punished according to the value society placed on the victim. A Babylonian slave was never personally compensated for wrong doing against him; he was the master's property, and if damaged the master would be compensated. While all judgments were rendered by the court, who you were in Babylonian society dramatically impacted the type of "justice" you received.

In Israel there were no classes of people who were afforded special privileges under the law because Israel's God has no favorites.[59] Under Mosaic Law, not only were judges called to provide justice to all, but every Israelite was called to a standard even higher than "an eye for an eye."

You shall not take vengeance or bear a grudge against the sons of your own people, but you shall love your neighbor as yourself: I am the LORD. You shall treat the stranger who sojourns with you as the native among you, and you shall love him as yourself, for you were strangers in the land of Egypt: I am the LORD your God. Leviticus 19:18,34 (ESV)

Taking revenge in Israel was against the Law, not just because justice was metered out by the courts, but because the Israelite was called to love his neighbor; even one who had offended him. Undergirding all of Mosaic Law was love – the call to love God and love others because God loves His creation. This was the basis for Hebrew relationships and Hebrew law. In contrast, Babylonian relationships were based on power, or the value a given person had because of his or her social class. As a result, justice was something only the powerful deserved to receive. In societies without belief in a loving God who values all His creation, "equal justice" is rare indeed.

Discussion Questions:

1. Both Hammurabi and Moses recorded laws that called for "an eye for an eye, and a tooth for a tooth." What positive things do these laws tell about the justice system of both cultures?

2. What were some of the differences between how these laws were applied in each culture?

3. What do these differences tell you about the quality of Mosaic Law?

So Mosaic Law really did provide justice for all, but wait – Israel had slaves too. How could God's people have slaves? Isn't slavery wrong? How can we suggest that Israel had a high standard of social justice when slavery was practiced within her borders and recognized by her law? This discussion requires that we define what we mean by the word slavery. When we use the word slavery we think of innocent Africans smuggled from their homeland to slave on cotton plantations where the owners grew rich off of their labors. This kind of slavery which played such an enormous role in the Civil War (or "War of the States") was terribly wrong. The denial of civil rights to African Americans after the Civil War was also wrong.

---

59 GALATIANS 2:6

A Comparitive Study using *Secret of the Scribe* · 115

However, the circumstances behind slavery in ancient Israel were much different than the slavery in America during the 1700s and 1800s. The Bible tells us of three types of slavery that existed in Israel: indentured servants, bond slaves and slaves of war. Indentured servants were people who had gotten into debt and had no way to pay off their creditors, so they sold themselves and/or their family members into servitude for money. As indentured servants, they served their masters for six years and then were set free having paid off their debt. There were many indentured servants in early America, whose servitude had nothing to do with the Civil War. The second kind of Hebrew slave may have initially sold himself into slavery, but when his six years were concluded, he chose to serve his master for life as a bond slave. However, to ensure that this was a free choice of the servant, the event was marked by a public ceremony and the involvement of the courts.[60] The last form of slavery involved prisoners of war.[61] Such was the case of the Gibeonites.[62] They were residents of Canaan who had tricked Israel into signing a treaty with them by portraying themselves as a people who lived in a far away land. As they had been marked for total destruction by God, their deceit saved their lives, but they were made slaves who carried water and chopped wood for the house of God.

It is true that in Israel slaves were also viewed as the property of their master[63] (for indeed most were in servitude because of debt); however, unlike Babylon, slaves were given protection as persons under the Law and compensated for serious wrongs carried out against them. If a slave had his eye put out or his teeth knocked out, he was set free.[64] Being given freedom for a slave would have been a better compensation then to have the eye of the wrong doer put out. If a slave was seriously wounded or killed by his master, the master would be tried by the courts.[65] If a slave ran away from his master, Israelite law provided refuge for the slave in the home to which he fled; it was assumed that the wrong doing was on the part of the master, and the slave was not forced to return.[66] In contrast, harboring a Babylonian slave was punishable by death (law 16). Slavery existed in all ancient cultures and in American and European history as well, but in Israel slaves were recognized as persons under the Law which granted them protection and compensation, and slaves like every other person in Israel were given a Sabbath rest.[67]

---

60 Exodus 21:2-11; Jeremiah 34:14
61 Numbers 31:25-47; I Kings 9:21
62 Joshua 9:23
63 Exodus 21:32
64 Exodus 21:26,27
65 Exodus 21:20,21
66 Deuteronomy 23:15,16
67 Exodus 23:12

$150 REWARD.

RANAWAY from the subscriber, on the night of Monday the 11th July, a negro man named

TOM,

about 30 years of age, 5 feet 6 or 7 inches high; of dark color; heavy in the chest; several of his jaw teeth out; and upon his body are several old marks of the whip, one of them straight down the back. He took with him a quantity of clothing, and several hats.

A reward of $150 will be paid for his apprehension and security, if taken out of the State of Kentucky; $100 if taken in any county bordering on the Ohio river; $50 if taken in any of the interior counties except Fayette; or $20 if taken in the latter county.

july 12-84-tf   B. L. BOSTON.

A POSTER LIKE THIS WOULD NEVER BE HUNG IN ISRAEL. WHY?

There is one final point of comparison regarding slaves. When you read the chapters in Exodus earlier, you may have noticed that daughters who were sold by their fathers as servants were not set free after six years of service. This is because a young female servant would also become the wife of the master or the master's son. The marriage relationship was the factor that required her to remain in the household to which she was sold. Only divorce would separate her from her master/husband. While being sold as a servant-wife would have been an unhappy situation for a young woman in Israel, Hebrew maidens were never "devoted" by their fathers to temple prostitution as they were in Babylon (law 181). So although poverty sometimes brought servitude, it did not bring the disgrace of prostitution. In Israel, laws for servant-wives ensured that they would be provided for and not separated from their children.

Discussion Questions:

1. Name some differences between the institution of slavery in Babylon and in Israel.

2. In both Babylon and Israel slaves were viewed as property, but slaves in Israel were also viewed as _____ who deserved _____ _____ under the Law. Why weren't slaves in Babylonian society ever given protection or compensation under Hammurabi's Code?

3. If you have learned about slavery in America, how were slaves in this country treated differently from slaves in Israel? What human rights were Israelite slaves given that African American slaves never received?

4. What might you say to a person who claimed that the Bible supports slavery?

Answer the fifth question of comparison on chart **CC-8**.

Parents and Children: Now let's compare Hammurabi's Code and Mosaic Law in regard to the rebellious child. Under Hammurabi's Code, if a son struck his father his hands were cut off (law 195). This was a terrible punishment indeed. But consider Mosaic Law; if a child attacked his father or mother he was put to death (Exodus 21:15). Both issue severe punishments for the same type of behavior; however, in contrast to thieves and murderers, it is the Mosaic Law that issues the more severe punishment of death. More surprising still is the law that follows just two verses later: "anyone who curses his father or mother must be put to death"[68] Wow! The punishment for cursing one's parent seems horribly excessive. Why would Mosaic Law contain such a shocking punishment? That's a question for your Jacob Journal! Rather than pausing now, we are going to jump into this discussion and look at some verses that may challenge our ideas of the goodness and justice of God and the significance of sin. If, after the discussion you still have questions, add them to your Jacob Journal. Below is a passage from Deuteronomy 21:18-21:

> "If a man has a stubborn and rebellious son who will not obey the voice of his father or the voice of his mother, and, though they discipline him, will not listen to them, then his father and his mother shall take hold of him and bring him out to the elders of his city at the gate of the place where he lives, and they shall say to the elders of his city, 'This our son is stubborn and rebellious; he will not obey our voice; he is a glutton and a drunkard.' Then all the men of the city shall stone him to death with stones. So you shall purge the evil from your midst, and all Israel shall hear, and fear." (ESV)

Rebellious youths, who would not heed the repeated instruction of their parents, snubbing their authority and stubbornly choosing to go their own way were put to death under Mosaic Law. It's a lucky thing for many twenty-first century children that they do not live under the laws of ancient Israel's theocracy! While these laws do not apply to us in our present-day American society, we should ponder why God issued such severe punishments in Israel's law. The first clue to this puzzle is provided in the last sentence of the scripture above: "So you shall purge

---

68 EXODUS 21:17

118 · Christian Theology & Ancient Polytheism

the evil from your midst, and all Israel shall hear, and fear." This idea is repeated throughout the books of the Law. When a person was harshly punished publically, it was a powerful deterrent for other people not to sin. Alternately, unpunished sin would have produced more sin. So what was one of the purposes of Mosaic Law? To deter the Israelite people from sinning. What was one of the most effective deterrents to sinning? The fear of punishment. What happened in the hearts of the Israelite people as a result? They feared punishment to such an extent that the need to carry it out was a very rare event. In fact, in the whole of scripture we find only one potential example of this law being enacted.[69]

Okay, you're probably thinking, "rare" is good. Teaching people to fear punishment and turn from sin is also good, but still – "stoning a rebellious son?" Does the punishment really fit the crime? Let's turn back to the Ten Commandments. As you will recall these laws start out with four commandments that deal expressly with a person's relationship with God: 1) God is to have first place above all else, 2) worshipping idols of any kind is forbidden, 3) God's name is never to be misused, and 4) the Sabbath is set aside as a day holy unto the Lord. Next, the Law turns to deal with man's relationship with his neighbor. Laws six through ten are listed as follows: do not murder, do not commit adultery, do not steal, do not tell falsehoods about your neighbor, and do not covet your neighbor's relationships or things. It is pretty apparent that the list of these laws is written in order of importance. While the breaking of any of these laws is sin, it is a greater sin to murder your neighbor than it is to crave the things he or she has.

You may have noticed that law number five was skipped in the list above. This fifth law actually transitions from the laws dealing with man's relationship with God to man's relationship with his neighbor: "Honor thy father and thy mother: that thy days may be long upon the land which the Lord thy God giveth thee." This is quite a contrast to what happened in Israel when children grossly dishonored their parents. Think about it: live long in the land, or be put to death. Hmmm ... it appears every Hebrew child had a choice to make; they could choose to honor their parents which brought life, or they could choose to dishonor their parents which brought death. Does this have a familiar ring? Like the choice God gave Adam and Eve in the Garden, Moses held out two choices to God's people: to obey God and live in the land or to disobey God and face exile and death. "Choose life or choose death" is one of the most dominant themes in the writings of Moses. To worship and obey God was life; to practice idolatry and disobey was death.

If the importance of obedience is the difference between life and death, we should contemplate when a person first learns to obey – as a child, from their father and mother. Thus honoring father and mother is actually placed in the scripture before the command "do not to murder". A murderer destroys a representative of

---

69 LEVITICUS 24:10-16

A Comparitive Study using *Secret of the Scribe* · 119

God. A child rebelling against his parent is rebelling against the representative that God has placed in his or her life. The parental authority figures represent God. So, rebellion against parents is rebellion against God. Therefore, the fifth commandment is the bridge between the first half of The Ten Commandments dealing with our relationship with God and the second half dealing with our relationship to others – through the fifth commandment the child is learning how to properly relate to both God and man.

From a biblical perspective, I hope you are beginning to see why honoring your parents brings life while rebellion leads to death. Questions may still linger in your mind about why the rebellious Israelite child received the death penalty when his behavior wasn't seemingly hurting anybody else. This line of questioning reveals what we do not fully comprehend about the nature of sin. Sin can be compared to a cancer cell. Cancer cells are characterized by uncontrolled growth of unhealthy cells. These cells grow in ways contrary to the cells' instructions and can attack and destroy the healthy tissues. If these mutant cells are not cut out or killed they can eventually destroy the entire human being. In the same way, the sin of rebellion is refusing to be controlled by the instructions given for successful living. Rebellion, like cancer, spreads and can infect those around it until it eventually corrupts an entire community.

Stop and think about our culture: teenage rebellion is practically viewed as a rite of passage, something every young person is entitled to do. Now overlay this attitude with the reality that far less than half of today's youth who profess to be Christians will end up holding on to their faith ten years from now.[70] Is it any wonder why? Rebellion is the path many kids choose in an effort to find themselves, but tragically they only end up finding "self" and leaving God behind. Rebellion corrodes our faith in God and in the Bible; faith in God is always linked with obedience. Please take heed: we cannot deliberately choose a path of disobedience and believe that our faith will be intact at the journey's end.

Discussion Questions:

1. How is the fifth commandment like a bridge that links the first set of commandments about our relationship with God to the second set of commandments about our relationship to people?

2. How is rebellion like cancer?

---

70 ADD REF FOR CHRISTIAN YOUTH LEAVING THE CHURCH

3. Are there any historians in your home who could give some examples from history about how rebellion of American youths has negatively impacted American culture?

4. The Bible tells a terrible story about a gang of youths mocking and ridiculing God's representative, Elijah.[71] He called down curses upon them and two bears advanced and mauled the young men. We do not know how many died. But it was clear that in the town where the youths came from rebellion was not being dealt with and the consequences for forty-two children were horrendous. Why would God allow Elijah to deal so severely with these rebellious boys? What kind of reactions do you think the town's people had? What kind of reactions do you have?

The Bible is a book of unfolding revelation; this means that certain truths must first be seen and understood before subsequent or deeper truths can be revealed. Through Mosaic Law, people first had to learn what sin is through its contrast to the character of God, as seen in the standard of His righteousness reflected in the Law. People had to learn that in striving to live according to God's standard they would experience life and blessing. Alternately, forsaking God's standard would bring curses and death. People also had to learn that the choices for life or death were not a private matter. After all, people do not float around in self-contained bubbles. When we bump into each other we don't bounce off; we can knock each other down. We can also help each other up. The Old Testament contains story after story in which the actions of one person or several people seriously impacted those around them. These stories among other things are here to teach us that sin is not a private matter; even secret hidden sins can affect the community around us. This idea matters immensely because God made man to live in community. Remember, the first thing in the creation account that was not good was "man being alone." We were not made to be great individuals; we were

---

71 II KINGS 2:23-25

made to be members of a great community of image bearers who represent God collectively everywhere we go. In the New Testament this community is called the Body of Christ. In the Old Testament this community was the nation of Israel and the goal of the Law was to make them a nation of priests, a holy people dedicated to God. Each and every person had to take seriously the job of dealing with sin. Everyone had to learn that innocent people suffer, even die, because of the sins of others. God's people must learn to hate sin.

One dramatic Old Testament story illustrating this point took place shortly after Israel had entered the Promise Land and began its conquest under Joshua.

Read aloud and discuss Joshua 7:1-26

1. The first verse begins by saying "... the Israelites acted unfaithfully in regard to the devoted things..." and in verse 11, "Israel has sinned ... they have been made liable to destruction." Wait a minute – this was not about Israel's sin but about Achan's. Why does God hold the entire nation responsible?

2. Was the purpose of the Law to develop some holy individuals or a holy people, a holy community where the collective body represents God? Do the sins of an individual family member reflect upon or impact the entire family? Do the sins of a church leader reflect upon or impact the entire church? Can the negative actions of a soldier reflect on his unit or even the whole military?

3. What were some of the consequences of Achan's sin for those other than Achan? Why do you think God allowed innocent people to suffer and held an entire nation responsible for one man's sin?

4. If you understood that innocent people were going to suffer because you refused to obey God, how do you think this would affect the choices you make?

5. What does this story teach us about the holiness of God and his expectations for the people made in His image?

The story of Achan's sin is not a "feel good" story. It is a dreadful story that called Israel and calls us to fear the holiness of God. God is not a nice old man who lives upstairs; He is the awesome righteous creator of the universe to whom all mankind must give an account. We must recognize that our sin dishonors both God and the community to which we belong. Like Israel, we must learn that sin for God's chosen people is a terrible choice with terrible consequences, sometimes even for innocent people. Indeed, the innocent life of our Savior was sacrificed on account of other's sin.

Taking God's holiness seriously means taking our own holiness seriously. As we are instructed in 1 Peter 1:14-16 (ASV) "as children of obedience, not fashioning yourselves *according to your former lusts in the time of your ignorance: but like as he who called you is holy, be ye also holy in manner of living; because it is written, Ye shall be holy, for I am holy."* If you are feeling a bit overwhelmed by all of this, and thinking things like "How can I be holy; I have trouble obeying my parents in the simplest things," keep reading. Before these lessons on the Law draw to a close you will find much as a believer in Christ to give you courage and confidence. It was Paul who said, *"Being confident of this very thing, that he which hath begun a good work in you will perform it until the day of Jesus Christ."*[72] We will address the reason for Paul's confidence in the following lesson.

Now let's wrap up our discussion on why the judicial Law of Moses decreed the death penalty to rebellious youths. As we already know, the Ten Commandments prohibit idolatry, immorality and murder, and by calling a child to honor his parents, they also prohibit rebellion. In the judicial rulings of Exodus 21-23, all of these sins are punishable by death. In the twelfth lesson in this guide, we looked at where idolatry – the worship of false gods – leads. We saw that idolatry always leads to three terrible sins: gross immorality, child sacrifice, and witchcraft. The Ten Commandments if followed enable a person to steer clear of all of these sins. To obey the first commandment to have "no other gods before the Lord" immediately calls us to shun all idolatry. To obey the sixth command "not to murder" would mandate that child sacrifice is never permissible. To obey the seventh commandment against adultery would imply that all immorality is unacceptable for God's chosen people. Interestingly, it appears that the only thing that the Ten Commandments do not directly or indirectly address is the sin of witchcraft, though it is a logical outcome of idolatry. You will recall that in worshipping false gods, gods who are obsessed with gaining and maintaining power, people figure out that they can steal some of this power for themselves through the cultic practices of witchcraft. Witchcraft is about people stealing supernatural demonic power, which in the legal rulings of the Law is clearly condemned and punished by death. In the following story, you will see that rebellion, which is also punishable by death, shares some startling resemblances to witchcraft.

---

72 Philippians 1:6

A story from the life of King Saul and the prophet Samuel provides more insight into what rebellion actually is. In lesson eight you read the sad story of King Saul being rejected by God as king over Israel because he did not obey the word of the Lord. In the conquest of the Amalekites, Saul was instructed by the Lord to destroy all those living there, including all the livestock. However, instead of obeying the Lord, Saul spared the best of what the Amalekites had, including sheep and cattle. When confronted by Samuel, he said these were sacrifices for the Lord. To this, Samuel replied:

> *"to obey is better than sacrifice, and to hearken (to listen) than the fat of rams. For rebellion is as the sin of witchcraft, and stubbornness is as iniquity and idolatry." I Samuel 15:22b, 23a (KJV)*

Saul had disobeyed the instructions God had given him through Samuel, and in doing so he had rejected God's authority. Saul's disobedience was called rebellion and his rebellion was equated with witchcraft and idolatry. What Saul took from the Amalekites were the symbols of a conqueror: the spoils of war and the defeated king. These symbols gave him power and prestige. Saul had stolen power for himself by stealing things that belonged only to the Lord. Saul's disobedience was rebellion, and rebellion, like witchcraft, is man's attempt to steal that which belongs to the supernatural.

Discussion Question:

1. For a Christian young person living after Christ, who fulfilled the law, why is obedience necessary in your walk with Christ?

2. How does rebellion against parents affect the life of a Christian?

3. What kind of power or authority do you think kids are trying to obtain through rebellion?

4. Do you think that Christian young people are more likely to view their sins as a private matter strictly between them, and God or do they recognize that individual sin can infect and inflict those around us?

5. Has this discussion about sin and rebellion affected your understanding about the significance of sin in general or rebellion in particular?

In reflecting on the differences between Babylonian and Mosaic Law, we must conclude that rebellion would not be viewed as a lesser crime in Babylon because their laws were not based on man's relationship with God. It is the double impact of simultaneously disrespecting both God and man that called forth the severest punishment in Israel. Given that the overarching purpose of the Mosaic Law was to cultivate a royal priesthood, a people who would represent God to the world, sin in their lives had to be curtailed. Punishment, even harsh punishment was metered out in Mosaic Law because the consequence for the nation of Israel to turn their back on the Law of God was exile and ultimately death. The law regarding rebellious sons could be viewed as a severe mercy. While it may have led to the death of some young men in Israel, all of Israel's laws were intended to save the community by calling them to life through obeying God.

Let's wrap this lesson up by expanding on an earlier thought – sin dishonors God. Think about it. As we learned in the story of Noah, our sins have an impact on God. Down through the centuries, nonbelievers have pointed at the gross sins of so-called Christians as evidence for why the idea of God is unbelievable. Knowing the disdain some would bring on God's name, He, nevertheless, chose to link His identity with ours for the purpose of making Himself known. We have been given a sacred trust with the God of the universe. As such, we cannot view issues of sin in our lives with little concern because Christ took care of our penalty on the cross; we must engage in the battle against sin for the honor of our great God and Savior, Jesus Christ.

Discussion Questions:

1. Why should a Christian, whose sins have been forgiven on the cross, be concerned about areas of sin in his or her life?

2. How does a child honor God? How does any Christian honor God?

3. What are some of the things God has given to the believer to enable him or her to have victory over sin?

> Go to chart **CC-8** and briefly answer the sixth question about how both laws handle the rebellious child.

A Comparitive Study using *Secret of the Scribe* · 125

LESSON XV

Love – the Fulfillment of the Law

GOD GIVES TO MAN, WHILE NEEDING NOTHING FROM HIM. MAN RECEIVES FROM GOD AND GIVES TO OTHERS, ESPECIALLY TO THOSE WHO CAN GIVE NOTHING BACK.

The previous lesson emphasized that sin is not a private matter. It adversely affects and infects others and sometimes a whole community. In this lesson we will look at the opposite of sin – love. We will discover that real love is not a private matter either. It is not just shared between God and us. Our love for God, if genuine, will always spill over into the lives of others. The first part of this lesson gives us three important questions to tackle. How does God love us? How do we love God? How do we love others?

We'll start with the easy one: how does God love us? For the sake of conversation we could say that God expresses His love to us in two ways: His guidelines and His gifts, both are different forms of God's provision for us. God's guidelines express his character and define the path that leads us to experience life in him. God's gifts include all the things he has given us that enable us to experience the life provided through His guidelines. In the beginning, His guidelines included: God's definition of man's purpose and meaning as "made in His image," and His instruction "do not eat of the Tree of the Knowledge of Good and Evil". His gifts were the Garden and the Tree of the Life. Adam and Eve were to obey God's guidelines and enjoy and share God's gifts with each other. God's guidelines for Israel were given through the Torah. This included man's meaning and purpose to represent God and the specific instructions given in the Law. God's gifts were the Promised Land and a long blessed life.

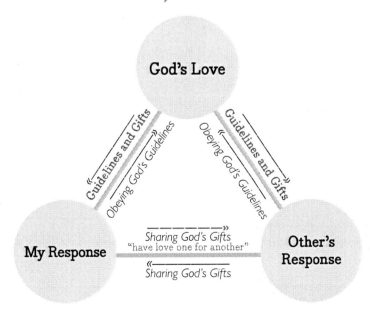

As we progress through this lesson we will examine Gods' guidelines and gifts for the church. For now let's look at how people love God. People respond to God's love in two ways: by obeying His guidelines and enjoying and sharing His gifts with others. Loving others is imitating Christ's gift of love for us. Look carefully at the diagram above. You might ask: why isn't there an arrow pointing to loving God. Obeying God's guidelines and loving others is how we love God. It is good to tell God we love Him, but obeying Him and sharing His love with others are the actions that give meaning to our words.

126 · Christian Theology & Ancient Polythesism

Discussion Questions:

1. What were God's guidelines to Israel, both their purpose and their instructions? What contained both?

2. What were God's gifts to Israel?

3. How were Adam and Eve, Israel and the Church to respond to God's guidelines?

4. How were all to respond to God's gifts?

5. Eve was called to share eternal life with Adam; what did she share instead?

We have taken the diagram, "Love God, Love Others," and turned it into a flower. The flower's center represents God's love of gifts and guidelines. Growing out of God's love are the petals that represent our response to God. The outgrowth of God's love is never just a single petal. His love always creates community – a family, a nation, or a church. The flower represents one of those communities in which we learn to experience and express the life and love of God. Together the community strives to represent both to the world. God's love for me and my love for God is expressed through loving others. This is because the Father's love for the Son and the Son's love for the Father were made manifest through Christ laying down His life for us.[73] Israel also received God's love through His guidelines and gifts long before God's ultimate gift of love was given. These earlier expressions of His love were all vital preparations for the "flower" of the church to bloom.

So, you may be thinking that if this lesson is about love then we must have changed subjects. Mosaic Law defines sin, not love. That's exactly what the Pharisees thought. Theirs was a serious mistake. Their lives were unfortunate examples of what it looks like to pursue obedience without love. To strive to obey God without striving to love others makes us what Paul called "a noisy gong". The modern equivalent of a noisy gong might be one of those blaster horns that people like to blow at sporting events. Everybody around notices the noise, but nobody has any desire to get close to the person making it. That's sort of how the Pharisees were in relation to others. Everybody noticed them and their show of their holy outward behavior, but they were insufferable. Who would want to get close

---

73 John 17:23-26

A Comparitive Study using *Secret of the Scribe* · 127

to people like that? Love has quite the opposite effect – people are attracted to and drawn in by love.

The Law both curtailed sin and cultivated love. Because the Pharisees of Jesus' day missed this second action, they got hung up creating all sorts of extra rules so they could make sure none of Moses' Laws were disobeyed. By focusing all their attention on not sinning they completely missed the "weightier" matters of the Law. The most powerful force behind the Law is love. The guidelines given to Israel were provided within the context of a relationship with God. The Ten Commandments begin, "I am the Lord your God, who brought you out of Egypt." (emphasis added). Out of love, God rescued them from slavery in Egypt and now the Law was being given to rescue them from the slavery of idolatry. The Law was His provision to keep the Israelites from being enslaved again. As such, the Law was also a gift of freedom. Missing the point again, the Pharisees created their own form of slavery. It's no wonder that they also failed to see the ultimate deliverance God would provide through Jesus Christ. Though the Pharisees were students of the Law, they were blind to its most fundamental principle of love.

By the time the Jews reached the first century A.D. Jewish scholars had been studying Torah for hundreds of years and debating about which were the greater and lesser requirements of the Law. When asked by an expert in the Law, Christ summarized and prioritized the Law this way:

"Master, which is the greatest commandment in the law? Jesus said unto him, Thou shalt love the Lord thy God with all thy heart, and with all thy soul, and with all thy mind. This is the first and great commandment. And the second is like unto it, Thou shalt love thy neighbour as thyself. On these two commandments hang all the law and the prophets."[74]

Christ reduced Ten great Commandments into two principles – love God, and love your neighbor – the two principles upon which all the Law and prophets were based. How can that be? If we separated all of the laws into fortune cookie strips they could be sorted into two categories, "how I relate to God" and "how I relate to my neighbor". In both of these relationships our number one obligation is love. Being loved becomes the deepest motivator by which God enables his people to obey Him. God's unmerited love enables me to love other unworthy sinners like myself.

---

[74] Matthew 22:36-40 (KJV)

In Israel a popular rabbinic teaching of the day understood the Law's requirement to "love thy neighbor", but neighbors and enemies were seen as two very different groups of people. All those laws regarding neighbors simply did not apply to enemies. It was this false teaching that Jesus confronted when he said,

> *"You have heard that it was said, 'You shall love your neighbor and hate your enemy.' But I say to you, love your enemies, bless those who curse you, do good to those who hate you, and pray for those who spitefully use you and persecute you, that you may be sons of your Father in heaven"*[75]

It was the same false teaching that allowed a Jew to hate his enemy that prompted the question, "Who is my neighbor?" In reply, Christ told the well known story of the "Good Samaritan". Perhaps not quite as well known is just who the Samaritans were. In short, they were enemies of the Jews. They were hated both because they were half breeds (a mixture of Jewish and pagan ancestry) and because they had betrayed the Jewish exiles who had returned under Cyrus to rebuild Jerusalem. No one was more despised by the Jew than the Samaritan. Thus the Samaritan was the very one Christ defined as the Jews' neighbor.

Discussion Questions:

1. Per Christ's definition of neighbor, who are your neighbors? Name the person or the types of persons that are most difficult for you to love and why this is.

   What are some specific responsibilities Christ gives us towards our enemies?[76]

2. Why do you think God's Word gives us instructions like this?

3. How does the fact that I am made in the image of God to be His representative impact this discussion about enemies?

4. Are our enemies made in the image of God? Think about the quote, "In as much as you have done it unto the least of these my brethren you have done it unto me." Who am I loving when I love my enemies?

---

75 MATTHEW 5:43-45
76 BEYOND THE MATTHEW 5 QUOTE ABOVE SEE ALSO MATTHEW 5:14,15; 7:12

A Comparitive Study using *Secret of the Scribe* · 129

5. Why is giving to those who give us nothing back, or even curses in return, the highest form of love?

6. Have you ever done any of these things Christ commands us to do for those who are difficult to love? If so, what happened?

The second great commandment really is like the first, because it is the natural result of obeying and imitating God. Loving our neighbor is the visible picture of God loving us, thus it is one of the evidences that the love of God really is present in our lives. "... *he who does not love his brother whom he has seen cannot love God whom he has not seen.*"[77] The objection might be raised, "But you don't know 'my neighbor!' You have no idea how unlovable he is!" Perhaps your neighbor is your difficult sister or brother or a bully who lives down the street, or someone who has hurt you in a far more significant way. Even in these cases, while God cares deeply about your pain, He does not allow you to use it as an excuse to disobey Him. When dealing with these very difficult issues in our lives we must look to our example, Jesus Christ. Remember it was His neighbors who cast Jesus out of His home town by trying to throw him off a cliff.[78] It was His "neighbors" who tried to stone Him for claiming to be God.[79] It was His "neighbors" in the city of Jerusalem who cried, "Crucify Him, Crucify Him!"[80] Yet, these were the very people he mourned over as he overlooked Jerusalem. He longed to gather them under his wings as a protective mother would cover her chicks, but they had rejected His provision. Jesus knew the price His neighbors would pay because of His rejection and he grieved over their destruction.[81] Even in the darkness of their rejection, he felt no hate; only a sad longing for His lost children.

As God's children, Christians have no freedom to hate. We are debtors to His love. This debt is worked out as we spread the love of Christ to others who are also undeserving. Paul summarized the teaching of Moses and of Christ this way:

"Owe no man anything, save to love one another: for he that loveth his neighbor hath fulfilled the law. For this, Thou shalt not commit adultery, Thou shalt not kill, Thou shalt not steal, Thou shalt not covet, and if there be any other commandment, it is summed up in this word, namely, Thou shalt love thy neighbor as thyself. Love worketh no ill to his neighbor: love therefore is the fulfilment of the law."[82]

---

77 I JOHN 4:20
78 LUKE 4:16-30
79 JOHN 10:39-42
80 JOHN 8:31-59;10:31-39
81 THE FALL OF JERUSALEM IN A.D. 70
82 ROMANS 13:8-10

Discussion Questions:

1. Christ said that he did not come to abolish the Law but to fulfill it.[83] How did Christ fulfill the Law?

2. If Christ fulfilled the Law what obligation do we have to the Law?

3. What does the verse above say that we owe?

So you might conclude from what we have covered that the Pharisees made the Law all about sin or how to avoid it and Christ made the law all about love? That's not exactly right either. In contrast to the Pharisees, Christ opened people's eyes to its deeper meaning. With the foundation of love laid, Christ began His teaching his disciples where the Tenth Commandment left off – "Do not covet." Coveting is not an sinful action, it is a sinful desire of the heart. The Law, as an external standard written on tablets of stone, primarily addressed outward actions. Yet outward actions are a manifestation of inward thoughts, feelings and intentions of the heart. Christ was preparing His people for the guidelines that would be written by the Holy Spirit. The Law said, "Do not commit adultery;" Christ pointing to the law of the Spirit said, "Do not lust." The Law said, "Do not murder;" Christ gave his followers no room to even harbor anger or delay resolving the smallest conflict with a brother. The judicial Law's "eye for an eye, and a tooth for a tooth" gave people the right to demand justice, but the deeper principle of the Law called for love, even towards one's enemy. In short, give up justice and turn the other cheek for the sake of love.

People may have thought that the laws of the Pharisees were tough, but Christ made obedience *alone* impossible. Later writers in the New Testament would focus obedience on all sorts of matters of the heart: forgiveness, patience, peace, gratitude, self control, and much more. In the Sabbath laws, man was called to imitate God's actions of creation. Under Christ we are called to imitate His very actions of redemption by dying to self and living to God.

Wow! Then Israelites had it easy, but they blew it. How can we obey an even higher set of guidelines? What gifts have we been given that the Israelites could only dream of? Remember that gifts were given to enable us to live by God's

---

83 MATTHEW 5:17

guidelines. We have received God's ultimate gift of love and we have been given the gift of the Spirit. Christ fulfilled the Law, and ushered in the Law of the Spirit, a law empowered by the presence of God in our hearts. Thus, through the work of Christ and the power of the Spirit, "the righteous requirement of the law might be fulfilled in us, who walk not according to the flesh but according to the Spirit."[84]

Discussion Questions:

1. What are the guidelines given to the church called?

2. How are they different from the Law given to Israel?

3. For a model to follow to fulfill our purpose, what were we given?[85]

4. What gifts have we been given to enable us to live by the law of the Spirit?

This discussion might be making you feel a little confused. You've surely heard sermons proclaiming the truth that we are not under the Law but under grace.[86] To be under grace means we have exchanged masters. No longer are we slaves to sin; we serve Christ, the Lord of righteousness. But grace is often confused with freedom, even what some call license. What is license? Let's start with the modern use of the word. A license gives you permission to drive. Driving gives a young person incredible freedom to do many things they couldn't do when they were dependent upon their parents for transportation. Because Christians live under grace and not Mosaic Law, sometimes people think that grace gives us license to sin. This is exactly what Paul warned the Romans about in chapter 6 verses 1 and 2. *"What shall we say then? Shall we go on sinning so that grace may increase? By no means! We died to sin; how can we live in it any longer?"*

Read Romans 6:15-18, and discuss the following questions:

1) What reason does Paul give for the necessity of obedience in the believer's life?

2) Where does slavery to righteousness lead as opposed to slavery to sin?

Grace is not a license that frees us from obedience; grace is God's gift that enables us to obey. Grace gives us a new master, Jesus Christ, and a new source of strength, the Holy Spirit.

---

84 Romans 8:4
85 Christ, the very image of God, in the flesh.
86 Romans 6:15-18

Even though our sin no longer results in our eternal death, the Christians still must deal with sin. When I exchanged my death for Christ's life my desire for sin henceforth must be put to death ... daily. To choose Christ's life is to choose not to sin! But you might say, "that sounds like Israel; they had to choose not to sin." Yes, and so do we, but we have been given ultimate grace. Here's another helpful definition from Paul:

> "For the grace of God that brings salvation has appeared to all men. It (grace of God) teaches us to say "No" to ungodliness and worldly passions, and to live self-controlled, upright and godly lives in this present age, while we wait for the blessed hope-- the glorious appearing of our great God and Savior, Jesus Christ, who gave himself for us to redeem us from all wickedness and to purify for himself a people that are his very own, eager to do what is good. These, then, are the things you should teach."[87]

Grace is God's gift of salvation and the gift of the Spirit. These enable our striving to say no to sin and yes to goodness. We must take very seriously the sin in our lives as it can hinder us from fulfilling the purpose for which we were saved. In Ephesians 2:8-10, again Paul says:

> "For by grace are ye saved through faith; and that not of yourselves: it is the gift of God: Not of works, lest any man should boast. For we are his workmanship, created in Christ Jesus unto good works, which God hath before ordained that we should walk in them."

Sin works in the opposite direction of grace. Grace gives us strength to fulfill what God has purposed for us, while sin debilitates us. What does it mean to be debilitated? Debilitation is a "serious weakening and loss of energy."[88] How can I walk in the good works God has called me to if all I can do is lie down on the sofa? Sin makes us "couch potatoes". It takes a great deal of energy to fight sin and do good, and the more I chose sin the less energy I have to serve Christ. This was indeed the very problem Israel had in fighting against the temptations of the cultures all around them. Though they had the very tablets of the Law, the miraculous works of God and the testimony of Moses, the poets and the prophets, they became overwhelmed by sin. After much patience by God they incurred the full consequence of their repeated rebellious sin – exile and death. But it was then while they were in exile that God gave His great promise. This Law, the very thing that has defined their just judgment, would one day be written upon the tablets of their hearts and man's very body would become a temple of God. No longer would the Law be an external reality of judgment stored in the Ark of the Covenant, housed within the Holy of Holies. Now it would live within mankind through the

---

87 TITUS 2:11-15
88 HTTP://WWW.GOOGLE.COM/SEARCH?HL=EN&Q=DEFINE%3ADEBILITATION&BTNG=SEARCH

A Comparitive Study using *Secret of the Scribe* · 133

power of the Spirit that not only imprints the truths upon our hearts but gives us the spiritual energy to make us holy. This is what grace is all about.

In the fullness of time, the redemption of Christ and the sending of the Spirit ushered in the fullest expression of God's grace. The incredible day that Christ sent the Holy Spirit was joined to the giving of Mosaic Law through a powerful testimony of history. The Holy Spirit descended on the feast of Pentecost. Several months after the Israelites were delivered from Egypt, Moses, on Mount Sinai, received from God the tablets of stone containing the Ten Commandments. As part of Mosaic Law, Jews were also commanded to celebrate a series of feasts. These feasts culminated in celebrating the giving of the Law 50 days after the feast of Passover. By the time of Christ it had became known as the feast of Pentecost. Fifty days after the Passover on which Christ was slain, and ten days after he had been taken into heaven, the disciples were gathered together in Jerusalem on Pentecost. Suddenly a mighty wind filled the room, tongues of fire appeared over each of the disciples' heads and they were filled with the Holy Spirit. They began to speak in foreign tongues and set off into the streets and preached to the people gathered there from lands all over the Roman Empire because of the great feast. Hearing the Gospel in their own tongues, three thousand people were added to the church that day!

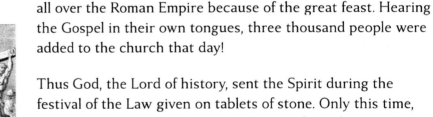

Thus God, the Lord of history, sent the Spirit during the festival of the Law given on tablets of stone. Only this time, after man's deliverance from the slavery of sin, the very Spirit of God inscribed His truth on hearts of flesh enabling us to love and obey. Thus obedience to the law of the Spirit is not accomplished through conformance to an external law, but through obedience to an internal law of love empowered by the very Spirit of God. We cannot be saved without the work of Christ and we cannot obey without the work of the Spirit. We are utterly dependent upon God for all things. As He has given us everything we need for life and godliness, we are called to respond to his bountiful goodness and grace by living unto God and dying daily to sin and self. We are like the bond slave of Israel of old – those who willingly chose to become servants for life. Recognizing the goodness and provision of their "master" and realizing that a life of "freedom" could never compare to the life provided through him, the servant gave up freedom to become a permanent member of the master's household.

134 · Christian Theology & Ancient Polythesism

Out of love, they chose servitude rather than liberty. Out of love we are invited to make the same choice.

This descent of the Spirit was also the beginning of the formation of a new people of God, not related in the flesh but related through the Spirit. By Him we have been made part of the Family of God. We are sealed and adopted as sons and daughters of God. A growing family resemblance or "likeness" will be seen in us as we strive through His power and strength to obey and to love all our "neighbors". Through the Holy Spirit, our pursuit of holiness is a pursuit of His life and love growing in us.

The sending of the Holy Spirit was the culmination of God's work among men; it was the final piece in the story that restored to people the full potential to be God's representatives. Thus in I Peter 2:9 we find the same purpose of the Law given to the Body of Christ:

> "But you are a chosen race, a royal priesthood, a holy nation, a people for his own possession, that you may proclaim the excellencies of him who called you out of darkness into his marvelous light. (ESV)

The Law based on a relationship of love between God and His people was never intended to remain an external standard. Christ took on flesh, so that the Spirit might live within our flesh enabling us to love the Lord our God with all our heart, with all our soul and with all our mind and our neighbor as our self.

Clearly, we have left our discussion of Babylonian law far behind, and this is part of the point. Though there are other comparisons we could make between Hammurabi's Code and Mosaic Law, the exercise would simply reveal more of the same. For these laws are as different from one another as the God of Israel is from the gods of Babylon. The laws of Babylon made nothing but dutiful slaves and haughty rulers. The Law of God makes sons and daughters and servant leaders who call us to lift up the name of our great God and Savior, Jesus Christ.

Go to chart **TC-1**. For Lesson XV answer the question, "Under the law of the Spirit how does God enable us to be His representatives?"

A Comparitive Study using *Secret of the Scribe* · **135**

136 · Christian Theology & Ancient Polythesism

LESSON XVI:

Israel's History and Our Lessons

As we explored in our last lesson, idolatry leads to destruction. Idolatry destroys our humanity by slowly transforming us into the likeness of who or what we worship. Idolatry is the great counterfeit of true worship – that which transforms us into the likeness of God. Idolatry leads only to death, while worshipping God leads to life, because God and God alone is the source of life. As we pick up Israel's history again, Moses is holding out this very choice – choose life or choose death. Unfortunately, much of Israel's future history will be about choosing badly. Nevertheless, God is proven faithful. There are valuable lessons to be learned from Israel's choices some 3000+ years later. Let's pick up Israel's history as she leaves the wilderness behind.

After forty years of wandering, Israel waits at the edge of the Promise Land. Manna meals have come to an end, and Israel is now eating off of the abundance of the land Moses is very old and knows his time is short. He sets himself to the tasks of completing the writing of the Law, establishing Joshua as his successor and urging Israel to remain true to her God – the One who brought her out of Egypt by His mighty hand.

Read aloud Deuteronomy 30:11-20 and discuss the following questions:

1 What were Israel's two options?

2 What would it look like for Israel to choose life? How about death?

3 What verse in this passage models the words God spoke to Adam in Genesis 2:17 about the consequences of eating of the Tree of the Knowledge of Good and Evil?

4 What will give Israel many years?

5 What is the source of Israel' life?

Following the passage just read, Moses instructed the people that during every seven years, while the land enjoyed its Sabbath rest, the people were to listen to the reading of the entire Law. Thus, each new generation would be taught to fear God. Despite this safeguard, God foretells Israel's tragic future of rejecting God and worshipping idols. Moses was given a terrible song to teach the people, calling them to fear God.

A Comparitive Study using *Secret of the Scribe* · 137

Read aloud Deuteronomy 31:30-32:47 and discuss the following questions:

1. Several students should try to summarize the message of Moses' song.

2. How could memorizing and singing a song like this help a person?

3. What is this song ultimately teaching about all other gods, for which Israel will eventually abandon God?[89]

4. There is not much "good news" in this song, but what hope does it contain in verse 43?

5. Look up what "atonement" means.

> For older students, fill in the question for lesson 16 on **chart TC-3**.

Standing on the edge of the Promised Land, Israel was faced with two options: to follow either the gods of the Canaanites or the God who freed them from Egypt and sustained them in the desert. To choose to follow God would mean she had to enter into His battle and wipe out the evil that disgraced the land they were about to possess. The book of the Bible bearing Joshua's name recounts this next era of Israel's history – an era wherein Israel generally chose to follow God. As they stood near the banks of the Jordan River, God told them to prepare themselves for His mighty deed. They would enter the Promised Land in much the same way that they had left Egypt.

It was spring, and the Jordan River, which marked the entrance into the Promised Land, was at flood stage. Joshua told the people to prepare to see a mighty deed of God. As soon as the priests bearing the Ark of the Covenant touched the River Jordan, the waters halted in their course and "piled up in a heap" before the Ark of the Lord. Before this mounding wall of water, the priests stood in the middle of the river until all the people had crossed over on dry ground. Then Joshua commanded a representative from each tribe to retrieve a stone from the middle of the river. When the priests left the bed, the river returned to its course with a thunderous crash.

---

89 DEUTERONOMY 32:39

138 · Christian Theology & Ancient Polythesism

Those twelve stones became the first of seven memorials that Joshua would instruct the people to build. As testimonies of God's faithfulness and of their faith and obedience to Him, these memorials were to be a permanent testimony of Israel's life in God – the One who rescued them from Egypt, who led them through the desert, and who kept His promises to Abraham by giving them this good land. Thus began the first major conquest of Canaan under the leadership of Joshua. Beginning in Jericho, Israel carried out God's judgment against the idolatrous inhabitants of each city, destroying them utterly. She served and feared the God of heaven and earth and kept her covenant with him by obeying God's Law and remembering His deeds The book ends with Joshua's recounting God's mighty deeds, and again holding out to the people God's offer, "choose you this day whom you will serve."

Read aloud Joshua 24 and discuss the following questions:

1. What deeds of God does Joshua recount, and why does he give the people this history lesson?

2. What choice does he give them?

3. The book of Joshua begins with memorial stones and ends with a memorial stone. What does the stone established at Shechem represent?

4. The first memorial altar of twelve stones commemorated God's mighty act at the Jordan River. The individual memorial stone represents the choice the people made that day to follow God. How would both of these memorials help Israel continue to choose God?

5. Is it necessary for Christians, as it was for Israel, to continue throughout their lives to choose to serve God?

Shockingly – despite the memorials, Moses' warnings, the Law of God, and the miraculous conquest of Canaan – the next chapter in Israel's history recounts her descent into idolatry. In the dark days of the book of Judges " there was no king in Israel, and every man did what was right in his own eyes". Now, rather than obeying God and wiping out the inhabitants of the land, Israel was worshipping their gods. Besieged by the Philistines, the Ammonites and other occupants of Canaan, Israel was suffering the consequences of her great sin. Judges 10:6 says,

> *"Again the Israelites did evil in the eyes of the Lord. They served the Baals and the Ashtoreths, and the gods of Aram, the gods of Sidon, the gods of Moab, the gods of the Ammonites and the gods of the Philistines. And because the Israelites forsook the Lord and no longer served him, he became angry with them. He sold them into the hands of the Philistines and the Ammonites who that year crushed and shattered them."*

It was not until Israel fully repented that God raised up a judge, a military leader. Would Israel once again take on the task to destroy the idolatrous nations whose land she had been given? Israel's problem was not that "there was no king in Israel", Israel was rejecting her King of kings. The book of Judges is the story of Israel's sliding back and forth between two worldviews – between worshipping the One true God and the gods of her powerful neighbors. She was oppressed by these nations when she worshipped their gods. When she finally repented of her idolatry, God raised up a judge to deliver Israel from her enemies. This cycle of idolatry, oppression, repentance and deliverance is repeated over and over again. The twelve judges recorded during this period include people like Gideon, Deborah, and Samson.

God sent both the oppression and the deliverance. Because she repeatedly broke her covenantal promises to God, Israel deserved to be wiped out completely. Yet Judges also encapsulates the story of a long suffering and merciful God who, despite Israel's faithlessness, would keep His covenant. The book of Ruth, which provides the ancestry of David, the forbearer of Christ, is set during the end of this dark period of Israel's history.

Israel's last judge was a man named Samuel, of whom numerous Bible stories are told. From his birth to ushering in the era of the kings, Samuel played a dramatic role in Israel's history. Like Moses, Samuel was Israel's judge, prophet and priest. It was to Samuel that Israel voiced loudly her demand to have a king.

Read I Samuel 8 aloud, and discuss the questions below:

1. What were the first reasons the people gave to Samuel for wanting a king?

2. How did God respond to Israel's request?

3. What reasons did Samuel give the people for why they shouldn't want a king?

4. What was the real reason Israel wanted a king?

Samuel anointed a reluctant, yet powerful-looking leader named Saul. In Samuel's farewell address,[90] he recounts the faithfulness of the Lord and convicts Israel of her great sin of rejecting God as Israel's king because they wanted to be like everyone else. The people repented, and thus the establishment of the Israelite kingship was subordinated to Israel's law. Everyone, including the king, must obey the Law of God. Thus, it was as a prophet that Samuel, and all those prophets who followed him, would confront the kings of Israel when they failed to obey God's Law. In the years ahead, the prophets of God would play a difficult role as the kings led the nation further and further from God.

As you know from earlier lessons, Saul did not obey God. He led Israel into battle but failed to destroy everything as God had commanded. He performed the role of priest which was never given to Israel's kings. For these acts, Samuel would anoint another king, a man after God's own heart.[91] It was David who took up God's call to drive out the idolatrous nations, and it was he who spread Israel's borders to their furthest extent. His wise son, Solomon, would establish peace in Israel and build God's temple. This was the high point of Israel's history which would never be reached again. Yet, Solomon, for all his wisdom, paved the way for Israel's eventual destruction. This man who built the glorious Temple of the Lord also built temples to pagan gods.

Solomon's kingship, like those of David and Saul before him, was subordinate to the Law of God. Moses strictly forbade Israel from intermarrying with the pagan peoples of the land. Despite his knowledge and wisdom, Solomon was a fool; he married numerous pagan princesses who turned his heart from following fully after God.

---

90 I SAMUEL 12
91 I SAMUEL 13:14

Read aloud I Kings 11:1-13 and discuss the following questions:

1. Why did Solomon end up worshipping pagan gods?

2. What does his choice say about his love for God?

3. What was the consequence of Solomon's choice?

4. Why didn't God cut off his line like He had Saul's?

Solomon did what was evil in the sight of the Lord. His idolatry was responsible for the next era of Israelite history known as the Divided Kingdom. Were it not for God's promise to David, Solomon's line would have been completely wiped out. The kingdom was split in two: Jerusalem and the tribe of Judah in the south would be left to the heirs of David, while ten tribes in the North would retain the name of Israel. The majority of kings from both regions "did what was evil in the sight of the Lord". This would become the constant refrain of the Book of Kings. It ends with the destruction of Israel – the Northern Kingdom – by the Assyrians. Those who survived were led away into slavery, never to be heard from again.

Stop and reflect: You have read and discussed several passages of Scripture, three of which capture watershed moments in Israel's history. All three have important relevance for any young person who wants to remain in Christ, who wants a faith that lasts. You have an enemy, who wants you to follow after him in the same way he wanted to lead Israel astray. You live in an idolatrous culture that will tempt you to worship its gods. Let's not miss the guidance that God has provided us in the Old Testament.

Lesson number one: Hard times are ahead, so do now what will help you remember then what and Whom you believe in. Many families have pages of photo albums, and souvenirs from family vacations. These help us remember precious moments of family life. Nevertheless, there are memories that are more important than the San Diego Zoo and the trip to Hawaii, but we often fail to memorialize them. These are the memories of God's faithfulness to you and your family. Many people keep a journal of their spiritual journey. In many ways, the Old Testament is like a journal of Israel's history: the good, the bad and the ugly – and the goodness and beauty of the Lord that transcended it all.

In the book of Joshua, there were two types of monuments: those that commemorated God's faithfulness, and those that commemorated Israel's belief in God and her promise to continue to act on that belief. Recently, a dear family friend told us a story of how he had taken his oldest son hiking in the mountains. They brought Quick Set Cement and found a place to build a memorial of stone.[92] In advance of the trip, father and son had worked together on a document that defined what this young man believed about God, his Word and the life that a Christian is called to. The son enclosed his written beliefs in a bottle which was cemented into the monument. In the future, the son will bring his children to this special place. Then he will pull it out and read to them what he believed when he was a young man. Testifying to God's faithfulness, he will be able to share stories of events that have proved his belief true over and over again.

Discussion Questions:

1   What do you think about the idea of building stone memorials?

2   How could they be beneficial to standing firm in your walk of faith?

3   Are there any examples of things in your own or your family's life that have demonstrated God's faithfulness or power to you?

4   If you were going to write down the things you believed about God, what are some of the things you would write about?

Lesson number two: Peer pressure isn't just an adolescent thing. Israel was led by God, but she wanted to trade Him in for someone she could see and for something that would make her look like everyone else. Israel's experience as described in the Old Testament can help us here as well. These weren't 13- and 14-year-olds wanting to look like everyone else; these were grown men and woman wanting to look like their pagan neighbors. These men and woman had witnessed some of the most amazing miracles God has ever performed on the face of the earth. Nonetheless, their desire to be like everybody else was more powerful than their desire to be like God.

---

92 This story of the father's account is called Memorial and Monuments by Doug Hansen. This forth coming book will be available for purchase in 2010. For purchase information please contact Brimwood Press at TFYH@brimwoodpress.com

A Comparitive Study using *Secret of the Scribe* · 143

You've probably already heard lots of talk about the dangers of the pressure to dress, behave or adopt certain attitudes, actions or outlooks on life that are acceptable to the "group". Dealing with peer pressure will run the course of your life, because the "group" is our idolatrous culture. It will call to you over and over again to do the things that it values, to believe the things it believes, and to worship the things it worships. In wanting to be like everyone else, Israel asked for a king. When we cave into the peer pressure inflicted by our culture in other ways, like Israel, this choice reflects a heart that has lost the desire to be like God. In its place is a heart that desires to be like everybody else. Succumbing to this desire is idolatry. Think about where Israel's desire to follow her king eventually led, and learn from her example.

Discussion Questions:

1 Name some things our culture wants you to indulge in that are contrary to the character of God.

2 Are you aware of ways in which you feel peer pressure?

3 Is it helpful to understand that the temptation you are facing is idolatry?

4 When does peer pressure turn into sin?

5 Why is it hard to follow God?

Lesson number three: Start planning for marriage young. What?! Some of you reading this may be as young as ten years old. Marriage is many years away. Why on earth is it coming up here? Preparing for marriage is one way to use the lessons of the Old Testament to strengthen yourself against the faithlessness of Israel. You should be astounded that the man who wrote the Proverbs and built the Temple lost his heart for God in his old age. Why did he? Because he married women who loved other gods. The Bible in both Old Testament and New tells us to marry someone who loves

144 · Christian Theology & Ancient Polythesism

God. Marry someone whose love for God inspires your own, because otherwise they will likely tempt you to forget your first love. You must think about this now, if you want to continually choose God your whole life long.

Do you remember what marriage is intended to represent – the life, love and unity of the Trinity. The man and wife love God, they love each other, and God loves them both. It's a three-way love relationship between two spouses and their God with God at the top of the triangle. If we love someone who doesn't love God wholeheartedly, that triangle grows increasingly lopsided. So purpose now to love God with all your heart and soul and mind and to marry someone many years from now who also loves God with his or her whole heart.

Discussion Questions:

1   How can you tell if someone loves God?

2   What character qualities would they possess?

3   How could someone tell that you love God?

4   Are there some character qualities that you may want to work on in the years ahead that would be attractive to another person who truly loves God?

5   Do you think it would be wise to start praying now that God would help you marry someone who loves Him too?

The history of Israel has so much to teach us about ourselves, as well as our God. Close by discussing what this lesson taught you about God.

> Consider closing this lesson in your **Jacob Journal** with prayer, and ask God to help you take these lessons from Israel's history to heart, so you can learn from their faithlessness. Plan ways you can set up memorials to God's faithfulness in your own life and ways you can capture what you believe about God; try to identify how peer pressure influences you, and commit yourself to marriage only with someone who is dedicated to the Lord.

A Comparitive Study using *Secret of the Scribe* · **145**

LESSON XVII:

The Bible's Main Characters – The Good, the Bad and the Ugly

Note to Parent/Instructor: This lesson contains some challenging content. If you are teaching children 10-12, highlight a few key paragraphs to read, and discuss the corresponding questions. Summarize the remaining content and help them fill out the comparison chart at the end of this lesson. Lesson 18 will review many of these ideas through the Bible story of Elijah and the prophets of Baal. For older students, lots of discussion questions have been provided to help them digest this content. As with all lessons, end the lesson at whatever point the students reach saturation and pick it up again the next day.

In lesson three when we first discussed the importance of theme, we talked about the Bible as a great work of literature. As a work of literature it is not just a great story; it has all the features of an epic narrative plus a whole lot more. Like every epic, it tells stories of extraordinary deeds, daring feats and battles won which would be impossible for anyone except the hero. God is the Bible's great hero – the protagonist. This is God's story, but there are two other characters that each play pivotal roles, which enable the reader to know what the hero is like. We have already talked about one of these at length – the character of man. His or her names change over the span of the epic, but the purpose and role this character plays stays pretty much the same. Mankind's purpose is to reveal God to the world through being like Him, and to worship Him alone. However, man is given freedom of choice.

The final character is the antagonist – the one who is against the hero and those the hero loves. This character is Satan – the bitter enemy of God and man. Yet in His powerlessness against God, he directs his hatred against men. Satan rebelled against worshipping God and tempts man to do the same; nevertheless, the darkness of his character still reveals the light of God. For indeed, all things in heaven and on earth serve the purposes of God. This lesson explores further the roles of all three characters and how man and Satan serve His purposes. This knowledge will add much to the dramatic story of the following lesson, as it powerfully illustrates the roles of these characters.

If you have taken BrimWood Press' worldview course, you know that the most important worldview question is who is God and what is He like. The Bible answers this question, but perhaps not in the way some might expect. The Bible could have begun with a list of facts about God. Genesis one could have started

146 · Christian Theology & Ancient Polythesism

something like this, "In the beginning God was there, because God always has been – God is eternal. God created all things. God is all-powerful and He knows all things. God is all-wise and all-good. In fact, God is holy. God is transcendent; that means He is above all things, yet at the same time He is present everywhere. God is Spirit. God is the Trinity. God is the Lawgiver and the Judge. God is love, etc, etc, etc. The list could go on and on and, frankly, would never end because God is so immense that any words we could use to describe Him will always be less than who He really is. Words as well as our minds cannot encapsulate or contain God. This is why the above list could also include the statement that God is incomprehensible. God is infinite (belongs to eternity) and we are finite – we live in the realm of a material, time-bound world that reveals but cannot fully make known the greatness of our immaterial, eternal God.

Now most of you are probably getting a little bored at this point. Aren't you glad this listing of God's attributes or character qualities is not the primary means God uses to teach us about Himself? When God chose to reveal Himself to man, and to capture that revelation through the written words of the Bible, what methods did He use? Much of what God shows us about Himself is in the context of the Bible's great stories. The first chapter of the Bible is the story of God's creation of the world and of mankind. We learn about God through what He makes, and we learn more about Him through how He relates to His creation, man. The story of God's relationship with us reveals some amazing truths about the Creator.

> "THE MAIN PURPOSE OF THE BIBLE'S STORIES IS TO REVEAL THE CHARACTER AND NATURE OF GOD."

Discussion Questions:

1. Why is any list of the character qualities of God always going to be less than what God is?

In a previous lesson we talked about how our humanity was given us by God, so the core of what makes us human is rooted in His identity. Our personhood is rooted in the Personhood of God. Yet, perhaps it is even more amazing that God revealed the nature of His personhood through us. In the Bible's first creation story there is a consistent refrain, "God said, Let there be ..." This refrain begins with God's creation of light and continues with each created thing, through the making of the animals. Then, suddenly, there is a major shift in the wording of the story, "Then God said, Let *us* make man in *our* image, in *our* likeness, and let *them*

A Comparative Study using *Secret of the Scribe* · 147

rule ..."[93] Just so the reader does not get confused about to whom this sudden plural pronoun refers, the text repeats the exact same idea again, only now it uses the singular form for both God and man. "So God created man in His own image, in the image of God He created him." Next the writer adds one more line to further clarify what is meant by "man/him". "... male and female He created them." The word "them" refers to man, just as the word "Us" refers to God. This is why in Genesis two, which gives a more detailed telling of the creation of man, it says, "it is not good for man to be alone". The man alone who is not united to his wife is not good, because alone his life does not portray the communal life of God. A single man can be referred to as "he" or "him", but not "them". Man was made to be "them" because God is "Us." This astounding revelation about God is first revealed in the context of the creation of man and woman.

Nothing else in all creation reveals this truth about God. Man and woman bear the likeness of God. The ocean and the storm reveal glimpses of God's power, the starry host offers a sense of the unfathomable nature of God, the sunrise and sunset display something of the beauty of the Lord, but the creation of man and woman united were to give the world a glimpse of the Personhood of God. Not even the angels reflect His Trinitarian nature. Perhaps this is what the Psalmist was reflecting on in Psalm 8 when he said, "You have made him a little lower than the angels, and crowned him with glory and honor." What is our glory and honor? We have been made to reflect the personhood of God. Thus we have been made for love, life and unity because this is what the Holy Trinity is and what the Triune God creates.

> This lesson could also be titled "The Good, the Bad, and the Beautiful." God is "the Good," Satan is "the Bad," and depending upon who or what we as humans worship, we are "the Beautiful," or "the Ugly". We were made for beauty and goodness.

Discussion Questions:

1   How was the world given its first clue about the Trinitarian nature of God?

2   What does the word Trinity tell us about the nature of God?

3   What is the result/by-product of the relationships of the Trinity?

4   Why do you think unity shares the same root word as Tri-une?

5   Why is it not "good" for man to be alone?

---

93 GENESIS 1:26,27

6   What is unique about the creation of people, as compared to the rest of creation?

There is one God who is Father, Son and Spirit. We know God through these three distinct Persons. When the first Bible story reveals that God is "Us", it doesn't elaborate on just who "Us" is talking about. As the Old Testament unfolds, it is God the Creator who plays the leading role in relation to man. In the Gospels, God is seen by people through the Son of man/God the Savior. Between the Gospels and Revelation, the focus is the power of the Spirit of God, who renews and transforms us into the likeness of the Son of God. In Revelation it is the Son of God who brings forth the final judgment and God's story to its glorious conclusion, ushering man into eternity. Yet from cover to cover we can find evidence of (or direct reference to) each Person of the Trinity. God is three in One.

Just as the leading member of the Trinity changes as the Bible's story unfolds, so does the community of man which God interacts with. We have already looked at man's purpose to image God through the marriage relationship. This was the first of three communal relationships meant to represent God to the world. But as we know, the first marriage failed, not because they got divorced but because they chose to be a god themselves rather than worshipping God alone. But God did not give up on marriages or the rest of the human race. He chose a man named Abraham and his wife Sarah to begin a special people, a nation who would represent Him to the world. Israel would represent God as Creator through imitating God's seven-day week. They would proclaim that God is the Provider by resting every seventh day and every seventh year. Israel would demonstrate that God is the lawgiver by obeying His commands and keeping His covenant. By wiping out the evil of the Canaanites, they would represent God as judge of the whole earth. By caring for the land – letting it rest every seven years – they were ruling the earth on behalf of the Lord of heaven and earth.

The third community is the Body of Christ, the one to which all Christians belong. While not the direct focus of these lessons, hopefully you have not missed that Christians imitate their sacrificing Savior who laid down His life for us. We in turn lay down our lives, our desires, our passions to take up the life of Christ. Through the Spirit of God we are empowered to carry on the work of the Son of God in which Christ fulfilled man's mission to represent God to the world in the flesh. To share God's life, love and unity within the Body of Christ and to reflect it to those outside of that community is the purpose of our existence.

How beautiful it is to realize that all of these communal relationships created by God have something to do with a marriage. The Bible's very first story culminates with the creation of the marriage. Throughout the Old Testament God refers to Himself as Israel's husband and Israel (much of the time) as His unfaithful wife. Nevertheless, God restores her purity (as you will see in lessons ahead). Finally

A Comparitive Study using *Secret of the Scribe* · 149

there is the Church – the Bride of Christ. The last book of the Bible, Revelation, celebrates the marriage supper of the Lamb, the feast of Christ and His Bride.[94] This marriage theme starts in the first chapter of the Bible and culminates in the last, making it perfectly clear from beginning to end that God created human beings to share in the life, love and unity of the Trinity. The Bible is a love story through which God holds out His proposal to free willed creatures who can choose to accept or reject Him. Marriage is the picture of the relationship we have been invited to share with our Tri-une God.

IN THIS PICTURE OF AN ANCIENT NEAR EASTERN WEDDING, THE BRIDEGROOM IS COMING FOR HIS BRIDE.

Discussion Questions:

1   We know God through what three relationships?

2   Through what three human relationships/communities is the world to see God?

3   Adam and Eve were told to be fruitful and multiply and fill the whole earth. Israel was told to possess the whole land of Canaan. Believers were told to spread the Gospel to the uttermost parts of the earth. What is similar about the ideas these commands express and why do you think this similarity exists?

4   Can you name some ways in which marriage, Israel and the Church were designed to reveal God to the world?

5   In today's culture, the individual is frequently made more important than the community. How do you think God's words, "It is not good for man to be alone" might apply to our world? Can you think of some things in our culture that isolate people from each other?

6   Why is community so important to God?

7   What does God invite us to share?

8   Why is the marriage, as a metaphor used throughout Scripture, such a good picture of the life we have been invited to share with God?

9   As Christians, what is the purpose of our existence?

94 REVELATION 19:7-9

150 · Christian Theology & Ancient Polythesism

From Genesis 1:26, 27, note the amazing truth first revealed about the Personhood of God through the creation of His representatives on chart **TC-2**.

Many times during these lessons we have talked about the theme of man made in the image of God, of man reflecting the image of God as His representative. This idea is actually part of a larger theme of Scripture – the idea that God reveals Himself *to* man *through* man. Thus far we have highlighted that revelation as seen through marriage, Israel and the Church. The Bible itself also reflects this same idea. Except for the Ten Commandments, God did not write the Bible alone. He wrote it through men. The Bible's truths are from God, but the arrangement and expression of those ideas were the job of the human writer. The Bible is the inspired Word of God, not the dictated word of God. (The latter is what the *Koran* claims.) Revealing Himself *to* man *through* man climaxed in the incarnation – the God/man Jesus Christ – a wonder we should never stop trying to comprehend. Amazingly, our incomprehensible God has revealed Himself in ways we can understand by working in and through us. God uses the known (ourselves) to make the Unknown (Himself) knowable.

Discussion Questions:

1 Name ways God has revealed Himself to man through man.

2 Would you agree or disagree with the statement, "the Christian life is meant to be incarnational." Think about the purpose of the incarnation of Christ and discuss whether, or not this idea could be applied to the Christian life. Try to formulate a reason why you agree or disagree.

All students should fill out the questions labeled A on chart **BN-1** called *Scripture's Three Main Characters*.

Through man God reveals His personhood. The Bible is the written account of this revelation. The rest of creatio n reveals other aspects of His nature. We could go as far as to say that all of creation reveals God. You might be thinking, *wait a minute, Satan is a part of that creation and God's creation has been corrupted by sin; how can Satan and sin have anything to do with revealing God?* Hold onto that great question, we'll come back to it in a minute.

First, let's look at the third main character of the Bible, Satan. Though the Bible tells us little about Satan's creation and fall, it seems he was once the most

A Comparitive Study using *Secret of the Scribe* · **151**

beautiful and powerful angel of light.[95] But Satan succumbed to pride, believing he should be made equal to God. Satan desired the worship given only to His Maker. He was the first who dared to ask *why God alone should be worshipped* and the first to commit the sin of idolatry.

Is it surprising that, having been cast from heaven, Satan should single out man for his ruthless attacks,? Down through the centuries, Satan's assaults have been especially evident on marriages, Israel and the Church. Man is hated by Satan because God made us like Himself to reveal and thus glorify Him. God also gave us rule over His creation. Satan has set out to make us like himself, thereby glorifying himself and stealing the rule given to man. The "father of lies" would succeed in his plot to get many men to disobey God. When man chose to reject the rule of God, man forfeited his very life along with his rights to rule God's world.

The Bible's condensed narrative of the first three chapters of Genesis is essentially told again and played out in historical detail through Israel. Will she – a people made by God – obey, worship Him and live? Will she resist the temptation of the evil one? Or will she fall and be like her first parents who were driven from the home God had provided? In the central struggle of Israel's story, the object of her temptation is the false worship of created things. The Old Testament tells the story of man waffling between two worldviews – the worldview of God and the worldview of Satan. Satan desired to be worshipped when God alone is to be worshipped. Satan's idolatry cost him the role of highest angel in the heavens.

Discussion Questions:

1. How would you describe the worldview of Satan?

2. What is the major conflict of the Bible that began with the fall of Satan?

3. Why does Satan hate man?

---

95 THE BIBLE IS VERY AMBIGUOUS AS TO THE CREATION AND FALL OF SATAN. EARLY CHURCH FATHERS TAUGHT AS DO MANY PROTESTANTS TODAY THAT THE FOLLOWING PASSAGES DESCRIBE IN POETIC LANGUAGE BOTH A HUMAN RULER AND SATAN, THE RULING POWER BEHIND THESE KINGS. SEE EZEKIEL 28:13-19; AND ISAIAH 14:12-17. REVELATIONS 12:7-13 ALSO DESCRIBES A FALL OF SATAN.

4   Give some examples from history and from today's world that demonstrate the attacks of Satan against marriage, Israel and the Church.

With this said let's go back to the question, *how could Satan possibly reveal God?* Man is to reveal God by being like him; Satan reveals God by being unlike Him. In any story in which good vs. evil is a part of the plot there is always an antagonist – the bad guy, who fights against the protagonist – the hero. Many of the actions of the hero are prompted by the evil actions of the antagonist. Whether the hero acts to save the world, the day, or the damsel we learn a great deal about his character, strength and motives through these actions. As the grand narrative of Scripture reveals our great God and Savior, should we be surprised that there is also a substantial villain, who is utterly evil, who hates the Hero and seeks to destroy that which is good, as all goodness is a reflection of God?

If all of creation is intended to reveal the character and nature of God, Satan unwittingly serves this purpose. God is made manifest through both light and darkness, even though there is no darkness in God.[96] In the first act of creation God said, "Let there be light!" Because there was darkness, that light burst forth is a powerful display. If you walk into a room already lit you probably take no notice of the light. But if the room is dark and you have to fumble around looking for the switch, when the light comes on, you are immediately grateful for its presence. The sad reality is most of us humans just wouldn't notice God were it not for the darkness in our world. Darkness drives us to look for the light. God is light!

As the antagonist, Satan led a rebellion of angels and then of mankind against God. Yet, unlike the superhero who must think quick on his feet when confronted with the latest diabolical plot, God's plan was prepared before there were angels or demons, universes or people. In full view of Satan, God set up this world and populated it with weak creatures (when compared to Satan) who would decide for themselves who should be worshipped. Satan had challenged God's sole right to worship. God would meet that challenge, but not by crushing this opponent with power. Ironically, power would prove to be Satan's downfall because God did not fight this battle with might. His victory would be procured through love – the greatest power in heaven and earth. The Creator God, unimagined by Satan, would Himself become the Savior of His fallen creature, man. The Savior would rescue from Satan's clutches them who had sold themselves into slavery. Satan made necessary this ultimate act and greatest revelation of the Hero.

> All students should fill out the questions labeled B on both charts **BNC-1 and 2**.

---

[96] 1 John 1:5

This discussion has touched on some major worldview ideas about the struggle between good and evil. Some careful clarification is necessary so that you don't end up thinking that the contest between God and Satan is like the cosmic battle between good and evil found in some *Star Wars Trilogy*. Here's some theology you have to keep straight as you think about the Biblical struggle between good and evil.

1   God is separate from His creation.[97] Angels, demons, people and the physical world are all part of God's creation, but none *are* God. ("The Force" is *not* separate from the material world.)

2   Satan was originally made good, but like man had free will. He chose to reject the dominion of His Maker and in his pride he corrupted himself.[98] Evil is a corruption of what was once good. ("The Force" has always been a mixture of good and evil.)

3   God is all good; there is no darkness in Him.[99] ("The Force" is a mixture of both good and evil.)

4   As creator, God gave angels initially, and man in an ongoing way, capacity for free will. Man chooses to obey and worship His maker or he can choose to disobey and die.[100] That death manifests itself in several ways both physically and spiritually, but it corrupts that which was once good. Unlike angels, man is given many opportunities to choose. (In the universe of "the Force", man is ultimately a victim of fate. He has no free will.)

5   God is all powerful.[101] Satan is not an equal foe. There is not an equal universal struggle going on between the powers of good and the powers of evil. All power belongs to God. Satan only has power that was given him by God. Satan's power does not proportionately reduce the power of God. (In Star Wars, the powers of good and evil are dueling foes, equally matched. Either has the potential power to overcome the other. Conflict occurs because one or the other has the upper hand.)

6. While the Bible is ambiguous about Satan's creation and initial fall, it is not unclear about Satan defeat. Christ triumphed over Satan through the cross.[102] His final end is the lake of fire; in which, he is eternally punished for his wickedness towards men.[103] God's story, as recorded in the Bible, begins with God, climaxes on the cross, and ends with Christ's final victory. (There will be no *Star Wars* like sequels.)

---

97 II Chronicles 2:6; Isaiah 57:15; Ephesians 4:6
98 Isaiah 14:14
99 I John 1:5; I Peter 1:16
100 Genesis 2:16-17
101 Genesis 18:14; Isaiah 14:24, 45:12,13; Matthew 19:26; Luke 1:37
102 Colossians 2:15
103 Revelations 2:10

7.   God will in His time destroy and separate from His creation all that is evil, restoring and renewing the perfect Kingdom of God for all eternity.[104] Satan, like sin and suffering, will be finished with the stories end when time and death shall be no more.[105] (In *Star Wars*, the ultimate goal of the universe is balance between the good and evil of "the Force".)

The list above separates the ideas of the worldviews of monotheism from pantheism. Yoda was fashioned after a teacher of Taoism, which is a Pantheistic religion. While Pantheism is not the subject of these lessons. These ideas have been included here because this dualistic understanding of the struggle between good and evil is so pervasive in our culture, especially our entertainment. To close this lesson, see if you can define the polytheistic ideas that would contrast each of the seven monotheistic points above.

Answers for this discussion follow and have been printed upside-down.

1   The gods comprise nature and are the forces of nature. They are not separate from the universe.

2   Evil is a part of the universe because the gods and goddesses are a mixture of good and evil.

3   The gods and goddesses are a mixture of good and evil.

4   Man is a slave. He must do the work of his master gods. Man has no free-will. He is a dictum of the whims of the gods.

5   Power is dispersed among the gods and goddesses. This power varies between the gods, and some are more powerful than others. Nonetheless, the power of each god must be maintained or the part of the created order that it sustains will evaporate.

6   The universe is eternal. Opportunities for a cosmic conflict between the gods of order (nature) and the demons of chaos are always present. Once the demons of chaos defeat gods of order, sooner or later the surviving gods will defeat the demons and some new form of life will begin again. This cycle is unending and the forces of "good" and "evil" are always present.

7   There is no end goal for the universe other than holding off the inevitable. Thus the only objective is to maintain the present created order through sustaining the power of the gods as long as possible.

---

104 Revelation 21&22
105 Revelation 21:1, 22-27

LESSON XVIII:

The Big Show-down – Is it God or is it Baal?

From the era of the Divided Kingdom (after the reign of Solomon) comes one of the most dramatic of all Bible stories: the show-down between Elijah, prophet of God, and the prophets of Baal. Ahab was Israel's notoriously wicked king, who had married an equally infamous wife – Jezebel. Raised by a pagan priest, Jezebel's influence led to the institution of Baal and Asheroth worship as Israel's state religion. Altars to God were torn down, and so many prophets of God were killed by the sword that Elijah believed he was the only one left. The story that ensues is at the heart of the Old Testament's central conflict.

You know the story: one man of God against 450 prophets of Baal, not to mention the 400 prophets of Asheroth – and the man of God wins. What you probably don't know is just how significant this show-down was.

Because we don't live in a polytheist culture it might be easy to assume that Baal was just another of the many nature deities that Satan used to lead people into idolatry and away from God. However, Baal was unlike any god we have discussed thus far. He was perhaps Satan's best invention of the day. Baal was not just the storm god, the sun god, the harvest god, or the fertility god; Baal was all of these and more. Baal was lord of the land. As lord of the land, he encompassed all the forces of nature necessary for production and fertility. A Baal idol could be cast as an image of the sun, or as a figure holding a lightning bolt depicting the storm, or a bull/calf representing the fertility of herds. Idols to Baal carved in many different forms abounded in Israel. Everything the land needed was believed to be provided through Baal. Baal was the closest thing in the mind of the polytheist to Israel's Lord of heaven and earth. But rather than Israel's one God, the pagans had many, many Baals. Each small area of land had its own Baal. Each Baal also had his own Asheroth, because his ability to provide productivity for the land was tied to his sexual relationship with Asheroth, the fertility goddess.

Despite these limiting factors, the idea of Baal was a direct affront both to God and to man. God was Israel's Lord of the land. She had been given the job to care for this land by letting it rest every seven years. This was what God assigned to

156 · Christian Theology & Ancient Polythesism

Adam when He placed him in the Garden to care for and till the soil.[106] Through "ruling" the earth man was imitating the Lord of all Creation. Instead of God as man's provider and man as God's appointed ruler/steward of the earth, now Baal with his consort, Asheroth, both provided and ruled. The gross immorality of temple prostitution tore apart both the sacred marriage covenant between husband and wife, and the sacred covenant between God and Israel. Israel's prophets would repeatedly call her an unfaithful bride because she had forsaken her Husband – the Creator and Redeemer.

In every immoral act unto the Baals, demons brought worship to Satan, who had claimed rights to the land that man had forfeited to him. Thus the contest between Elijah and the prophets of Baal, was not a story about one man facing down hundreds of men. This was a showdown between the power of God and the power of Satan – a contest facilitated by a weak prophet who believed that God is the only Lord of the land.

Discussion Questions:

1   Who were the Baals, and why were they "Satan's best invention of the day"?

2   In what ways were claims about the Baals like and unlike the one true God of Israel?

3   How did people's worship of Baal displace both the role of God and of man?

4   Who promoted the worship of Baal in this period of Israel's history?

A nobody from Tishbe, Elijah was a man who struggled with frequent bouts of depression, yet he had become a thorn in the side of wicked King Ahab. Elijah was one of the few remaining prophets of God who had eluded the clutches of Ahab and Jezebel, despite a massive manhunt that had been undertaken to kill this "troubler of Israel". Why the manhunt? He had prayed, asking God to withhold the rain, even the dew. God had answered Elijah's prayer and there was a severe famine in the land of the Baals. For some unexplainable reason, Baal and Asheroth had been unable to produce a single crop in all of Israel for three dry, dusty years. The people had faithfully prostituted themselves before their god and goddess, yet still the rain did not come and Baal's land did not provide for their needs.

When Elijah finally came out of hiding and showed himself to the king, he presented an opportunity for Ahab to stage a prize fight, a show down between

---

106 GENESIS 2:15

the Baals and the One who had been Israel's God. Jumping at the idea, Ahab must have thought this would win back the credibility of Baal and Asheroth – 850 pagan prophets against one prophet of God. Little did Ahab know that God was once again giving His people a choice, while He confronted and exposed the lies of the evil one who had enslaved His people.

Read I Kings 18:16-40 aloud and discuss the following questions:

1. What two opinions were the people wavering between?

2. What did Elijah propose to the crowd?

3. What does the fact that the Baals and Asheroths did not answer their pleading prophets demonstrate about the power of Satan?

4. What did Elijah have to do before he could present his offering to the Lord?

5. What three things does Elijah pray for?

6. How did the people respond to the mighty display of God's power?

7. What act demonstrated that they had chosen to follow God?

The show-down proved to be no contest for God – for there is no comparison between the power of God and the power of Satan. Satan's Baals were exposed as frauds, and God was glorified as the King of kings and Lord of lords. In the same way that the Lord of heaven had shut up the skies, now He – and He alone – sent down a consuming fire and the prophets of demons were destroyed. At the center of this contest was one weak and weary man whose faith in the Lord of all the earth had silenced Israel's foe.

> Note the role Elijah played as God's representative and how his weakness was used to display God's power and His defeat of Satan on theme chart **TC-2**. Answer all C questions on chart **BNC-2** and the question for Lesson 18 on **TC-3**.

About the same time that the prophet Elijah lived there was a very popular myth[107] told in Babylon about a cosmic conflict that began before the world was made. The story is a part of the Babylonian creation myth called Enuma Elish.

---

107 MYTHS ARE MADE-UP STORIES THAT ANSWER A CULTURE'S RELIGIOUS QUESTIONS.

158 · Christian Theology & Ancient Polythesism

MARDUK, TAIMUT AND MAN

THE MOTHER GODDESS AND FATHER GOD BIRTHED MANY NATURE GODS AND GODDESSES. BUT AFTER A WHILE, THE FATHER GOD GOT TIRED OF HIS OFFSPRING'S NOISE AND HE TOLD HIS WIFE OF HIS PLAN TO KILL THEM ALL. ONE OF THESE OFFSPRING OVERHEARD THE PLOT AND DECIDED TO KILL HIS FATHER INSTEAD. HE DID THE DEED. THE MOTHER GODDESS NAMED TAIMUT WAS ENRAGED. WHILE SHE HAD NOT BEEN KEEN ABOUT HER HUSBAND'S PLAN TO KILL ALL THE CHILDREN, IN REVENGE SHE WAS INTENT ON WIPING THEM ALL OUT. WITH THE AID OF HER MILITARY GENERAL, KINGU, SHE CREATED A HIDEOUS ARMY OF DEMONS, GODS OF CHAOS. THROUGH JOINING FORCES, THE DOOM OF THE OFFSPRING GODS AND GODDESSES WAS SURE. ANNIHILATION OF ALL WOULD BE THE PUNISHMENT FOR THE CRIME. WHEN WORD OF THEIR MOTHER'S PLOT REACHED THE GODS AND GODDESSES, THEY IMMEDIATELY MOURNED THEIR FATE. THEN A YOUNG GOD NAMED MARDUK, GOD OF THE WIND AND

A Comparitive Study using *Secret of the Scribe* · 159

STORM, CAME FORTH. MARDUK BOLDLY PROCLAIMED THAT HE WOULD TAKE TAIMUT ON IN SINGLE-HANDED COMBAT. HIS BROTHERS AND SISTERS SCOFFED. MOTHER WAS THE GODDESS OF RAGING WATERS; HE COULD NEVER STAND BEFORE SUCH A FOE. DESPITE THEIR JEERS, MARDUK INSISTED THAT HE WOULD BE VICTORIOUS AND WHEN HE PREVAILED THEY MUST MAKE HIM KING OF ALL THE GODS. DECIDING THEY HAD NOTHING TO LOSE, MARDUK'S PROPOSAL WAS SENT TO TAIMUT. SNEERING, SHE ACCEPTED AND THE DAY OF THE BATTLE WAS SET.

THE DEMONS OF CHAOS LINED ONE SIDE OF THE FIELD; THE GODS AND GODDESSES OF NATURE LINED THE OTHER. TAMUIT, WHOM BABYLONIANS DEPICTED AS A TOWERING DRAGON, ROARED ONTO THE TURF. MARDUK, WITH NOTHING BUT A BOW AND QUIVER OF ARROWS, STRODE OUT TO MEET HIS ENORMOUS FOE. THE BATTLE BEGAN. WITH TOOTH AND CLAW AND LASHING TAIL, TAMUIT MADE QUICK WORK OF HER YOUNG OPPONENT. WITHIN MINUTES SHE WAS READY TO FINISH HIM OFF BY OPENING HER GAPING MOUTH TO SWALLOW HIM WHOLE. BUT AT THAT VERY MOMENT, MARDUK CALLED FORTH THE FOUR WINDS AND DROVE THEM DOWN HIS MOTHER'S THROAT. WITH HER MOUTH

AGAPE, THE WARRIOR DREW FORTH HIS BOW AND ARROW AND SHOT INTO HER THROAT, PIERCING HER VERY HEART. WITH A MIGHT THUD, TAMUIT WAS DEAD!

ASTONISHMENT LED TO JOYOUS CELEBRATION, BUT THAT WAS QUICKLY HALTED WHEN THE GODS AND GODDESSES REALIZED THAT THE DEMON ARMIES WERE FLEEING. THOUGH THEY PERSUED AND KILLED MANY, NUMEROUS OTHERS ESCAPED. BUT ON THAT DAY OF MARDUK'S VICTORY, THEY CARED LITTLE, AND ENDED THEIR PURSUIT TO CROWN THE VICTOR KING. AS HIS FIRST ACT, MARDUK CUT HIS MOTHER'S BODY IN HALF, AND WITH IT HE FORMED THE WATERS OF THE EARTH AND THE WATERS OF THE HEAVENS. THEN ALL THE GODS AND GODDESSES TOOK THEIR PLACES IN THE CREATED ORDER. BUT THE THREAT OF THE DEMONS OF CHAOS WAS EVER PRESENT IN THE MINDS OF ALL THE NATURE GODS. IN A LATER ATTEMPT TO DESTROY THEIR FOES, MARDUK SLAYED THE EVIL GENERAL KINGU, BUT MANY DEMONS STILL ROAMED. THE POWER OF THE GODS AND GODDESSES HAD TO BE MADE SURE. FROM THE BLOOD OF THE EVIL GOD KINGU, MARDUK FORMED MAN. MAN WOULD BE THE SLAVE OF THE GODS, MADE TO ENSURE THE STRENGTH OF THE GODS. THROUGH THE CONSTANT WORK OF THEIR SLAVES, THE GODS AND GODDESSES OF THE CREATED ORDER WOULD REMAIN STRONG, NEVER TO BE OVERTHROWN BY THE GODS OF CHAOS.[108]

Pretty good story, huh?! In the first Babylonian empire the god of the wind and the storm was Enlil, whose escapades caused the flood. In the second Babylonian empire, he was called Marduk and was the chief god of the capital city of Babylon.[109] *In Babylonian society, this story of Marduk and Taimut served to explain*

---

108 *Creation and Chaos* BY DR. BRUCE WALTKE, PAGE 9. THIS STORY IS FROM *Enuma Elish*, THE NEO-BABYLONIAN CREATION MYTH.
109 NEBUCHADNEZZAR LIVED ABOUT 200 YEARS AFTER ELIJAH AND WAS A KING OF THE NEO-BABYLONIAN EMPIRE

why Marduk was the most powerful god in the pantheon. Babylonians reenacted this story each year to renew the strength of the gods.

Let's simplify the plot of this story: The first creator god is threatened with possible overthrow by a lesser god(s). To defeat this rival a powerful army is made to bolster the might of the creator god. Nevertheless, the creator god is overthrown by a move of skill and cunning of the lesser god. The lesser god becomes the most powerful god and assumes the role as creator. To ensure the power of the new creator god and the rest of the gods of nature, he makes slaves so they do not become tired and vulnerable to a future foe. Man ensures the ongoing power of the nature pantheon.

This is probably the story that Satan wishes was true – God as Taimut, Satan as Marduk, and man as slave. Instead, the plot of the real story goes something like this:

{Before the story begins: *The Creator God has made angels to worship and serve Him. The most powerful angel has rebelled and in his pride demanded to be worshipped and served like the Creator. The Creator has cast him down.*} The Creator makes a beautiful world and a creature called man to represent the Creator in that world. The fallen angel, in a move of skill and cunning, tricks the creature into worshipping and serving him. The creature becomes a slave. Chaos enters the creation. Out of love for His creation, the Creator takes on His creature's form and rescues him from slavery. The rescued creature loves his Savior and gladly worships and represents his Creator to the world. The fallen angel is judged for his treachery; order is restored to the creation; the love of the Creator and creature is celebrated; God is worshipped forever more.

Discussion Questions:

1   What purpose did the story of Marduk and Taimut serve in the Babylonian society?

2   Unlike the purpose of the Babylonian creation myth, the Bible's creation story is not about a clash of power, nor is the primary purpose of the Bible to prove the power of God. Why do you think this is?

3   Does God's story have higher ends than the defeat of Satan? Is Satan's defeat ever in question throughout the entire story? Why not?

4   What is the purpose of the Bible?

5   In the last lesson we discussed that Satan's role, like man's, actually serves the purpose to reveal God. In understanding that the lies of polytheism

were an invention of Satan, what does the Old Testament reveal about his character?

6   In revealing the character of God and the contrasting character of Satan, is the question of who is worthy of worship naturally answered?

Unlike the story of Marduk, the Bible never sets out to prove the superior power of God. In the beginning, there is no conflict, no mention of Satan. When he shows up in Genesis 3, God puts in motion His plan to save His creature. God is not motivated by power or vengeance. What the Bible does set out to prove is the love of God. In many ways it is not until we come to the end of the Bible's story with its epic battle that we realize the magnitude of the war that Satan has been waging against God. But by then, the reader can see that Satan's doom has long been sure.

Even though the creation of man had nothing to do with ensuring the strength of God, he does play a role in displaying the power of God and in answering the question who should be worshipped. The fact that man is weak in comparison to Satan is necessary in the role he plays. In the contest of Elijah and the prophets of Baal, God certainly showed that Satan was powerless before Him, but this great work of God was facilitated by a weak and grossly outnumbered man. When the majority of those in Israel had fallen for Satan's Baals, the faith and humility of one man led to a decisive triumph for God. The same is true in stories like David and Goliath and Gideon and his little army; the power of God is displayed through a weak man or woman who is faithful. Some verses from I Corinthians 1:27-29 provide some understanding into the heart or even the strategy of God.

> "...God chose the foolish things of the world, that he might put to shame them that are wise; and God chose the weak things of the world, that he might put to shame the things that are strong; and the base things of the world, and the things that are despised, did God choose, yea and the things that are not, that he might bring to naught the things that are: that no flesh should glory before God." (asv)

God is glorified by foolish and weak things and Satan is ultimately defeated by the same. God chose the lowly and the despised to bring to nothing those who are proud and strong. The "foolish things" this verse is talking about is the message of the cross – God's love for man endured the humiliation of the cross.[110] Christ's death and resurrection sealed the doom of Satan while it displayed the character of our great God and Savior – the *only* One worthy of worship.

The "weak things" in this verse refers to man. Elijah has demonstrated how the weakness of a faithful man serves to display God's glory, but how does mans'

---

110 I Corinthians 1:18

weakness serve to defy Satan's claim to worship? Perhaps the following analogy will help:

Imagine you were gifted with amazing speed. In fact, in every race you had ever run, you were always the decisive winner. As your confidence grew, so did your pride. One day you declared that you were the fastest runner in the world! Only two people challenged your bodacious claim. The first was an adult who was eight inches taller than you, with well developed muscles bulging from his thighs. Nevertheless, you went to the starting line as cocky as ever ... you had never been beaten. The gun fired; you leapt from the starting block, but to your utter amazement the adult athlete left you in the dust. Crossing the finish line, you immediately raised a string of protests. That wasn't fair! Look at all his advantages. You held to your claim, "I'm still the fastest runner in the world ... at least of all the children ... and in a few years, I'll come back and beat that guy." Then a second challenger stepped forward – a six-year-old. You scoffed. Now you were the one who's a head taller. At the starting line you boasted and bragged, but to your total astonishment she broke the ribbon at the finish line. You were completely humiliated. Your boast was proven absolutely false by a little girl. You walked away in shame, never to brag again.

This simple analogy illustrates what may have happened if God made a creature who was stronger than Satan, whose resolve to worship God was never shaken. Satan could have cried foul. But God made a weak man and a weak woman with genuine free will. They were so free, in fact that the majority chose to worship Satan or themselves. Nevertheless, humble men and women across the pages of human history have chosen to worship God. They chose to deny themselves and all the temptations of this world to proclaim that God alone is God. Someday, these men, women, boys and girls will come from every tribe and tongue proclaiming the glory of God. This will be Satan's final humiliation – man, despite his weakness, testifying that God and God alone is Creator, Savior and Lord of all the earth. Man's faithful testimony and God's sacrificing love declare that only the Maker and Redeemer is worthy of all worship and praise. The last book of the Bible prophesies Satan's final defeat and the worship given to God throughout all eternity. Revelation 5:12 -14 proclaims:

"... with a loud voice, Worthy is the Lamb that was slain to receive power, and riches, and wisdom, and strength, and honour, and glory, and blessing. And every creature which is in heaven, and on the earth, and under the earth, and such as are in the sea, and all that are in them, ... saying, Blessing, and honour, and glory, and power, be unto him that sitteth upon the throne, and unto the Lamb forever and ever. And the four living creatures said, Amen. And the elders fell down and worshipped." (KJV)

God's glory and strength are revealed through the life of weak men or women who trust and obey Him. The revelation of God in and through man is recorded in the scriptures as the written testimony culminating in the worship of God. Answering Satan's challenge, *Who should be worshipped?* is not the primary purpose of the Bible's story, but it is the logical conclusion. In revealing the character and nature of God, this question is naturally answered – the One who is worthy. Thus the Bible ends with the worship of God – the sole Source of love and life. As the God who Provides, He alone is worthy of all praise, honor and glory.

Discussion Questions:

1 How does the story of Elijah reveal the truth that God uses weak things?

2 Give two ways God uses "weak things" to win His victory?

3 What do the odds of Elijah's battle display about the power of God?

4 How is man like the "little girl" who silenced the boast of the runner?

5 What is the difference between God's power and the power of Satan?

6 Why didn't God need to make any "soldiers" in his battle against Satan?

7 Why do you think Satan put so much effort into turning Israel away from God?

8 What does the story of Elijah teach about the three main characters of the Bible?

9 Do you think it is most important to know the Bible's main characters or the Bible's main struggle? Why?

10 Is God more likely to use you in spite of your weaknesses or because of your weaknesses? Why?

From our story of Elijah, the three main characters of the Bible, and the Bible's main struggle we have jumped to the end of the whole story. Unfortunately, we still haven't wrapped up the story of Israel; so it's back to the Northern Kingdom. Now it would be wonderful to be able to say that after God's amazing display of power on Mt. Carmel the people repented, rejected their idol worship and choose to steadfastly love God. They did, for a while. Ahab and Jezebel were soundly defeated. Ahab's linage was brought to a screeching halt and a new king named Jehu rounded up most of the remaining prophets and worshippers of Baal and put them to the sword. But in time, other kings ruled Israel whose hearts worshipped pagan gods. Israel fell

A Comparitive Study using *Secret of the Scribe* · 165

headlong into idolatry with all its grossest manifestations of sexual immorality, child sacrifice and witchcraft. Israel had tried the limits of God's patience. At long last, in the year 721 B.C., God "removed Israel from His presence."[111]

The nation of Assyria, rulers of the same land from which God had called Abraham,

swooped down and destroyed the nation who had chosen death. Assyria claimed the land God have given Israel because of the idolatry of the Canaanites who lived there before her. Now Assyria was God's tool of judgment. Israelites who survived were carried captive to Assyria, and lived out their lives in slavery, never to be heard from again.

God judged His people the same way he had judged the Canaanites before her, and the same way he would later judge the Assyrians, the Babylonians and all pagan peoples who chose to worship the creation rather than the Creator. From the beginning God warned Israel that the judgment that befell Canaan would also be hers if she degraded herself before idols. God's judgment does not discriminate. Sin is defined, and men are judged according to God's standard, not according to race. Israel chose destruction, slavery, and death, yet the nation survived because God was faithful to His covenant. God's faithfulness, mercy and redemption are the subjects of our next lesson – the last lesson from Israel's history.

Answer question D on chart **BNC-2** and return to chart **CC-1** to answer the question for Lesson 18.

---

111 II Kings 17:20,23

166 · Christian Theology & Ancient Polythesism

LESSON XIX:

Judah's End and New Beginning and the Never-Ending Faithfulness of God

A False Perspective on a True Story

A Jewish Polytheist's View on a Prophet of God:

HE'S AN ODD OLD MAN. SOME SAY, "HE'S CRAZY!" OTHERS SAY, "HE'S A TRAITOR!" THEY'VE TRIED TO KILL HIM MORE THAN ONCE. IN FACT, THEY'VE LOCKED HIM UP MORE TIMES THAN I CAN KEEP TRACK OF. HE'S ALWAYS DISTURBING THE PEACE – WHAT LITTLE THERE IS THESE DAYS, AS THE THREAT OF BABYLON BREATHS DOWN OUR NECKS. THAT'S THE PROBLEM: HE'S A PROPHET, AND HE SAYS THAT WHILE HIS GOD, YAHWEH, IS THE GOD OF JUDAH, HE'S FIGHTING FOR BABYLON. WHAT KIND OF MESSAGE IS THAT? WHAT KIND OF GOD IS THAT? IF HE WERE REALLY OUR GOD, THEN HE'D WANT TO MAKE SURE HIS CITY, JERUSALEM, AND HIS TEMPLE WEREN'T DEFEATED LIKE SO MANY OTHERS. DEFEAT MAKES THE GOD LOOK BAD; THERE GOES HIS CLAIM TO POWER. WHO'S THIS JEREMIAH TRYING TO FOOL? HIS GOD CAN'T EVEN TAKE CARE OF HIM. THERE HE IS – UNDER ARREST, HELD IN THE TEMPLE COURT YARD, STILL A MESS FROM THE STINKING MUD PIT THEY TRIED TO DROWN HIM IN. HE WOULDN'T STOP PREACHING THAT DREARY MESSAGE OF JERUSALEM'S DOOM. HE'S EITHER MAD OR A

RUTHLESS TRAITOR. BUT NO MATTER WHAT THEY DO TO HIM, THERE'S NO DISSUADING JEREMIAH.

FOR A WHILE THERE, HE WALKED AROUND WEARING A CATTLE YOKE, PREACHING THAT BABYLON WOULD DO THE SAME TO JUDAH. THEN ANOTHER PROPHET STEPPED FORWARD, YANKED THE YOKE OFF OF JEREMIAH'S NECK, AND BROKE IT INTO PIECES. HE ANNOUNCED, "YAHWEH WILL BREAK THE YOKE OF THE KING OF BABYLON WITHIN TWO YEARS. THE STOLEN TEMPLE TREASURES, THE KING AND ALL THE EXILES WILL BE BROUGHT BACK FROM BABYLON." THE LOOK ON JEREMIAH'S FACE WAS SO STRANGE. AT FIRST HE SAID HE'D BE GLAD IF THAT CAME TRUE, BUT THEN HIS EYES CLOUDED OVER WITH TEARS. LATER, JEREMIAH SAID THE PROPHET WAS A LIAR, OFFERING NOTHING BUT FALSE HOPE. BUT I LIKED WHAT THE MAN SAID. I SLEPT BETTER THAT NIGHT THAN I HAD FOR A WHILE. BUT NOT LONG AFTER, THAT PROPHET DIED. THOSE "TWO YEARS" HAVE LONG COME AND GONE, WITH NO RETURNS FROM BABYLON. NO RETURNS, THAT IS, EXCEPT THE BABYLONIAN SOLDIERS, WHO CAME BACK TO TAKE THE REST. JERUSALEM WAS PUT TO SIEGE BY THE MOST POWERFUL MILITARY IN THE WORLD. THEN WHAT DID JEREMIAH DO? HE BEGGED ISRAEL TO SURRENDER TO THE ENEMY. THE OFFICIALS HAD HAD ENOUGH OF JEREMIAH'S TRAITOROUS WORDS. THEY THREW HIM IN JAIL TO ROT. MEANWHILE, NEBUCHADNEZZAR KEPT ON WITH HIS SIEGE, UNTIL IT WAS RUMORED THAT EGYPT MIGHT GET INTO THE FRAY. THOSE BABYLONIANS LEFT RIGHT IN THE MIDDLE OF THE FIGHT TO GO TAKE CARE OF THE MARCHING EGYPTIAN SOLDIERS ... BUT NOT BEFORE LETTING US KNOW THEY'D BE BACK. THAT WAS SOME MONTHS AGO.

EVER SINCE THE SIEGE, THINGS HAVE GONE FROM BAD TO WORSE. LOTS OF PEOPLE ARE SICK. MOST FARMERS ARE AFRAID TO GO OUT OF THE CITY WALLS AND TEND THEIR FIELDS, FOR FEAR THAT THE BABYLONIANS WILL SHOW UP. THE BREAD SUPPLY, ALONG WITH MOST THINGS, IS RUNNING LOW. YET THERE GOES JEREMIAH AGAIN – HE ATTRIBUTES ALL THE DISEASE AND FAMINE TO HIS GOD. HE KEEPS SAYING BABYLON WILL BE BACK IF WE DON'T REPENT AND WORSHIP ONLY YAHWEH IN THE TEMPLE THAT SOLOMON BUILT. BUT HE IS WORSHIPPED THERE, ALONG WITH A LOT OF OTHER GODS. THAT'S A REAL BIG TEMPLE, AND THERE JUST WASN'T ENOUGH SPACE IN JERUSALEM TO KEEP BUILDING TEMPLES. BESIDES – JEREMIAH MUST HAVE FORGOTTEN – OUR WISE KING SOLOMON ALSO BUILT OTHER TEMPLES TO OTHER GODS JUST DOWN THE STREET. IF SOLOMON WORSHIPPED MANY GODS DURING THE GOLDEN YEARS OF ISRAEL, HOW CAN JEREMIAH BLAME ALL OUR CURRENT TROUBLES ON THE SAME THINGS SOLOMON DID THEN?

SOMEONE TRIED TO POINT THIS OUT TO JEREMIAH. YOU SHOULD HAVE HEARD HIM RANT AND RAVE ABOUT SOLOMON'S FOOLISHNESS. IF YOU LISTENED TO THE PROPHET FOR VERY LONG, YOU'D END UP THINKING THERE WAS ONLY ONE GOD. CAN YOU IMAGINE?! THE WORK OF THE ENTIRE UNIVERSE DONE BY ONE GOD?! IMPOSSIBLE! HE EXPECTS US TO BELIEVE THAT YAHWEH IS RESPONSIBLE FOR EVERYTHING, WHEN BABYLON IS CONTROLLING JUST ABOUT EVERY COUNTRY I CAN THINK OF. I DON'T THINK THE BABYLONIANS EVEN WORSHIP THIS YAHWEH GOD. BUT AT LEAST WE DO, ALONG WITH EVERYBODY ELSE'S GOD. SHOULDN'T WE GET SOME CREDIT? BUT DON'T ASK JEREMIAH. HE'LL JUST SAY THAT'S THE PROBLEM – THE WORSHIP OF MANY GODS.

A Comparitive Study using *Secret of the Scribe* · 169

WHERE DOES HE GET SUCH STRANGE IDEAS? HE KEEPS BRINGING UP SOMEONE NAMED MOSES (I WAS NEVER VERY GOOD IN HISTORY). JEREMIAH'S TIRADES ALWAYS INCLUDE CURSES WRITTEN BY MOSES ABOUT WHAT WOULD HAPPEN TO US IF WE WORSHIPPED OTHER GODS. I GUESS UNDER MOSES OUR ANCESTORS MADE SOME AGREEMENT TO WORSHIP ONE GOD AND SERVE HIM ALONE. WHAT WERE THEY THINKING? IF ALL THESE BAD THINGS THAT ARE HAPPENING TO US ARE BECAUSE WE DON'T WORSHIP YAHWEH ALONE, THEN WHY DO ALL THOSE GOOD THINGS HAPPEN IN BABYLON? THEY WIPED OUT ASSYRIA AND JUST KEPT ON GOING. I HEAR THEY ARE BUILDING JUST ABOUT THE FINEST EMPIRE IN WORLD ... HANGING GARDENS, PALACES THAT ARE GRANDER THAN THOSE OF EGYPT. THEY WORSHIP TONS OF GODS. HOW COULD JEREMIAH BE SO CONFUSED? EVERY GOD DESERVES HIS DUE.

HE IS SO OUT OF STEP WITH THE TIMES. HE MUST BE CRAZY. WE'VE SEEN HARD TIMES BEFORE. THE GODS MUST JUST BE A LITTLE BUSY THIS TIME OF YEAR. THEY'LL TURN THINGS AROUND, YOU'LL SEE. BUT THAT OLD GLOOMY JEREMIAH WOULD BE BETTER OFF PACKING HIS BAGS AND LEAVING FOR THAT "BABYLONIAN VACATION" HE KEEPS INSISTING WE SHOULD ALL TAKE. REALLY, JUST WHO DOES HE THINK HE IS?

Discussion Questions:

1 In this account, told by a Jewish polytheist, what were some of his arguments for Israel's worship of many gods?

2 How does not knowing about Moses, and the truths of Genesis through Deuteronomy lead to his false view of the world?

3 The chief god of the city of Babylon was Marduk. To whom was the polytheist likely to ascribe Nebuchadnezzar's military might?

4   If God had been concerned about proving His power to the people of Israel and the surrounding nations, do you think His Temple would have been destroyed?

This fictitious account, told from the viewpoint of a polytheist Jew, expresses many historical details of the life of the faithful prophet of God – Jeremiah. Mocked and mistreated, he was hated by most of the people he ministered to. This account also tells us a great deal about Judah – the Southern Kingdom. She had not, like Israel had under Ahab, completely rejected the worship of God. He was worshipped right along with other nature gods like Baal, Asheroth, Molech and many more.[112] This fact only made Jeremiah's message all the more difficult to communicate.

To understand the conclusion of this period of Israel's history, you may be surprised to learn that worshipping God as one of many gods is actually *worse* than not worshipping Him at all. As you learned in the previous lesson, man can worship God, or man can worship Satan, or man can worship himself. Worshipping man and worshipping Satan are both sins of idolatry, but it is yet another sin to include the worship of God with the worship of nature gods. This act calls God a liar, because it is contrary to everything God has revealed about Himself. In God's first revelation of Himself, God is creator, not creature. God is one, not many. God is all powerful, not a limited power. God is the provider, not just a contributor. God is not a part of the created order; He is separate from it. To worship or even associate Yahweh alongside the likes of idols like Baal or Molech grossly demeans and distorts the revealed identity of God.

This sin is a gross insult to God. The insult is called "blasphemy". To blaspheme is to reduce or devalue the sacred nature of God. The root words for blasphemy come from the Greek *blaptein* – to injure and *pheme* – reputation. To injure the reputation of the only One who is worthy of all glory, honor and praise is a contemptuous act of the gravest disrespect. Man can reject God, but to demean God is another sin altogether, as it represents to the world a totally twisted image of God.

Judah probably thought she was better than her relative Israel, because at least she still worshipped God. But in truth her worship of God along with other nature gods and goddesses was a hideous distortion of the true nature of the One, all-powerful Creator God. As Israel was before her, Judah was about to be "thrust out of the presence of God".[113]

"THEY SET UP THEIR ABOMINABLE IDOLS IN THE HOUSE THAT BEARS MY NAME AND DEFILED IT. THEY BUILT HIGH PLACES FOR BAAL IN THE VALLEY OF BEN HINNOM TO SACRIFICE THEIR SONS AND DAUGHTERS TO MOLECH, THOUGH I NEVER COMMANDED IT, NOR DID IT ENTER MY MIND, THAT THEY SHOULD SO SUCH A DESTABLE THING AND SO MAKE JUDAH SIN."
JEREMIAH 32:34-35

---

112 BLENDING THE WORSHIP OF THE ONE GOD WITH THE WORSHIP OF MANY GODS IS CALLED SYNCRETISM.
113 JEREMIAH 7:15; 15:1-2

In the last book of the Bible, the Apostle John records the judgment of Christ against one of the seven churches "I know your works, that you are neither cold nor hot: I would you were cold or hot. So then because you are lukewarm, and neither cold nor hot, I will spew[114] you out of my mouth. (Revelation 3:15,16) This church was not worshipping other gods, but she had put her confidence in things other than God. God must have first place in our life; to value God like other objects, be they other human relationships or achievement or pleasure or money or fame, is to devalue God. God will not be just one of many important things in the life of a Christian. In treating Him so, we blaspheme our Maker.

There are sobering implications here for the Christian. A Christian who says he loves God but strives hard after things like popularity, relationships or money has made these things into idols. For a Christian to have idols is like Judah setting up altars to Baal and Molech in the Temple of God. As the temple of the Holy Spirit, we should shudder at the thought. The first love of our hearts must be given to God. The person who says he is a Christian, but rather than striving after Christ-likeness strives after *things,* will not become like God. Thus the "image of God" that he presents to the world is false. In saying he is a Christian, he does great damage to the cause of Christ. There is a trite saying: "You may be the only Bible some people will ever read." The lukewarm Christian distorts the character of God. This is why God would rather have us "hot" or "cold."

Discussion Questions:

1. To whom and through whom does God reveal Himself? Why was it so wrong to worship pagan gods in the Temple dedicated to God?

2. Why was Judah's worship of both the true God and other false gods worse than the worship of false gods only?

3. Why is it worse to be someone who claims to be a Christian, yet strives after things other than God, than it is to deny the existence of God altogether?

4. When a Christian is convicted of striving after things rather than wholeheartedly seeking God, what should they do? Can God forgive such a terrible sin?

5. The following lesson is about the terrible judgment that God brings upon Judah because of her great sin. Name some reasons why Judah deserves God's punishment.

---

114 To *spew* MEANS TO SPIT OR VOMIT

6   The following lesson is also about God's great mercy – how God forgives Israel's sin and the future hope she is given. Based on your current Bible knowledge, how do you think God's mercy, forgiveness and hope will be given to Israel?

> Go to **chart TC-2** and note the implications of Revelations 3:15-16 for those who strive to represent God.

Let's turn back now to the prophet Jeremiah, who was given by God the unenviable task of confronting Judah with her odious sin. Unlike the opinion of the observer in our earlier story, Jeremiah was not mad, but he was angry. He expressed the anger of the Lord when he said,

> *"They have followed worthless idols and became worthless themselves ... my people have exchanged their Glory for worthless idols. Be appalled at this, O heavens and shudder with great horror."*[115]

Jeremiah was called by the Lord Almighty to speak judgment to his people through the reigns of Judah's last four kings, who had continuously worshipped other gods. His father was the high priest under Judah's last good king, Josiah. Jeremiah mourned the death of this king, whose spiritual revival came too late. Despite Jeremiah's constant warnings, Judah fell headlong into idolatry, committing all the sins of Israel. Even watching Israel's tragedy did not motivate Judah to leave the path of destruction down which she was careening.

FOR OLDER STUDENTS: READ LEVITICUS 26 AND JEREMIAH 12, NOTING THE SIMILARITIES BETWEEN MOSES' WARNING AND JEREMIAH'S HISTORICAL ACCOUNT OF THE FALL OF JERUSALEM. WHY WERE THESE HORRIBLE CONSEQUENCES A JUST SUFFERING FOR JUDAH'S IDOLATRY?

For many long years Jeremiah warned God's people about the consequences of breaking her promises to God – in short, doom and destruction. Many of the words spoken by Jeremiah were originally written by the prophet Moses, through whom Israel had made her covenant with God. In the desert, Israel had been entrusted with the Law of God. At the heart of Israel's laws were the Ten Commandments, which God Himself had written upon tablets of stone. Two of these laws were at the center of Israel's commitment to God. Israel had pledged not to bow down to idols and to keep the Sabbath laws,[116] the sign of her covenant. Receiving a land flowing with milk and honey was

115 JEREMIAH 2:5,11
116 LEVITICUS 26:1,2

A Comparitive Study using *Secret of the Scribe* · 173

contingent upon keeping her promises. She did not. Jeremiah foretold in warning (and in witness) God's terrible judgment upon His idolatrous people. (If older students are doing this study, pause the lesson here, and read and discuss the two chapters noted in the margin note on the previous page.)

However, in the years leading up to Judah's destruction, Jeremiah was not just a prophet of doom; he also preached the never-failing mercy of God. Almost up until the time the Babylonians had built their siege ramps against the walls of Jerusalem, Jeremiah continued to preach that God would restore His people if they would repent (turn from their sins).[117] Stubbornly, Judah refused to change her ways and return to her covenant with God. So Jeremiah, at God's instructions, did the next best thing; he pled with Judah to surrender to the Babylonians, rather than undergoing the nightmare of a siege. But Jerusalem officials branded him a traitor and arrested him, then plunged into battle with the mightiest nation on earth. While under arrest, Jeremiah endured the final tragic days of the siege of Jerusalem. God indeed brought sword, famine and disease and fulfilled the worst of the curses prophesied by Moses.[118] Solomon's Temple was utterly destroyed. Jerusalem was burned; the walls were torn down. Most of those who survived were led away to Babylon in chains.

Despite the people's rebellion and stubborn pride before, during and after the siege, Jeremiah spoke words of comfort. He promised that the inevitable Babylonian captivity would have a time limit – seventy years. God would bring the exiles back from Babylon.[119] Israel had been unfaithful to her God, but God would be faithful to Israel.[120]

Jeremiah wrote letters to those already in Babylonian captivity, telling them to settle in the land, live peaceably, marry, have children and believe that God would return them to their land.[121] After Israel suffered for her sins, God would bring His people home. Those that returned would be called the *remnant*. God would purify them, wipe away all their sins, and restore them to the land. Jeremiah prophesied

---

117 JEREMIAH 26:13
118 LEVITICUS 26:1,2
119 JEREMIAH 16:14; 33:7
120 JEREMIAH 31:1-4
121 JEREMIAH 29:3-7

this gracious restoration by God. Through suffering and through grace, the people of God – the remnant who returned – would never again be characterized as idolaters. From the time of the return of the exiles, Israel – by God's grace – would keep covenant with her God and worship Him alone.

Read aloud II Chronicles 36:15-23 (written after the return by a later writer) **and Jeremiah 50:17-20** (written after the destruction before the return) **and discuss the following questions:**

1   What was the destruction of both Israel and Judah?

2   Why was this destruction just?

3   What hope did Jeremiah's prophecies give to the people?

4   How did God show His people grace – unmerited favor – before, during and after the fall of Jerusalem?

God's faithfulness, as prophesied by Jeremiah, included the promise of a new covenant which one day God would establish with the house of Israel. You will remember that the sign of the old covenant, the agreement Israel made with God under Moses, was the Sabbath laws. Central to the Sabbath laws was letting the land rest every seventh year. This was as an expression of Israel's trust in God's provision and her role as steward of His land. Because she did not keep this vital sign of her covenant, the length of her captivity was determined by the number of Sabbath rests the land had not received – that number of years was seventy. While these years were noted by the writer of Chronicles after the exiles returned, Jeremiah had sent word to the captives living in Babylon that they must be out of the land for 70 years.[122]

Rather than seeing this as a terrible judgment, the exiles received the news with great hope. In breaking her pledge to God, Israel had forfeited any right to the blessings of God. She deserved to be put out of His sight forever. Today Israel should be nothing more than one in a list of many obscure nations who occupied Palestine before Greek rule. Instead, God would fulfill the promise that Israel failed to keep; God gave the land its Sabbath Rest for 70 years, while Israel stayed in Babylonian captivity. God did what man was purposed to do. In Israel's darkest hour, it was God who provided a way for Israel to be redeemed out of slavery and restored to fellowship with her Creator.

Below, you will read a portion of the book of Jeremiah that foretells both the return of the exiles and God's establishment of a new covenant. As with many words of the prophets, there was an immediate meaning as well as a future

---

122 JEREMIAH 25:11; LEVITICUS 26:43-45

A Comparative Study using *Secret of the Scribe* · 175

meaning. We are familiar with verse 15 as it applies to Herod's murder of the innocent children in Matthew 2:16. The weeping that Jeremiah would have understood was Judah's grief while watching her young men and women being led away in chains to Babylonian captivity. On the route to Babylon, Ramah is just five miles north of Jerusalem. Depending on when these children went into captivity, some would actually be a part of the exiles who would return to the land under the Persian King Cyrus.

Read aloud Jeremiah 31:15-37 and discuss the following questions:

1   In verse 18, is it possible to be disciplined, but not affected by the discipline? From verse 18 and 19 how do you know Ephraim (one of the chief tribes of the Northern tribes) has been changed by God's discipline?

2   The road signs are an invitation for Israel to what?

3   What is amazing about God calling Israel "Virgin daughter"? What does this name signify?

4   What characterizes the era of this new covenant?

5   How will the new covenant differ from the old covenant?

6   With whom will the new covenant be made?

7   How long will this covenant last?

The new covenant would be a covenant of grace. It would be marked not by external action, but by the transformation of the heart. Only this time, God and God alone would suffer. Through the old covenant, God had brought a means of forgiveness to His people; through the new covenant, God would bring both a lasting forgiveness and eternal life.

You read in Jeremiah 31:22 that "The Lord will create a new thing on earth – a woman will surround a man." One of the writers from the early Church era, Jerome, said that this verse referred to the Virgin Mary. With Christ in her womb, she was the woman who surrounded a man. As such, this is actually a prophecy of the coming Messiah, who would be born of a woman. Jesus Christ, God incarnate, would usher in this new covenant which Jeremiah foretold. "This is the covenant I will make with the house of Israel ... I will forgive ... their sins."[123]

Hours before Jesus was betrayed, he was eating the Passover feast with his Jewish disciples. In their presence, Christ took the cup of wine and said, "This is the *blood of the new covenant, which is poured out for many for the remission of sins.*"

---

123 JEREMIAH 31:33A,34C

176 · Christian Theology & Ancient Polythesism

(Matthew 26:28) To those who believed, this covenant gave forgiveness of sins and the Holy Spirit, who would empower the man of God to fulfill His purpose. Recall that the tablet of stone containing God's Ten Commandments was placed within the Ark of the Covenant, and the Ark was placed inside the Holy of Holies at Solomon's dedication of the Temple. Under the new covenant, we become the temple of God and are indwelt with the Holy Spirit who writes God's laws upon the tablets of our hearts. We Christians not only have the gift of conscience given to all men; we have the very life of God indwelling and enabling us to obey the words of God.[124]

Also, the new covenant would address more than man's need for a lasting forgiveness;[125] and a power source enabling him to fulfill his purpose. Under this covenant, Christ would suffer on man's behalf. Through His suffering, Christ shed his blood. Through His blood, we gain eternal life. Thus the sign of the new covenant is the life blood of Jesus Christ. In the same way that Israel's practice of the Sabbath Rest was intended to distinguish her from the cultures around her, sharing the broken body and shed blood of Jesus Christ unites believers and distinguishes us from those who do not have the life of Christ. Participating in the Lord's Supper is the Church's sacred celebration and the sign of the New Covenant. (See Some Final Words on Rest at the end of this lesson).

Finally, through the new covenant we have the supreme example of Christ, the God/man. Christ came to show us the Father and to show us ourselves. This revelation culminated in the love of God as demonstrated through the death of Christ. In dying, Christ displayed the depth of the Father's love, and in rising again, the breath of His power. Christ's death also fulfilled man's purpose to reveal the love of God to the world; through the accounts of Christ's life, we have a living model of what God looks like in the flesh. Through the Spirit we are given the power to live His life in our flesh. As we strive to love and obey Christ, we reveal the Creator and Savior to the world.

Read aloud I John 4:9-12 and discuss the following questions:

1 For what three reasons was Christ sent into the world?

2 Why does our love matter?

The one who ushered in the new covenant also fulfilled another great promise God made with the house of David. Jeremiah anticipated God's fulfillment of this promise.

> WHILE GOD CHOSE TO WRITE HIS WORD IN AND THROUGH MAN, THE TEN COMMANDMENTS STAND APART FROM ALL OTHER TEXTS OF SCRIPTURE. GOD HIMSELF WROTE THESE COMMANDMENTS UPON TABLETS OF STONE, WITHOUT HUMAN AGENCY. THE LAW ORIGINATES IN THE CHARACTER OF GOD ALONE. AFTER MAN BROKE GOD'S FIRST LAW IN THE GARDEN, GOD MERCIFULLY PROVIDED HIS STANDARD AGAIN. THIS PERSONAL ENGRAVING OF GOD FORESHADOWED THE INSCRIPTION HE WOULD WRITE IN THE NEW COVENANT. THE HOLY SPIRIT WOULD WRITE THIS LAW UPON THE TABLETS OF HUMAN HEARTS, FOR THE PURPOSE OF RE-MAKING OUR CHARACTERS TO BE LIKE HIS.

---

124 HEBREWS 10:15,16
125 IN CONTRAST TO THE CONTINUAL SACRIFICES OF ANIMALS. HEBREWS 10:8-14

A Comparitive Study using *Secret of the Scribe* · 177

Read aloud Jeremiah 33:15-18 and discuss the following questions:

1. How is the branch of David described?

2. What is His name?

3. What two things will He do?

Despite the unfaithfulness of David's descendants, God had preserved his line and established it forever through Christ. Both Mary and Joseph were descendants of King David. Christ is the king who sits on David's throne, but unlike any Israelite king, Christ is both king and high priest as our mediator between God and man.[126]

As we close this final lesson on Israel's history that anticipates her return to the land, we have seen the steadfast love of her Redeemer and the amazing faithfulness of her God. What Jeremiah saw was the terrible destruction of Jerusalem, the survivors marched off into captivity, and even his own death outside of the land he loved. Jeremiah saw much that would necessitate the title he is best known for – the weeping prophet. Yet despite all the tragedy he experienced, he foretold and believed in the faithfulness of God. Jeremiah by faith believed that God would keep His promises despite His people's unfaithfulness. Jeremiah by faith told the captives that they would return to the land and that God would forgive their sins and re-establish His covenant with them. By faith, Jeremiah foretold that someday God would establish a new covenant and a new king, who would sit on the throne of David forever and ever. Jeremiah believed all of this, even when he saw nothing but the ruin and desolation of Jerusalem. Sometime after the fall of the city of God, Jeremiah wrote these words:

Read aloud Lamentations 3:13-26 and discuss the following questions:

1. Who is the "He" Jeremiah is talking about in verses 13-18?

2. Despite his wretched circumstances, what is it that gives Jeremiah hope?

3. From verse 22 forward, how does Jeremiah describe God?

---

126 Zechariah 6:13; Hebrews 1:1-14; 7:11- 8:1

4   What did Jeremiah content himself with doing?

Jeremiah knew that God could be trusted even when his own experience seemed to reflect the opposite. History has confirmed that Jeremiah's faith was well placed. Despite our circumstances, may we cling as Jeremiah did to the God who is faithful.

Some Final Words on Rest

The first day of rest – the rest God took on the seventh day – symbolized the fact that He had provided everything man needed in order to have life in Him (this included the Tree of Life). The Sabbath Rest was Israel's sign of her commitment to depend on God's provision for her life. Like her first parents, she failed to rest in God. Nevertheless, Israel would be greatly used by God to provide rest to the whole world. Through her, God became incarnate and again provided everything we need to come unto

Him and find rest for our souls. Rest symbolizes salvation, through which we are given life. This life is made possible through Christ, who conquered death through His death and resurrection. Thus the Christian's sign of her covenant with God is partaking in the body and blood of Christ. The Lord's Supper is to the Church what the Sabbath Rest was to Israel. Both proclaim the only source of life that was made evident from the beginning.

Older student should note what God provided for Judah and the land during the captivity on chart **TC-1**. Then add a second entry to chart **TC-2**, noting the ways Jeremiah represented God to his unfaithful people. On chart **TC-4**, record the suffering of God, Jeremiah, and Judah.

A Comparitive Study using *Secret of the Scribe* · **179**

LESSON XX:

Suffering of the Babylonian & Biblical Job

This lesson and the one that follows will delve deep into the topic of suffering. The Bible has an enormous amount to say about this subject, but the most intense teaching about suffering is provided in the Old Testament story of Job – a righteous man who undergoes extreme affliction. Unsurprisingly, the Bible is not the only piece of ancient literature that examines the subject of unjust suffering. In fact, there are four Sumerian and Babylonian stories that, like the story of Job, try to make sense of why good people suffer. For the overarching purposes of this guide, Job gives us another opportunity to compare and contrast the worldviews of ancient polytheists and Hebrew monotheists and how each were shaped by the problem of pain.

The ancient peoples of Mesopotamia believed that the gods punished those who did not please or obey them. Suffering was a consequence for sin. What they did not understand was why the gods sometimes punished people who did please them. Struggling to comprehend the suffering of a just man – one who offered sacrifices, obeyed the gods' laws, and prayed faithfully – they asked, "Why would this man suffer?" Sumerians and Babylonians wrote poems similar to the some of the Bible's psalms and more lengthy narratives like Job that dealt with the worldview question, "Why do good people suffer?" To understand how the Sumerians and Babylonians wrestled with and reconciled this issue, let's begin with a portion of *Secret of the Scribe*.

Read the story of the queen's death in *Secret of the Scribe* and discuss the questions below:

> Page 4 – start reading at the bottom of page 4, "Our trouble started..." and end on page 8 with "... the queen died an hour after dawn."

Discussion Questions:

1   Who was the ashipu?

2   What methods did the ashipu use to save the queen's life?

3   What did he conclude had made her sick?

4   Who was the asu?

5   What methods did the asu use?

6   While the ashipu's methods were different from the asu's, what were they both trying to accomplish in order to save the queen?

7   To what two supernatural powers were the queen's suffering and death attributed?

The queen was a powerful, rich woman. The story in subtle ways indicates that she was a good woman. She was like "a mother to me and also to my child, Tabni." The king was experiencing sincere grief at the thought of losing her. The gentle lamb slept peacefully beside the queen. Yet in her last hours she experienced terrible sufferings, gross disrespect from the "wicked goat," and a vile potion rubbed upon her belly. This story only briefly hints at one of the great themes of ancient wisdom literature – the question of why good people suffer. Nevertheless, it introduces two characters – the ashipu or asu – both of whom play major roles in ancient literature that involves righteous sufferers. While the ashipu and asu were unable to identify the reason the gods caused the queen to suffer, they sought to solve the problem through the use of sorcery. Both the ashipu and the asu used magical spells or potions to give them supernatural power over the demon that must be driven away. In the *Secret of the Scribe*, they failed, and the queen died. But in the great ancient Mesopotamian stories, the sufferer, through the help of a sorcerer, is always restored to health and wealth.

In these ancient stories, a man who is righteous by the standards of his religion, full of wealth and respect, is suddenly stripped of everything and endures horrific suffering. Unlike the queen, who suffers briefly and dies, these men suffer on and on, until they are finally healed and restored to their original position. During their great suffering they each ask, "Why have such evil circumstances befallen me? In the earliest of these stories, the sufferer admits that he has sinned and therefore justly incurred the wrath of his god. However in later accounts, the sufferer, like the biblical Job, is convinced of his own right standing before his god and thus the injustice of his suffering. In all of these stories two important questions are asked: Why do the gods deal unjustly with men who strive to please them? How can a person convince the gods to change their minds and relent from inflicting pain?

For the Mesopotamian stories, no ultimate answer is provided for the first question above. The characters simply conclude that the ways of the gods cannot be understood by their slaves. Yet, in regard to the second question, the characters did understand that the loss of favor from one's gods could result in the gods' leaving and demons coming to torment the defenseless person. Thus, these stories do develop a means for the characters to persuade the gods to change their minds and look again with favor upon their slave. So, how can a human persuade a god or gods? The answer – find a mediator, someone who can go between the worlds

A Comparitive Study using *Secret of the Scribe* · 181

of men and of gods. That person was the exorcist, sorcerer or the witchdoctor (the ashipu and even the asu) – the one who had some secret knowledge of supernatural power. This man or woman could help a person in pain. He could determine what god or demon was inflicting the suffering, what sacrifice or song would appease the god, and what kind of magical spell or incantation would cast the demon out. These stories point out again how central witchcraft was to ancient Mesopotamian culture.

Below is a story about one such sufferer that was pressed in cuneiform clay by a Babylonian scribe some 3,700 years ago. The story the scribe recorded is actually much older, as its main character, Tabu-utul-Bel, was a Sumerian official who lived in the city of Nippur, possibly before the great flood. Written in first person, Tabu-utul-Bel, the Job character, describes his suffering and dismay in detail. Pay special attention to why he thinks his suffering is unjust. What brings him relief from his suffering? What does he believe about the gods?

Read aloud and discuss the poem entitled "The Ludlul Bel Nimequi"[127] (This is also called "Poem of the Righteous Sufferer" or the "Babylonian Job")[128]

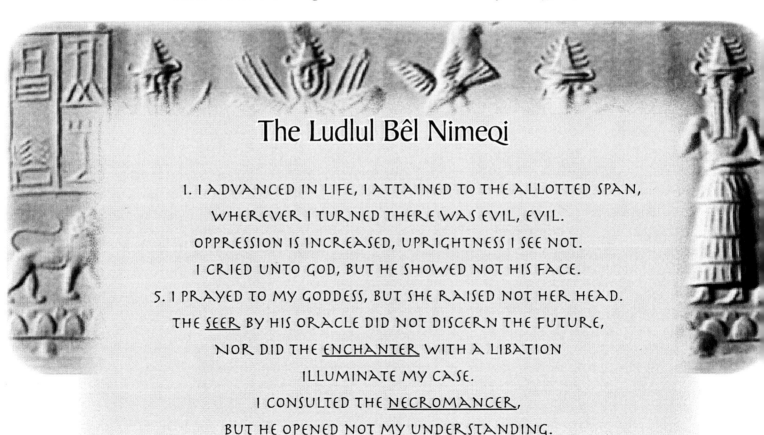

The Ludlul Bêl Nimeqi

1. I ADVANCED IN LIFE, I ATTAINED TO THE ALLOTTED SPAN,
WHEREVER I TURNED THERE WAS EVIL, EVIL.
OPPRESSION IS INCREASED, UPRIGHTNESS I SEE NOT.
I CRIED UNTO GOD, BUT HE SHOWED NOT HIS FACE.
5. I PRAYED TO MY GODDESS, BUT SHE RAISED NOT HER HEAD.
THE SEER BY HIS ORACLE DID NOT DISCERN THE FUTURE,
NOR DID THE ENCHANTER WITH A LIBATION
ILLUMINATE MY CASE.
I CONSULTED THE NECROMANCER,
BUT HE OPENED NOT MY UNDERSTANDING.

---

[127] From: George A. Barton, Archaeology and The Bible, 3rd Ed., (Philadelphia: American Sunday School, 1920), pp. 392-395
[128] Encyclopedia Britannica at http://www.britannica.com/EBchecked/topic/350791/Ludlul-bel-nemeqi

THE <u>CONJURER</u> WITH HIS CHARMS DID NOT REMOVE MY BAN.

10. HOW DEEDS ARE REVERSED IN THE WORLD!

I LOOK BEHIND, OPPRESSION ENCLOSES ME

LIKE ONE WHO THE SACRIFICE TO GOD DID NOT BRING

AND AT MEAL-TIME DID NOT INVOKE THE GODDESS,

DID NOT BOW DOWN HIS FACE, HIS OFFERING WAS NOT SEEN;

15. (LIKE ONE) IN WHOSE MOUTH PRAYERS AND

SUPPLICATIONS WERE LOCKED,

(FOR WHOM) GOD'S DAY HAD CEASED, A FEAST DAY BECOME RARE,

(ONE WHO) HAS THROWN DOWN HIS FIRE-PAN,

GONE AWAY FROM THEIR IMAGES,

GOD'S FEAR AND VENERATION HAS NOT TAUGHT HIS PEOPLE,

WHO INVOKED NOT HIS GOD WHEN HE ATE GOD'S FOOD;

20. (WHO) ABANDONED HIS GODDESS AND BROUGHT

NOT WHAT IS PRESCRIBED,

(WHO) OPPRESSES THE WEAK, FORGETS HIS GOD,

WHO TAKES IN VAIN THE MIGHTY NAME OF HIS GOD,

HE SAYS, "I AM LIKE HIM".

BUT I MYSELF THOUGHT OF PRAYERS AND SUPPLICATIONS.

PRAYER WAS MY WISDOM, SACRIFICE, MY DIGNITY;

25. THE DAY OF HONORING THE GODS WAS THE JOY OF MY HEART,

THE DAY OF FOLLOWING THE GODDESS WAS MY

ACQUISITION OF WEALTH,

THE PRAYER OF THE KING, THAT WAS MY DELIGHT,

AND HIS MUSIC, FOR MY PLEASURE WAS ITS SOUND.

I GAVE DIRECTIONS TO MY LAND TO REVERE THE NAMES OF GOD.

30. TO HONOR THE NAME OF THE GODDESS I TAUGHT MY PEOPLE.

REVERENCE FOR THE KING I GREATLY EXALTED

AND RESPECT FOR THE PALACE I TAUGHT THE PEOPLE,

FOR I KNEW THAT WITH GOD THESE THINGS ARE IN FAVOR.

WHAT IS INNOCENT OF ITSELF, TO GOD IS EVIL!

35. WHAT IN ONE'S HEART IS CONTEMPTIBLE TO ONE'S GOD IS GOOD!

A Comparitive Study using *Secret of the Scribe*

WHO CAN UNDERSTAND THE THOUGHTS OF THE GODS IN HEAVEN?

THE COUNSEL OF GOD IS FULL OF DESTRUCTION;

WHO CAN UNDERSTAND?

WHERE MAY HUMAN BEINGS LEARN THE WAYS OF GOD?

HE WHO LIVES AT EVENING IS DEAD IN THE MORNING;

40. QUICKLY HE IS TROUBLED; ALL AT ONCE HE IS OPPRESSED;

AT ONE MOMENT HE SINGS AND PLAYS;

IN THE TWINKLING OF AN EYE HE HOWLS LIKE

A FUNERAL-MOURNER.

LIKE SUNSHINE AND CLOUDS THEIR THOUGHTS CHANGE;

THEY ARE HUNGRY AND LIKE A CORPSE;

45. THEY ARE FILLED AND RIVAL THEIR GOD!

IN PROSPERITY THEY SPEAK OF CLIMBING TO HEAVEN.

TROUBLE OVERTAKES THEM, AND THEY SPEAK OF GOING

DOWN TO SHEOL.

At this point the tablet is broken.
The narrative is resumed on the reverse of the tablet.

46. INTO MY PRISON MY HOUSE IS TURNED.

INTO THE BONDS OF MY FLESH ARE MY HANDS THROWN;

INTO THE FETTERS OF MYSELF MY FEET HAVE STUMBLED.

47. WITH A WHIP HE HAS BEATEN ME; THERE IS NO PROTECTION;

WITH A STAFF HE HAS TRANSFIXED ME;

THE STENCH WAS TERRIBLE!

ALL DAY LONG THE PURSUER PURSUES ME;

IN THE NIGHT WATCHES HE LETS ME BREATHE NOT A MOMENT.

THROUGH TORTURE MY JOINTS ARE TORN ASUNDER;

48. MY LIMBS ARE DESTROYED, LOATHING COVERS ME;

ON MY COUCH I WELTER LIKE AN OX.

I AM COVERED, LIKE A SHEEP, WITH MY EXCREMENT.

MY SICKNESS BAFFLED THE CONJURERS,

AND THE SEER LEFT DARK MY OMENS.

49. THE DIVINER HAS NOT IMPROVED THE CONDITION

OF MY SICKNESS;

THE DURATION OF MY ILLNESS THE SEER COULD NOT STATE.

THE GOD HELPED ME NOT; MY HAND HE TOOK NOT.

THE GODDESS PITIED ME NOT; SHE CAME NOT TO MY SIDE.

THE COFFIN YAWNED; THEY [THE HEIRS] TOOK MY POSSESSIONS.

50. WHILE I WAS NOT YET DEAD, THE DEATH WAIL WAS READY.

MY WHOLE LAND CRIED OUT: "HOW IS HE DESTROYED!"

MY ENEMY HEARD; HIS FACE GLADDENED.

THEY BROUGHT AS GOOD NEWS THE GLAD TIDINGS;

HIS HEART REJOICED.

BUT I KNEW THE TIME OF ALL MY FAMILY.

Between verses 51 to 59 the damage to the surviving tablets make an exact translation confusing to read. These lines have been rearranged and somewhat enhanced to aid the readers understanding:

51. WHEN AMONG THE PROTECTING SPIRITS

THEIR DIVINITY IS EXALTED.

I, TABU-UTUL-BEL[129], LAY DOWN AND A DREAM I BEHELD;

THIS IS THE DREAM WHICH I SAW BY NIGHT.

[HE WHO MADE WOMAN] AND CREATED MAN – MARDUK

HE ORDAINED THAT I BE ENCOMPASSED WITH SICKNESS.

BUT HE SENT ME A MAN TO HELP ME

IN THE DREAM UR-BAU[130] APPEARED

A MIGHTY HERO WEARING HIS CROWN

HE IS A CONJURER, CLAD IN STRENGTH,

MARDUK INDEED SENT HIM;

HE SAID: "HOW LONG WILL HE BE IN SUCH GREAT AFFLICTION

AND DISTRESS?"

IN HIS PURE HANDS HE BROUGHT ABUNDANCE.

AND CALLED FORTH MY GUARDIAN-SPIRIT.

---

129 TABU-UTUL-BEL IS THE NAME OF THE MAN WHO IS SUFFERING. HE IS THE JOB CHARACTER OF THIS POEM.

130 THE NAME OF THE SORCERER SENT BY MARDUK TO HELP THE SUFFERING TABU-UTUL-BEL.

THIS SEER HE SENT A MESSAGE:
"THROUGH IT MARDUK'S ANGER WAS APPEASED,
MY LORD, HIS HEART WAS SATISFIED;
MY LAMENTATION WAS HEARD.
UR-BAU APPROACHED ME WITH THE SPELL WHICH HE HAD
PRONOUNCED, INCANTATIONS TO DRIVE AWAY
THE TORMENTING DEMONS.

59. HE SENT A STORM WIND TO THE HORIZON;
TO THE BREAST OF THE EARTH IT BORE A BLAST,
INTO THE DEPTH OF HIS OCEAN
THE DISEMBODIED SPIRIT VANISHED.
UNNUMBERED SPIRITS HE SENT BACK TO THE UNDER-WORLD. THE
HAG-DEMONS HE SENT STRAIGHT TO THE MOUNTAIN.
60. THE SEA-FLOOD HE SPREAD WITH ICE;
THE ROOTS OF THE DISEASE HE TORE OUT LIKE A PLANT.
THE HORRIBLE SLUMBER THAT SETTLED ON MY REST
LIKE SMOKE FILLED THE SKY.

WITH THE WOE HE HAD BROUGHT, UNREPULSED AND BITTER, HE
FILLED THE EARTH LIKE A STORM.
61. THE UNRELIEVED HEADACHE WHICH HAD
OVERWHELMED THE HEAVENS
HE TOOK AWAY AND SENT DOWN ON ME THE EVENING DEW.
MY EYELIDS, WHICH HE HAD VEILED WITH THE VEIL OF NIGHT
HE BLEW UPON WITH A RUSHING WIND AND
MADE CLEAR THEIR SIGHT.
MY EARS, WHICH WERE STOPPED, WERE DEAF AS A DEAF MAN'S.
62. HE REMOVED THEIR DEAFNESS AND
RESTORED THEIR HEARING.
MY NOSE, WHOSE NOSTRIL HAD BEEN STOPPED
FROM MY MOTHER'S WOMB.
HE EASED ITS DEFORMITY SO THAT I COULD BREATHE.
MY LIPS, WHICH WERE CLOSED HE HAD TAKEN THEIR STRENGTH,
HE REMOVED THEIR TREMBLING AND LOOSED THEIR BOND.
63. MY MOUTH WHICH WAS CLOSED SO THAT I
COULD NOT BE UNDERSTOOD,
HE CLEANSED IT LIKE A DISH, HE HEALED ITS DISEASE.
MY EYES, WHICH HAD BEEN ATTACKED
SO THAT THEY ROLLED TOGETHER,
HE LOOSED THEIR BOND, AND THEIR BALLS WERE SET RIGHT.
THE TONGUE, WHICH HAD STIFFENED SO THAT
IT COULD NOT BE RAISED,
64. HE RELIEVED ITS THICKNESS, SO ITS WORDS
COULD BE UNDERSTOOD.
THE GULLET WHICH WAS COMPRESSED, STOPPED AS WITH A PLUG,
HE HEALED ITS CONTRACTION, IT WORKED LIKE A FLUTE.
MY SPITTLE WHICH WAS STOPPED SO THAT IT WAS NOT SECRETED,
HE REMOVED ITS FETTER; HE OPENED ITS LOCK.

A Comparitive Study using *Secret of the Scribe* · 187

Discussion Questions:

1. What are some of the various terms used for people who deal in some form of magic? (These words have been underllined.)

2. To what kind of person does the sufferer contrast himself?

3. What examples does he give to demonstrate that he was an upright man before his gods?

4. What does he conclude about his god in verses 35 to 45?

5. Based on his dream, who caused the suffering of this man?

6. How did Marduk help the sufferer?

7. Who was Ur-Bau?

8. What was the cause of Tabu-utul-Bel suffering that was blown away by a rushing wind?

9. What are some of the terms given to evil spirits?

> Go to chart **CC-9**, "The Babylonian and Biblical Job", and answer the first four questions.

Now let's turn to the story of Job. Job was not Jewish, but he served the God of the Jews. He lived in the land of Uz, which was located in Southern Arabia. The human author and the period of history in which Job lived is not known. Additionally, when his story was incorporated into the writings of Old Testament is not known. Nevertheless, like the story above, the problem confronted in the story of Job is known to all. You don't have to live very many years before you realize that despite all the good that exists in this world, bad things do happen. Some of these bad things happen to good people. This is the story of Job. Job, a good man, a blameless man in fact, endures what for most is unimaginable suffering. Job does not understand why. Knowing nothing of the reasons behind his suffering, he is convinced that his suffering is unjust.

Below are references for your first reading from the book of Job. As you read, listen for similarities to the Babylonian Job. The passages here come toward the end of the book and contain Job's last words of defense about the injustice of his suffering and his plea to stand trial before God. For the last 22 chapters, Job has been fending off the accusations of three friends, who had come to him to be his comforters. However, rather than comfort, their words have proved to be salt

188 · Christian Theology & Ancient Polythesism

rubbed in an open wound. They insist that God has justly brought this suffering upon Job as retribution for some hidden sin. In defending his integrity, Job sincerely questions and even challenges the justice of God. This was his downfall. While Job sounds rather proud in these texts, he is not exaggerating his goodness. Job was blameless, and his friends were deeply mistaken about the reasons behind his suffering. Even so, Job's perplexity revealed his profound lack of understanding about the ways of God. Anyone who looks thoughtfully at this story of Job will learn much about the nature of God, suffering, and His purposes for mankind.

Read Job chapters 29:1-20, 30:15-31, 31:24-40 and 38:1 aloud and answer the following questions:

1. What similarities do you see between the biblical Job and the Babylonian Job?

2. What examples does Job give that support his righteousness? (Name some things he did and some things he did not do.)

3. What does Job conclude about the source of his suffering? (For example, see 31:23)

4. In 31:35-37, what is it that Job wants?

5. In both the beginning and towards the end of the Babylonian Job story, the sufferer appeals to or receives help from a sorcerer. Do the passages in Job mention any type of magic used to drive away the source of "evil" in his life?

6. In the last reference, who comes to Job?

Both the Babylonian and biblical Job ask, "Why do You cause me to suffer so, when I am a blameless man?" Despite this bewilderment, in the end Job's wealth is reinstated and multiplied. His health returns. His reputation is restored. In these regards, the story of Job shares many similarities with the Mesopotamian story you read earlier, and other stories you may chose to read later.

Despite the similarities in the sufferers' plights and the stories' outcomes, there are several dramatic differences in the biblical story that share no parallels with any ancient literature. First, the biblical book of Job has a prologue, in which Job's life is discussed between God and Satan. In this cosmic conversation, the reader is given insight into Job's suffering. Satan himself is granted permission to test and afflict him, but Satan's treachery is never revealed to Job. Ultimately,

A Comparitive Study using *Secret of the Scribe* · 189

Job knows it is God who has allowed his suffering, and it is God himself, not some conjurer who finally comes to Job. In the Babylonian story, the sorcerer sends a violent storm that blew the "hag-demon" and the "unnumbered spirits" back to the underworld. However, Job is given something no Mesopotamian sufferer ever received – a revelation of God cloaked in a whirlwind. Job's encounter with God in the midst of the storm silences his need for vindication. Indeed, God's appearance and the purpose for Job's suffering as revealed in the prologue are two staggering differences that set the biblical narrative apart from all its pagan counterparts.

The story of Job is about the *significance of suffering* and *an encounter with the Almighty* that is worth any and all earthly sorrows. These will be topics of our next lessons on Job.

"But man is born to trouble, as the sparks fly upwards."
Job 5:7

LESSON XVIII

The Significance of Suffering

Job's suffering played an epic role in God's grand narrative. Job's suffering was part of God's plan in thwarting the conquest of evil and silencing the boasts of Satan. The story of Job speaks both to the worthiness of God's exclusive right to our worship and our worthiness to rule as his representatives! In previous lessons, we looked at these two scriptural themes separately. In this lesson, suffering links together God's right to worship and our worthiness to rule. Suffering reveals the nature of both God and man and routs the power of the evil one. This idea is huge! Through Job, we get a glimpse of just how significant the purpose of suffering is to the plan of God.

Understanding why suffering is so central to the plan of God requires a return to The Garden – to the story of Adam and Eve and the contrasting origin stories of the pagans. In our very first lesson, the polytheistic stories of the creation account were compared to the Bible. In the pagan story, relational problems existed among the gods right from the start. The gods were at war amongst themselves. They hoped that fashioning a slave (called "man") could make things better either by ensuring the continued strength of the gods of creation or by relieving the work of the lesser gods. Since man had been designed to relieve the actual or potential suffering of all the gods and goddesses, these ruling deities could at last live a life of ease.

In contrast, the Bible's account tells us that the world was made perfect by a perfect, self-sufficient God – a God with no needs. God gave the Garden to a man and woman to sustain them as they walked in perfect relationship with Him. It also provided Adam and Eve with meaningful work: tending the Garden as God's representatives. Conflict and suffering did not exist "in the beginning".

But God gave His representatives free will. Man could choose to eat of the Tree of Life and represent God, or he could chose death by eating of the Tree of the Knowledge of Good and Evil and represent himself.[131] When man sinned, he was rejecting both God's life and his own God-given purpose. This rebellion against his Maker brought suffering into the world. Nevertheless, man's treachery did not surprise God. Long before this first act of sin, it was God's plan to use suffering as the means to restore man to His love and life. But redeeming man through suffering meant both God and man would know immense pain.

---

131 Genesis 2:16-17, 3:22

A Comparitive Study using Secret of the Scribe · **191**

Read Genesis 3 aloud and discuss the following questions aloud. (There is much to discuss from this passage, but for our purposes we will focus here on the consequences given to Adam and Eve for their sin.)

1. What consequence was Eve given for her sin?

2. What consequence was Adam given for his sin?

3. Name some ways in which these consequences would cause people to suffer.

4. The prophecy, "He shall bruise you on your head, And you shall bruise him on the heel" refers to two beings. One will be crushed, but the other will suffer. Who would be crushed? Who would suffer?

5. Compare the consequences given to Adam and Eve to their God-given purpose in Genesis 1:26-31 and Genesis 2:18-25. How many parallels can you find between Adam and Eve's consequences in Genesis 3 and their original callings?

In both the story of Creation and the story of Job, Satan instigates the suffering, but it is God who is still in control of all things. In the beginning, it was not Satan who laid down the consequences for man and woman's sin; it was God. Remarkably each of these consequences relates to the purpose God has given man. Man was to rule over and care for the earth, but now the earth would not be the source of instant provision for man, as was originally intended. Instead, man would toil through sweat and hard labor to assert his right to eat from the fruits of the ground. Adam in his role to image God by providing for his family would now know suffering and frustration in this endeavor. Eve in her role to image God by being her husband's helper would now desire her husband's rule. Sorrow, frustration and disunity

192 · Christian Theology & Ancient Polythesism

would enter the marriage relationship – the same relationship that was originally designed to mirror the unity of the Godhead. God had commanded Adam and Eve to lay claim to the whole earth by filling it with people who would be God's image bearers. But now, child bearing and (by implication) child rearing would be filled with suffering. Birthing children and shaping image bearers would be tasks filled with great pain. Man's ability to lay claim to God's gifts and fulfill God's purposes had been greatly compromised. Why? Surely God could have come up with any number of consequences for Adam and Eve's sin, if indeed the purpose of God's pronouncement was punishment. So, why would God wrap suffering around the very purposes for which He had made man? Stop for a moment and ponder this question as a group.

> Unless you were able to come up with a satisfying answer in your group discussion, take a moment to write the above question in your **Jacob Journal**. We will come back to this question later in a later lesson, but it's important for you to spend some time wrestling with it.

Satan must have been quite pleased with himself in his deception of Adam and Eve. With a single piece of fruit and a few smooth words, the Deceiver corrupted the very ones made to represent the Creator and rule over His world. Now they would represent or be slaves to Satan, and by default the earth would fall into his hands. Slaves own no property; what the slave has belongs to his master.

In previous lessons, the major conflict of Scripture has been defined as Satan's attempt to claim God's worship for himself. This conflict is clearly seen in the opening chapters of Job, where Satan demeans the worship Job gives to God. Satan also lays claim to God's world. God gave the stewardship of the earth to man, but since the fall, Satan has been asserting that man forfeited his dominion when he chose to worship created things rather than his Maker. Who will be worshipped? Who will rule the world? The Prologue of Job, chapters one and two, answers both of these questions. The plot is simple: Satan, tries to steal God's world and His worship by attempting to discredit both God and man. This conflict is not resolved by the voice of God silencing Satan's claims. Rather, a desperately weakened man (Job) defeats both of Satan's accusations.

Read Job 1:1-12 aloud and discuss the questions below: For this exercise, select three people to read aloud. The first person is to be the narrator and will read verses 1-6 and 12b. The second person will read the verses in which Satan speaks. The third will read the verses where God speaks. Then discuss the questions below:

1. How is Job described?

A Comparitive Study using *Secret of the Scribe* · 193

2. Which of Job's actions demonstrate that he is a godly man?

3. Any ideas about why Satan, in response to God's question, said that he was roaming over the face of the earth?

4. Satan begins his accusation of Job with a question: "Does Job fear God for nothing?" What is Satan suggesting?

5. According to Satan, why does Job fear God?

6. How is the fear of God revealed in Job's life?

7. What does God give Satan permission to do? Does this surprise you?

In the face of Satan's claim that he is roaming over the face of the whole earth, God presents Satan with a challenge regarding a man named Job – a righteous man who worships and fears God. Satan rises to the challenge and sets his sights on discrediting Job. He first slanders Job and accuses him of obeying and worshipping God only because of the earthly things God provides for him. According to Satan, if God were to remove His provision from Job, Job would reject Him. Here again is the craftiness of Satan. In a single accusation, Satan boldly suggests that God blesses man only in exchange for man's worship. And alternately, that man worships God only to gain His favor of provision (instead of worshipping God for who He is). Satan challenges the very natures of both God and man, and attempts to twist both for his insidious purposes.

This course has looked at one of the great themes of Scripture – God Provides. Indeed He does. But this truth alone does not encompass all of who God is. God is always much greater than any single role that endeavors to describe Him. In the story of Job, Satan attempts to squeeze God into this single role of Provider. Evidently, like some cosmic vending machine, God spits out a treat when we put in our worship quarters. Is God worthy of worship, obedience and love even when He seemingly fails to provide His goodness to us? Is man a trustworthy image bearer; will he represent God even when God seemingly does not provide? These are two great questions that are answered in the prologue of Job.

Read Job 1:13-22 and discuss the following questions: (If you enjoyed reading the previous text like parts in a play, choose people to read the roles of narrator, Job and the four messengers who bring the terrible news.)

1. What did Job lose?

2. What methods did Satan use to bring about his destruction?

3. How did Job respond?

4. How was Job's response a decisive blow to Satan's challenge?

5. What does Job's response to his great personal tragedies teach us?

Job, who has just lost everything – his children and his wealth, does not curse God as Satan projects he will. Falling on the ground, he worships God. Job blesses God and routs the accusations of Satan. What a contrast to Adam and Eve's response to Satan's temptation in the Garden! While having everything bountifully provided for them, Adam and Eve fell headlong into sin. After losing everything, Job clung to God. But Satan was not finished yet. Job's body was still whole.

Go to **BSC-2**, and answer the question labeled "E".

Read Job 2:1-10 and discuss the following questions. (Again the characters are: narrator, God, Satan, Job's wife and Job.)

1. As in the first heavenly setting, where does Satan say he has been? Do you think there is something significant here?

2. God says that there is no one like Job on earth. Where else could Job be? What is significant about God saying that Job is on the earth?

3. Does Satan acknowledge in any way that God and man clearly won round one of this showdown?

4. Can you identify any similarities between this battle with God, Satan, and Job and the conflict with God, the Baals and Elijah?

5. What does this second win say about God and Job and the claims of Satan?

6. What is Satan saying about man in verse four? What does man, according to Satan, cherish above all else? Is he right?

7. Both God and Job's wife use the word "integrity" to describe the man. What do you think integrity means in this context?

A Comparitive Study using *Secret of the Scribe* · **195**

8   Why it is that Job does not accept the advice of his wife?

9   Why do you think Satan wasn't interested in harming Job's wife?

10 Where does Job believe his trouble is coming from? Is he correct?

In this second heavenly scene, Satan presents himself before God. Rather than acknowledging his defeat by Job, he still claims to be roaming over the whole earth. What's so significant about his roaming? Satan was laying claim to the earthly dominion God gave to man. Man cast away his authority over the earth when he chose to be a god unto himself; Satan is attempting to steal the territory man has failed to claim. Taking possession of our God-given dominion seems to be linked to the physical presence of image bearers everywhere who represents the Lord of all the earth.

To understand this from scripture, let's take a brief look at God's instruction to man about the land and think about the implications of these instructions. God told Adam and Eve as His image-bearers to multiply and "fill the earth" – this was the first great commission. After the destruction of the world in a flood, Noah and his family are re-commissioned and told to fill the earth.[132] Abraham, after being given the land by God, was told "everywhere you walk the land will be yours".[133] Christ told his disciples in the "third" great commission to take the Gospel to every nation.[134] Sadly, this job was made more difficult by another Old Testament story -the Tower of Babel.[135] In rebellion against their God-given purpose to fill the earth, people built a tower to keep everyone together. God confounded their languages, forcing them to scatter. Today this language barrier poses a significant challenge in accomplishing the great commission. Nevertheless, the Bible still gives us confidence that God will, through the power of His Spirit, enable us to accomplish His purpose. Is it not interesting that the sign of the coming of the Holy Spirit was the flaming tongues of fire and the diverse crowd in Jerusalem hearing the Gospel in their own language? Through the work of the Son and the power of the Spirit, we will accomplish His purpose to demonstrate the lordship of the Creator across the whole earth. When Christ returns, every nation, tribe and tongue will have representatives worshipping before the throne of God.

---

132 Genesis 9:1
133 Genesis 13:17
134 Mark 16:15
135 Genesis 11:8,9

From the beginning, image bearers of God were to roam the face of the whole earth, proclaiming His Lordship through making the Creator known. Since Adam and Eve fell prey to Satan's temptation, the Deceiver has been parading about, claiming that man forfeited his rule and his very life. The devil's primary mission has been to enslave men, steal the earth and rob the worship due only to God. Through Christ's sacrifice, man was redeemed from slavery, and His sacrifice proclaimed the One "who is worthy of worship". Through man's sacrifice the earth will be restored to its rightful Ruler.

In Job's prologue, Satan asserts his right of lordship. God disregards his claim by holding up the man Job. "Have you considered my servant Job?" What could Satan do when he ran into this man? Even after losing all his children and his wealth, Job was still representing and worshiping God. Satan's claim to the whole earth was thwarted by this faithful image bearer. This silencing of Satan by the suffering Job cannot be overstated.

This story sheds remarkable light on the character of God. Willingly, He entrusted his reputation and His world to weak human beings who would answer Satan's challenge – even when this didn't always work out so well for God. In the beginning, God entrusted his world to the first man and woman who were given everything, and they broke that trust. Yet in Job, we see that a suffering man, stripped of everything, still continues to be trustworthy. Though Adam and Eve fell, the story of Job proclaims that God still puts trust in man. God knowingly gave His beautiful world to people whom He would teach to be like Himself.

Discussion Questions:

1. Did God know that Adam and Eve would rebel against God before He ever made man?

2. What does God's continued trust in man say about God?

3. What do you think God's trust in man does for man? How does knowing someone trusts you affect how you feel about yourself?

4. How should a person feel when they break that trust? Does God give repentant people another chance? How do you know?

5. How does knowing that God has entrusted you with His reputation and His world affect you?

A Comparitive Study using *Secret of the Scribe* · **197**

6. What does it look like to be entrusted with God's world? Read Matthew 28:18-20

God trusted Job. God knew that Job was a man of great integrity whose trust in God would not be shaken. This word, "integrity," is actually one of the great themes of the book of Job. Understanding the meaning of integrity is foundational to understanding this story. Saying a person has integrity implies that they are trustworthy; they can be depended upon not to turn their back on a trust or a pledge even when it does not work to their advantage.[136] Job did not renounce God; Job's response denounced Satan's claim. Even though he had lost almost everything, Job did not turn his back on God, much to his wife's displeasure. Unlike Adam, who succumbed to his wife's temptation, Job resisted his wife's suggestion to curse God and die. Though Job was incredibly weakened by enormous trials, he continued to trust in God, proving Satan a liar. Job worshiped God because He is God, not just because He provides. Job had great integrity.

In Satan's second challenge, Job's integrity was tested through his flesh: "And Satan answered Jehovah, and said, Skin for skin, yea, all that a man hath will he give for his life. But put forth thy hand now, and touch his bone and his flesh, and he will renounce thee to thy face. And Jehovah said unto Satan, Behold, he is in thy hand; only spare his life." Job 2:4 (ASV)

"Job will reject you as his God if you harm his flesh. Nothing matters more to man than his own body." This accusation of Satan would certainly prove true for many living in our society. We are in large measure obsessed with our appearance, our health, our strength and our personal well-being. Job lost it all. In misery he was reduced to sitting on an ash heap and scraping his sores with broken pottery. Grieving, he accepted the ruin of his body as from the hand of God and refused to abandon his trust in Him. "Shall we receive good at the hand of God, and shall we not receive evil?" Job's integrity withstood Satan's claim. The contest was finished; the enemy was driven back.

Wow! Job thwarted the claims of Satan, gave glory to God by accepting his suffering from God's hand, and continued steadfastly to worship God in the midst of his horrendous pain. Satan was defeated and God glorified! Surely the story has reached its satisfying conclusion. Job's health can now be restored, his wealth can be returned, and he can get started on another family. Wait! There's a problem here. We've only finished chapter two. Satan disappears and is never mentioned in the story again, but the book doesn't end until chapter 42. Why on earth does our hero Job wallow in his suffering for another forty chapters? The short and shallow answer – Job's friends. There's a lot of confusion about suffering in this story.

---

136 THIS IS A PARAPHRASED DEFINITION FOR INTEGRITY FOUND ON-LINE AT HTTP://WWW. MERRIAM-WEBSTER.COM/DICTIONARY/HONESTY.

> Go to **TC-2** and note how, in the first two chapters of Job, man's role as representative is put to the ultimate test, how Job responds, and the significance of that response. Go to **BSC-2** and answer the questions labeled "F".

Job's friends were baffled. They knew nothing of the cosmic contest going on in the heavenlies. Upon seeing Job's misery, his friends sat in silence, grieving his losses for seven days. So far, so good. Then each of his friends in turn made a terrible mistake: they tried to explain *why* Job was suffering. Their conclusions could not have been more erroneous. Job's friends suggested that in some way, Job must have been unfaithful to God. He sinned--probably secretly, and because of this sin, God was justly punishing Job. Job's friends called into question the integrity of Job. As the reader, this should upset us. God has already praised Job for his integrity. Job is suffering because he is a righteous, blameless man, who had been chosen to do battle with the Evil One and who won! Job is our hero, but his friends are insisting that in some way Job deserves his pain. We can only imagine how Job felt. He was angry, disgusted, depressed. He quickly sets out to marshal his defense for his own integrity. It's not long before he is so disgusted with his companions that he stops caring about what they think. His conflict is not with these faithless friends; it's with God himself. How could God bring such suffering on a righteous man? In Job's zealous defense of his own integrity, he calls into question the integrity of God. *How can God be trusted when He lets the righteous suffer?* Here is a great irony of Job: the man whom God trusts falters in his trust of God.

Why didn't someone step in here and set Job's friends straight? Why didn't someone tell Job the divine significance of the great battle he has just fought and won? Why didn't someone remind Job that God was trusting in him? While Job was in the midst of so many trials, he wasn't made aware of these things, but in reading his story, we are. If we press on into Job's story and strive to learn from his suffering, we will be called both to trust God and to be trustworthy.

Discussion Questions:

1. To be falsely accused is a terrible thing. Imagine a war hero, someone who had risked his life for his country, coming home to face a military tribunal

in which he is accused of being a traitor. How would he feel? What other analogies can you think of that might describe how Job felt?

2. Have you ever had an experience in which you were facing difficulty, and someone (in trying to help you) actually made things worse? Share the event or the feelings you experienced.

3. What is most difficult for you when you are trying to comfort someone who is hurting?

4. Why is it important for Christians to reach out to people who are suffering?

5. What do you think about the fact that readers of Job are given far more insight into his situation than Job was?

For a sampling of the dialogue between Job and his friends, read aloud and discuss the following passages. They contain speeches by two of his friends, Eliphaz and Bildad and some of Job's responses. You may wish to select three different people to read the parts of each character.

Read Job 22; 23:1-7; 25; and 27:1-6 and discuss the following questions:

1. Name some of Eliphaz' and Bildad's arguments for why Job's claim to be blameless is impossible.

2. Of what sins do Job's friends accuse him?

3. What does Job refuse to give up?

4. What does Job accuse God of?

With a better understanding of what's going on between Job and his friends, the first passage you read in the previous lesson may make a little more sense. Job's friends knew of only one reason that could explain Job's suffering – Job had sinned. Even Bildad said outright, "Your idea that you could be blameless before God is preposterous! Men are maggots! How could you claim to be righteous before God?" Obviously, Bildad knew nothing about Noah, whom God described using the same language He used for Job.[137] God saved the world through righteous Noah. Blameless Job defeated the claims of Satan. Both men are types of Christ. Both are Old Testament pictures of the work Christ will do through his suffering on the cross. Both are prophetic of the work God would do in the flesh. Further, they reveal the shared purpose people have been given – to bring

---

137 GENESIS 6:9

salvation to the ends of the earth and to extinguish the fiery darts of the Evil One.[138]

Job's friends could not imagine that it was possible for a righteous man to suffer. They assumed that God, who controls the affairs of men, would never allow the truly righteous to suffer because that would discredit the character of God. Does it? This was the assumption and sin of Job's friends. They projected a false picture of God by inferring that God would never allow something that seemed unfair in man's judgment. Job's friends only proved that they did not know God – the God who suffers. God suffers unjustly because of man's sin. We too will suffer like God. Unjust suffering is sharing in the very work of God. The affliction of the righteous offers them a means to reflect the love and goodness of a God who willingly suffers for men. It is also one of the tools God uses to make us like Himself--not to mention that it's a powerful weapon in refuting the claims of the Evil One. And it is the necessary path by which the Gospel of Jesus Christ will be spread around the world. Suffering is central to God's plan of redemption.

Take turns reading the following verses aloud: II Corinthians 1:5; Philippians 3:10,11; John 15:20; Romans 8:17; Colossians 1:24; II Timothy 3:10-12; I Peter 4:12,13,19

1. What similar idea do all these verses share?

2. What's your response to these verses?

> Go to chart **TC-4** and note the unjust suffering of Job, why he suffered, and the outcome of his suffering during the 1st two chapters.

---

138 EPHESIANS 6:16

LESSON XXII:

Suffering Central to the Plan of God

Suffering – central to the plan of God? What part of "God loves me and has a wonderful plan for my life" includes suffering? Now, you've probably always understood that there is some measure of suffering that we experience for wrong-doing. Perhaps it was getting a spanking when you were little, or a loss of privileges as you've grown older. Typically parents are a reliable source of "suffering" when it comes to correcting sinful behaviors. But suffering as a result of correction has nothing to do with the kind of suffering that God endures. Reading the verses at the end of the previous chapter, you couldn't miss the idea that we are called to share in God's suffering (something Job's friends knew nothing about). These ideas may be new to you too. Before exploring the book of Job further, let's pause and give a brief overview of the three major types of suffering that the Bible talks about.

The Suffering Pyramid: The Bible gives essentially three reasons why people suffer, which we have arranged here in the shape of a pyramid. The most common-place suffering is on the bottom and the most powerful suffering on the top.

All people suffer, but not all suffering applies to the suffering pyramid which we will discuss here. In the suffering pyramid, each level represents suffering that people willingly accept. This doesn't mean that the suffering person approved of it ahead of time. But it does mean that at some point the sufferer accepts the affliction as from God and willing responds to the circumstances that the suffering brings. He does not fight against it or deny its reality, but embraces the pain, knowing it is a part of God's work in and/or through him.

Level I: Corrective Suffering

This is suffering as a teaching tool to correct error or sin in our life. This was the type of suffering with which Job's friends were quite familiar. It was also the tool God used most frequently with Israel. If Israel obeyed, she was blessed; if she disobeyed, she was punished. Deuteronomy 8:5 " ... as a man chasteneth his son, so the LORD thy God chasteneth thee." (KJV) The same idea is repeated in the New Testament.

202 · Christian Theology & Ancient Polythesism

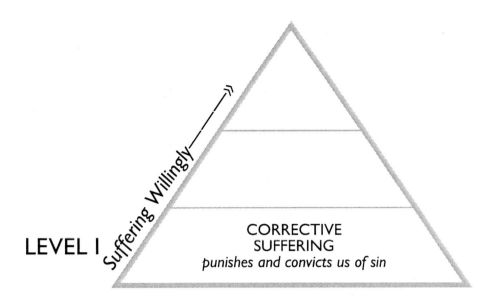

Read aloud Hebrews 12:7-11

The purpose of this suffering or discipline is to help us love the rewards of goodness more than we enjoy the pleasures of sin. It is designed to draw us toward "right-doing" and away from wrong-doing. This suffering gives us a reason to want to obey – to avoid pain. However, not all people disciplined by the Lord are actually corrected. The person suffering discipline must willingly receive the correction. This starts with repentance – acknowledging our wrong-doing and accepting punishment as our just consequence. Without repentance, the pain of discipline will not bring about correction and future obedience. Thus we are destined to repeat the same sins over and over again. God in his mercy may apply increasing amounts of pain until the sufferer is willing to accept and be trained by God's discipline.

Correction is the reason for the vast majority of the suffering recorded in the Old Testament. This is probably the greater part of the suffering in our personal lives. But this was not the reason for Job's suffering. Job did not suffer because of His sins.

1. Why do Christians still sin?

2. How does suffering help us stop sinning?

Level II: Transformative Suffering

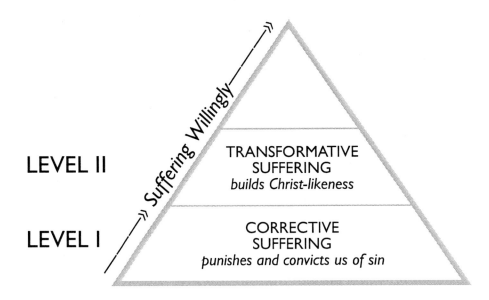

This second level of suffering is virtually absent from the Old Testament, but comes into clear focus in the New Testament. The purpose of this type of suffering is to help believers become more like Christ. This suffering is sent not to chasten sinful acts, but to stimulate godly ones. In contrast to Level I, where suffering teaches us not to sin, here suffering is designed to teach us to do good. This is the difference between weaning yourself off of an old habit and adopting a new habit. The first part – the forsaking of sin – is negative. The second – the increase of virtue – is positive. This is the pursuit of holiness. For example, in Christ's life, He not only refrained from doing evil against his enemies, but He prayed for them and He forgave them –in fact, in love He laid down His life for them. To learn to do good, we may find ourselves suffering at the hand of an "enemy". God may have allowed this enemy to teach us forgiveness, kindness, compassion, patience, or even love. The fruit of the Spirit is the by-product of these trials.[139]

Often this suffering is the result of willingly choosing to lay down our lives as living sacrifices – sacrificing our desire for sin and self-interest for the choices that honor God. This is what was referred to in the "Eight Great Sacrifices" in Lesson 7. When we present our bodies to God as a living sacrifice, He calls us to put aside our own desires. This can be painful. However, as in Level I, in order for this suffering to result in lasting character change, we must have a willing spirit. Here "willingness" does not manifest itself in repentance, but in perseverance. We must steadfastly desire to become like Christ and not grow faint when the road becomes difficult. Often what is most discouraging is just how slowly this change occurs in our lives. Satan would love to use these feelings of defeat to tempt us

---

[139] TITUS 2:11-14; HEBREWS 13:15,16

into believing that becoming like Christ is a hopeless endeavor. He'd like you to believe, "You'll never become like Christ." Do not be faint-hearted. Remember in Whom you have been empowered.[140] Do not grow weary in doing good, for in due season you will reap a reward if you do not give up.[141]

Several years ago a Christian pastor named Eugene Peterson wrote a book entitled *A Long Obedience in the Same Direction.* This interesting title comes from a passage written by a man who was anything but Christian. Nevertheless, Friedrich Nietzsche wrote these words, *"The essential thing 'in heaven and earth' is...that there should be long obedience in the same direction; [which] has always resulted in the long run, [in] something which has made life worth living."* The words of this staunch atheist captured one of the God's truths. Christ-like character is not developed after one difficult trial, any more that a single strenuous sprint makes you an Olympic runner. Virtue is the result of persevering obedience unto Christ.

Read aloud and discuss Romans 5: 3-5 and James 1:2-4:

1. How does a mature believer behave?

2. What shapes Christ-like character in a Christian's life?

3. Using Nietzsche's words, how does becoming like Christ make "life worth living"?

4. Can you describe the two levels of suffering discussed thus far?

This suffering that transforms our character, while powerfully relevant to living the Christian's life, was not the reason for Job's suffering. Job was not suffering to become more like God ... at least not at this point in the story.

> This would be a good time to get out your **Jacob Journal** and spend a few moments reflecting on some of the suffering that you have experienced in your life. Consider whether it belonged to Level 1 or 2, how God used it, and what purpose it served. How have you generally responded to suffering? Have you tried to blame it on others? Or have you willingly accepted it as intended by God for your growth and His glory?

---

140 Ephesians 3:16-19; Colossians 1:9-14
141 Galatians 6:9

A Comparitive Study using *Secret of the Scribe* · **205**

Level III: Representative Suffering

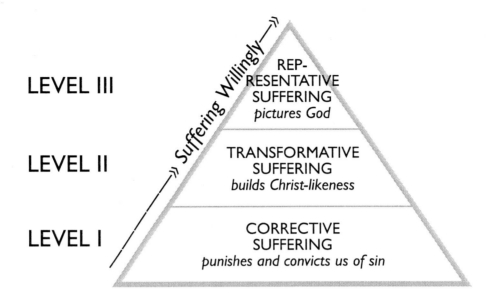

The third and highest level of suffering has nothing to do with discipline for our sin or trials that develop Christ-like virtues. This is the level at which people suffer because they are representing God, furthering His perfect will and bringing Him great glory. Here man's suffering shares in the suffering of God. Christ who knew no sin suffered on our behalf. This suffering for both God and man is always unjust. This is the suffering that represents God to the world. This type of suffering has a very different motive than those of the other types of suffering – sin and spiritual growth. The motive for this type of suffering is man's purpose to represent God.

To review: we have discussed how God in creating free-willed human beings willingly choose to inflict suffering on His own perfect, innocent Self, since He knew that people would disobey Him. We have noted many times the fact that God created people to bear His image and represent Him. We have also examined how people become like what they worship. Thus when humans worship God, they become like Him and represent His character. Through Job, we have seen that the highest form of worship is choosing to worship in the midst of suffering. When that suffering is undeserved, the innocent Christian represents the innocent God who suffers on our behalf. In enduring unjust affliction, we are a living picture of God. We offer the deepest worship to God by acting out God's own actions. Of course, we cannot like God know, see and choose the suffering in advance. Graciously, God does not give us that burden to bear, but we can willingly accept affliction when it comes.

Learning to willingly suffer often involves wrestling matches with God. Nowhere is this more clearly demonstrated than in the Garden of Gethsemane. Christ in his humanity pled with the Father to take away the suffering of the cross. Yet, after sweating great drops of blood, he willingly resolved, "... not my will, but thine be done." Out of obedience and love, He was at that moment both yielding his human flesh to God the Father and modeling for us the path that we too may be called to walk. As the Son of God, He was suffering innocently for the sins of man. In becoming like Christ, we too may be called to suffer for the plan of God. Unjust suffering requires great trust and great yielding to the will of our trustworthy God.

This level of suffering is frequently undertaken for the growth of the Body of Christ. In this affliction, we are "co-laboring with Christ", building up His Church, and defeating the power of the Evil One through suffering. The suffering believer at this level is a powerful foe against evil and a mighty warrior for the cause of Jesus Christ.

Previously we covered the fact that the Bible's primary conflict is Satan's challenge: "who should be worshipped?" We have already explained the Bible's answers to this question – "the one who is worthy." Who is the one who is worthy? The "Lamb that was slain." Christ silenced Satan not through power, but through suffering. We add to the silencing of Satan through worshiping the Lamb in the midst of our suffering. But there is also a second challenge: "who has dominion of the earth?" Should we be surprised that man's dominion and Satan's silencing will be proved through our suffering?

Adam and Eve in their sinless state simply had to bear children to fill the earth, spreading the Lordship of Christ through his image bearers across the face of the whole earth. Israel had to possess the land by wiping out its evil inhabitants. The church must bring the Gospel to the whole world, making disciples of all nations, baptizing them in the name of the Father, Son and Holy Spirit. How will the church accomplish this task to restore the rule of God across the whole earth? Not through political power or military might – she is not battling against flesh and blood, but against spiritual powers and authorities [142] that have set themselves up against God. Like Christ's work on the cross, she must triumph over them through her faithful suffering unto God, proving that she is a faithful image bearer of her Creator and Savior. From the beginning, the life of man was given special purpose. Should we not consider fulfilling our purpose as necessary before

LIKE JOB, CHRIST HAD THREE FRIENDS WITH HIM DURING HIS GREATEST HOUR OF SUFFERING. CHRIST ASKED FOR THEIR EARNEST PRAYERS. HIS FRIENDS FAILED HIM TOO.

---

142 EPHESIANS 6: 12

Christ, our righteous Judge, returns and wipes out all physical and spiritual evil? If so, then suffering has and will play a significant role in man's ability to fulfill his purpose.

In the New Testament, in history, and in modern times, nowhere is this seen more clearly than in the lives of the martyrs. Beginning with the martyrdom of Stephen in Acts, believers spread from Jerusalem into the furthest parts of the Roman Empire. Throughout the Empire, they faced persecution and martyrdom in varying degrees of intensity for the next 250 years as Rome tried to eradicate Christianity from its world. But persecution did not smother the spread of the Gospel. Instead, it fanned the flame as pagans encountered a God who was worth dying for – a God who had died for them. By the early 300s, a strong Christian presence existed everywhere in the Empire, until one of its most powerful emperors embraced the faith that none of his predecessors had been able to destroy. He died wearing the simple white robes of a baptized believer, rather than the royal purple toga of a Roman emperor.[143]

It was an early church theologian named Tertullian who wrote, "The blood of the martyrs is the life-giving seed of the Church." Following the examples of Christ, the chief corner stone of the church, the martyrs gave up their flesh for the cause of building the church of Christ. Wherever the Gospel has spread, there have been martyrs who have prepared the soil and planted the seed. Martyrs were innocent men and women and sometimes even boys and girls who suffered the ultimate injustice and willingly gave up their physical lives for the cause of Christ. Because of their testimony, many embraced the gospel.

Every Christian martyr down through the centuries and those of this century triumph afresh over Satan's charge against Job:

> *"Skin for skin, yea, all that a man hath will he give for his life. But put forth thy hand now, and touch his bone and his flesh, and he will renounce thee to thy face."*

Martyrs denounce this claim of Satan, shrinking the size of the territory to which he can lay claim. In light of Genesis 1, the first great commission, and Matthew 28, the last great commission, we can conclude that when there are image bearers spanning the globe, their presence like Job's will refute Satan's claim to be god of this earth. This future reality will undoubtedly require the continued sacrifices of great men and women of God, who willingly suffer through the power of the Holy Spirit to make disciples of all nations.

Martyrs are only one example of "representative suffering" that furthers the purposes of God. However, the martyr is perhaps the closest picture of our

---

143 THIS EMPEROR WAS CONSTANTINE.

innocent God giving up his life for the salvation of man; the martyr chooses to imitate Christ in sacrificing his life for the life of the Church.

The witness of "Level III sufferers" not only spreads the Gospel, but it is vital to the maintenance of the Gospel in lands that have embraced Christ for centuries. Each new generation must grasp the life of Christ for themselves. Godly representatives who suffer from poverty, the death of loved ones, or the destruction of their flesh through illness, disease, deformity, or an accident can be used to mightily build up the Church of Jesus Christ. Through their worship of God in the midst of their tragedies, they, like Job, testify to the worthiness of our great God and Savior.

Discussion Questions:

1. Do you know a story from the life of a martyr? What happened as a result of his or her death?

2. What suffering have you experienced in your life?

3. In what level of the pyramid would that suffering belong?

4. Could that suffering could belong in more than one level?

5. In what ways has your own suffering resembled (even in a very small way) that of Job?

6. What have been the outcomes of suffering in your life? Have you ever had a chance to see God use your suffering to develop your character, reveal something about Himself, or further His kingdom?

> In concluding this discussion on the special kind of suffering that represents God, consider adding some of your responses to the questions above to your **Jacob Journal**.

A Comparitive Study using *Secret of the Scribe* · **209**

LESSON XXIII:

An Encounter with the Almighty

Earlier in this course, we talked about how the primary purpose of the Bible's story is to reveal the character and nature of God. The last lesson looked at how suffering people can reveal God and further His plan. In this lesson, God reveals Himself to the sufferer.

When confronted with Job's affliction, his friends could have acknowledged their own ignorance about God's ways in relation to Job's suffering and pondered the mysteries of God. Instead they discredited God's representative. Job, too, lost focus on representing God and turned instead to representing himself. The more Job's friends sought to tear him down, the more determined he was to justify himself, even if it meant accusing God of wrong-doing. At this point in the story, Job had fallen into grave sin, and he was no longer representing God. Suddenly a new character enters the scene – Elihu, a younger man who has been quietly listening to the debate between Job and his three friends. Elihu rebukes Job "for justifying himself, rather than God," and he rebukes Job's friends for their baseless accusation of Job's sin. He then lifts up the mysterious and marvelous nature of God. Finally, after long chapters of seemingly pointless argument, someone represents God! As soon as Elihu finishes his speech as God's representative, God rapidly brings the story to its powerful conclusion.

Take turns reading a bit of Elihu's authoritative rebuke of Job and his powerful introduction of God in Job 34:1-12, 36:1-3, 15-17, 22-33, 37:1-5, 19-24 and discuss the questions below:

1. Elihu charges Job with what sins?

2. In contrast to Job, what does Elihu ascribe to God in the first few verses of chapter 36?

3. In what way have "judgment and justice" taken hold of Job?

4. In the later verses of chapter 36 and the first reading from chapter 37, what does Elihu say twice about God?

5. What do you think Elihu means when he says in verse 19, "we cannot [present] our case because of our darkness"?

210 · Christian Theology & Ancient Polythesism

6. Can you describe some of the different imagery Elihu uses to describe God? Why would these be particularly powerful given the polytheistic cultures (Egypt included) that surrounded Israel?

It is difficult to see our hero Job being rebuked, even though he deserved it. Our Level III sufferer has tumbled down and received a verbal thrashing for his sin. Ironically, while Job defeated the accusations of Satan, the accusations of his friends defeated him. Job's sin was ultimately his failure to cling to the trustworthiness of God. He doubted God's goodness, and in doing so he sinned greatly. It is now, after Job has failed, that God comes to him and reveals Himself. It is not the victorious hero that sees God; it is the humbled and defeated man.

In the passage that you are about to read, you will see that God does not come to Job on Job's terms. It is not Job who questions God. Instead, God does the questioning. Job learns more through God questioning him than any questions he might have asked of God. The answers Job wanted are things we know from the prologue, but the truth Job needed was a larger understanding of the character and nature of God. In the Babylonian story, the sufferer needed to find a powerful man – the sorcerer; in the biblical story, Job needed to discover the power and wisdom of God. Job was about to be confronted with the heights of God's wisdom, the depth of his knowledge, and the breath of His power; and through it, his perspective on unjust pain would be completely transformed.

Read Job 38 and discuss the following questions:

1. What did God "clothe" himself in when he spoke to Job? Any thoughts on why God choose this expression of his creation from which to communicate with Job?

2. God's questions of Job here, and in the two chapters that follow, contain some of Scripture's most stunning poetic language. Pick an example of a question you think is worded beautifully, and share what you think God was teaching Job through the question.

3. What character traits of God are His questions designed to help Job see? (This is the most important discussion question. Be thoughtful about your answers.)

A Comparitive Study using *Secret of the Scribe* · **211**

4. What do you think Job was thinking or feeling during this encounter with God?

Towards the end of chapter 38 and in the chapters that follow, God presents Job with the wonders of his animal creation and the object lessons they provide. He questions Job about His joyful empty-headed ostrich that abandons her eggs in the sand but was given speed that enables her to outrun horse and rider. Did God make a mistake when he "failed" to give the ostrich the wisdom to sit tight on her eggs? Or consider the wild donkey and ox ... God provides them food in the desert where they escape the plow and the burdens men could make them carry. Was God wrong to delight in the freedom of the donkey and the ox, rather than make them man's docile servants? For an entire chapter, God describes the power and might of the leviathan, the most powerful creature on earth that is feared by men and by beast alike. No one can capture him, nothing can subdue him; he will not be tamed. Yet, he is but a tiny portrait of the power and might of his Creator.

Read aloud Job 40:1-14 and discuss the following questions:

1. Upon being confronted with the power and might of God's creation, why doesn't Job put forth his case before God when given the opportunity to speak?

2. In this passage, which of God's questions do you think would have been most painful for Job?

3. In verse 8, God confronts Job with his sin. How would you define Job's sin?

Read Job 42:1-9 and discuss the following questions:

1. Is Job able to answer any of God's questions? Why not?

2. What did Job learn through the questions?

3. In verses 5 and 6, Job gained humility, repentance and what?

Throughout this entire story, Job has been "suffering in the dark". He knows nothing of the cosmic significance of his suffering; all he knows is that he is in intense pain and that he is blameless. He doesn't know that he has validated God's trust in him; he doesn't know that he has refuted Satan's claim to the fealty of creation; and he doesn't know that his innocent suffering is a portrayal of the suffering experienced by an innocent God. While readers get to see these aspects of the story, Job does not. Thus Job becomes resentful and falls into sin. At this point God comes to him. The revelation of Himself that He gives Job is enough to satisfy Job for all the suffering he has endured. In a series of heart-breaking and convicting questions, God reveals to Job how much greater, wiser, grander, powerful and knowledgeable He is than Job. His thoughts and purposes are mysteries which are too awesome for Job to comprehend. It is wrong for Job to demand an answer from this sovereign, omniscient Lord. When Job receives this revelation, he responds in repentance. Job may not know why he had to suffer, but he came to acknowledge his own poverty before the vast and limitless nature of the Lord.

It is not our understanding of the ultimate reasons behind our suffering that will pull us through dark days. Rather, in the midst of the storm, it is believing that God is all-powerful, all-wise, and all-good whether or not we have eyes to see him there. More than Job's need for vindication, more than his desire for restored health, more than his longing for his children brought back to life, Job needed an enlarged understanding of his Maker. He needed a God whom he could "wrestle with"– a God big enough to trust in, even when all his personal understanding failed.

So here again is great irony in the story of Job: Satan's accusation that God is only worshipped because he provides is turned on its head, not once but twice. In the beginning of our story, Satan is silenced through Job's worshipful response to a God who did not provide. At the end of the story, Job is silenced by God's heart-rending questions that provide him with an enlarged view of God. Job learns that all his great losses and all his indignation are an insignificant price to pay for the priceless gift of this revelation of God. All Satan's craftiness and all man's sinfulness can never ultimately thwart the Lord who Will Provide.[144]

In the story of Job, we, believers down through the ages, have a masterpiece to read in the midst of our suffering. We know the supernatural significance behind Job's suffering. We are given a glimpse of a God who can be trusted even when all our circumstances would tempt us to believe Satan's lies. We too can defeat Satan by choosing to worship the God who sometimes seemingly does not provide, because we know that *God is greater than all his gifts. It is God, not his gifts that we cling to.* Glory be to his everlasting name!

Discussion Questions:

1. Name some of the specific "gifts" God has provided in your life.

2. Pick one of these gifts (a big one), and try to imagine what your life would be like without it.

---

144 GENESIS 22:14

3. Can you imagine how easy it would be to assume that God has stopped caring for you, or how easy it would be to start doubting the goodness of God? What have you learned from the story of Job that could give you an anchor to hold onto in the midst of your storm?

4. If a friend experienced some terrible loss, such as a health crisis or the death of a family member, would that be a good time to sit down and try to assess, perhaps using the pyramid of suffering, why God had taken these things from them? Why or why not?

5. Job's friends did one good thing – they sat in silence with Job for seven days. Why was that good?

6. Why is it bad to offer other people explanations for their suffering? Who is the only one who knows why His children are suffering? How can we help a person in suffering hold on to their trust in God?[145]

In the end of the story, God restored everything and more to the repentant Job. The restitution began with God reestablishing Job's role as priest – representing God to man and man to God. God tells Job to offer sacrifices for the sins of his friends. Yes, the story goes on, covering Job's restored health and wealth and family, but God's greatest mercy and blessing is to restore Job as His representative. This was Job's purpose in life, and we share this same calling.

Few of us will ever face Job-size suffering, but his story calls us to embrace the suffering we experience in our lives as directly from the hand of God. It calls us to integrity – to maintain a steadfast trust in God, even when He seemingly doesn't provide. In the end Job learned to trust God as God trusted Job. For those knowing Job's outcome and the epic stage that set the story, he is a great hero and powerful teacher. His story gives us reason to cheer. Job is one of Scripture's many examples to teach us to rejoice in our affliction because we know and trust the Author of our salvation – the one who suffered/s for us. Suffering, willing suffering, will make us like God. Innocent suffering will make God known.

> Go to **TC-1** and note what God provided to Job and why this provision was more valuable than all of God's previous gifts. Also add to **TC-4** and note what Job thought he needed in regards to his unjust suffering – answers and the value of the questions he got instead.

---

145 THINK ABOUT BEING GOD'S REPRESENTATIVE. HOW CAN YOU SHOW HIS COMPASSION TO OTHERS WHO ARE SUFFERING? HOW CAN YOU SHOW HIS LOVE? HOW CAN YOU SHOW HIS TRUSTWORTHINESS? DON'T TELL OTHERS TO READ JOB. INSTEAD, BE THE FRIEND JOB NEVER HAD.

214 · Christian Theology & Ancient Polythesism

Before this topic of suffering is concluded, let's revisit a couple of questions from this lesson. Let's start with the one you recorded in your Jacob Journal. Why did God make it so much harder for man to accomplish his God-given purpose through the suffering defined by the "Curse"? Can we see any of God's wisdom in the Curse? Think about this: pain is our tutor. Paradoxically, it teaches us to value what is worth suffering for. It teaches us to prize what Adam and Eve traded away for a bite of forbidden fruit. The "Curse" that God pronounced contains all three levels of suffering: it is a corrective for sin, it is a source for transformation, and it is the means by which man will represent God to the world.

God freely showered His goodness upon Adam and Eve, but they rejected Him; thus God provided suffering, so we could learn the value of His love.

In the Curse, we find everything God would use to ultimately redeem and restore all of creation. Because of the Curse, the Messiah would suffer death. Through Christ becoming a curse for us, Satan was defeated, and his power over our destiny in death is no more. Through man's struggles to provide daily for his family's needs, he learns to value the God Who Provides. Through the pain of childbirth, woman is taught to value life, no matter what suffering must be endured. Through the conflicts now built into the marriage relationship, we are taught to value love and unity. As the Trinity is abounding love and indivisible unity, marriage is the tutor that teaches us the central character and nature of God.

Through all these sources of pain, both God's and man's, it is possible for us to become fit to fulfill our purpose to represent the image of God across the face of the whole earth. Indeed, when the last drop of innocent martyrs' blood is shed, and it bears fruit in the life of a true image bearer worshipping God from every nation, tribe, and tongue, the end will come. Christ will return to receive a bride who has been made ready by the blood of the Lamb and has sacrificed her own for the love of the bridegroom. Thus the curse is actually our blessing; it is the pathway that leads us back to paradise.

Discussion Questions:

1. In the 1970s, almost every state in the Union passed "No Fault Divorce Laws". These laws dramatically simplified the process of getting a divorce. Either husband or wife who was unhappy in the marriage could file to have the marriage ended without any need to establish just cause, such as adultery. Divorce rates significantly increased after the passage of these

laws. While there are many problems associated with couples having access to an easy divorce, these laws did make the process of getting a divorce less painful. Based on the purpose behind the suffering in marriage brought about with the curse, what are divorced couples missing out on?

2. In 1973, the Supreme Court passed Roe vs. Wade, the law which, among other things, guaranteed women the right to have an abortion in all 50 states during the first trimester of pregnancy. A woman who carries and gives birth to a child out of wedlock will suffer. She has painful choices to make about whether or not to relinquish the baby for adoption, marry the father whom she may not love, or try to raise the baby on her own. None of these choices are easy. If the pain of childbearing was intended to teach women to value life, how could opting out of this suffering through an abortion impact the young mother?

3. The 1970s waerealso the height of the Women's Liberation Movement, which sought to end an array of discriminations directed at women. One focus of the movement was to get women out of the home and into the work place, and provide opportunities equal to those of men. As a result, many married women went to work, sharing the role of provider in the home. The man's burden to provide was lightened. Relative to the intentions of the "curse", how might this be damaging for a man?

4. There were other social changes during this time that sought to give individuals more control of their lives by reducing the burdens of married life and childrearing. While touted as a means to reduce human suffering, what do all the examples sighted here do to the human understanding about life, love and our purposes on God's good earth?

5. Why do you think Christ promised us that in this world we would have tribulation rather than relief from suffering?

6. Can you think of reasons to rejoice even in the midst of suffering?

> If this discussion has given you some resolution for the question of why God "cursed" the purposes He gave to people, return to your **Jacob Journal**. Add the insights that were helpful to you about why God made the path to fulfill our purpose full of suffering.

If someone asked you why God "cursed" His creatures, and you didn't have time to discuss the blessing of suffering, you could answer with the obvious: "because Adam and Eve sinned". This answer is technically correct, but it begs another question, "why did they sin?" The ultimate answer is because God gave them free will. Why did God give them free will? We've covered this before, but let's turn now to Christian author, C.S. Lewis of Narnia fame, and learn from his wisdom.

Below is an excerpt of a book called *The Screwtape Letters*. The story is a series of letters between a "wise" old uncle, Screwtape, and his young nephew, Wormwood. They happen to be in the same business, working for the devil, "Our Father Below". As demons, their job is to dissuade people from making that most "disastrous" choice of heaven over hell. Screwtape gives all sorts of helpful advice warning his nephew about the ways of the "Enemy" (God) and schemes for foiling His purposes. This excerpt looks at the down-side for demons when people, using their free will, choose to obey God, and the type of relationship this obedience fosters with the "Father Above".

"But the obedience which the Enemy (God) demands of men is quite a different thing. ... He really does want to fill the universe with a lot of loathsome little replicas of Himself – creatures, whose life on its miniature scale, will be qualitatively like His own, not because He has absorbed them, but because their wills freely conform to His. We want cattle who can finally become food; He wants servants who can finally become sons. We want to suck in, He wants to give out. We are empty and would be filled; He is full and flows over. Our war aim is a world in which Our Father Below has drawn all other beings into himself; the Enemy wants a world full of beings united to Him but still distinct.

... you now see that the Irresistible and the Indisputable are the two weapons which the very nature of His scheme forbids Him to use. Merely to over-ride a human will ... would be for Him useless. He cannot ravish. He can only woo. For His ignoble idea is to eat the cake and have it; the creatures are to be one with Him, but yet themselves; merely to cancel them, or assimilate them will not serve.

We can drag our patients along by continual tempting, because we design them only for the table ... He cannot "tempt" to virtue as we do to vice. He wants them to learn to walk and must therefore take away His hand; and if only the will to walk is really there, He is pleased even with their stumbles. Do not be deceived, Wormwood. Our cause is never more in danger than when a human, no longer desiring, but still intending, to do our Enemy's will, looks around upon a universe from which every trace of Him seems to have vanished, and asks why he has been forsaken, and still obey."[46]

---

146 THE SCREWTAPE LETTERS, C. S. LEWIS, CHAPTER 8

A Comparitive Study using *Secret of the Scribe* · **217**

Discussion Questions:

1. What does Screwtape say that God wants?

2. To get what God wants, men have to what?

3. Why is man's free will so important to God?

4. In the second paragraph, it says, "God cannot ravish, He can only woo." What does that mean?

5. What kind of relationship does God want?

6. What kind of human circumstances are being described by "looks around upon a universe from which every trace of Him seems to have vanished, and asks why has he has been forsaken..." (by God)?

7. Why is this circumstance so dangerous to the cause of the devil when a person still chooses to obey God?

Obedience, especially obedience in the midst of suffering, transforms the world for Christ. God's world set right will be a place in which men and women walk with Him, sharing a love relationship with the God who is love – a love that is worth any and all suffering.

One final question: we asked earlier why you thought God came to Job in a storm? You might have remembered that the storm god was typically the most powerful god of Israel's Canaanite and Babylonian neighbors, so it could be that God was showing Job what the real God of the storm looked like. This would be a thoughtful answer and may very well be correct. It's also possible that God was honoring his representative, Elihu, using his imagery describing the power of God in the rain and storm.[147]

This is also a thoughtful answer. Perhaps God picked this motif because He knew Job would remember. In the days to come, or even long after his ordeal, Job would remember his own powerful words that he had spoken about the glories of God in the midst of the debates with his friends. In chapter 26, Job declared:

> *He bindeth up the waters in his thick clouds; And the cloud is not rent under them. He incloseth the face of his throne, And spreadeth his cloud upon it. He hath described a boundary upon the face of the waters,.... The pillars of heaven tremble and are astonished at his rebuke. He stirreth up the sea with his*

---

147 JOB 36:27-37:18

power,... Lo, these are but the outskirts of his ways: And how small a whisper do we hear of him! But the thunder of his power who can understand.[148]

When Job would recall his own words, do you think he might remember the God of the storm and perhaps hear Him softly say, "Job, what I showed you was just a whisper of my ways!"

Discussion Questions:

1. What did you learn about the power and wisdom of God through the story of Job?

> Return to chart **CC-9** and finish the last question. It asks you to compare and contrast God's use of power in Job's epilogue and the sorcerer's use of power in the Babylonian Job (Lesson 17, verse 59-61). Remember that Satan was not driven away in the Job story by power; Satan was vanquished by a powerless yet trustworthy man.

Author's note to parents: A few years ago I was speaking at a homeschool conference where I strongly emphasized the importance of teaching our children about suffering. In the back of my mind, I hoped that no one would ask for a resource suggestion for such a task. While this "reader's guide" was in the planning stage, I had no idea of the significant role suffering would play in this work of theology. During the writing of these lessons, the Lord used two Christian resources to powerfully confirm the truths taught to me through the story of Job. Now both are tremendous resources I can recommend as a follow-up to these lessons on suffering.

The first included in the back of this book. It is a CD of a Focus on the Family broadcast between Dr. James Dobson and Dr. Ken Hucherson entitled, "A Privilege to Suffer for Him". Dr. Hucherson is a pastor dying of cancer. By medical accounts, he should be long dead, but the trust and yielding of this "Level III" sufferer will challenge your faith and cause you to give glory to God. Man can truly embrace suffering not just as God's permissible will, but as His perfect will. He can revel in his weakness as he represents the power and love of God to a sick and dying world. Dr. Hucherson's testimony is the story of a modern-day Job, whom we should hold up to our children as a hero of the faith. This man lives with great integrity the lessons to be learned through the story of Job. Listen to this CD with your children as soon as these lessons on suffering are finished. Dr. Hucherson's shares more of his story and perspective on life in Christ in his upcoming book *Hope is Contagious*, scheduled for publication spring 2010 by Zondervan.

---

148 Job 26:8-14 (KJV)

A Comparitive Study using *Secret of the Scribe* · **219**

About the time I finished these lessons on suffering, I began reading the book, The Heavenly Man, by Paul Hattaway for our evening read aloud. It is the true life story of a modern day Chinese Christian called Brother Yun and his involvement in the Chinese House Church movement. It is an amazing story of suffering and of the mighty acts of Christ our Savior. Brother Yun is another modern day Job. Through him and thousands of Chinese Christians like him, the message of the Gospel is spreading not only in China but to Muslims, Hindus and Buddhists. It is the number one goal of the Chinese House Church movement to take the Gospel to the 90% of the unreached peoples who live between China and Jerusalem. I cannot recommend highly enough that you read this story with your children. In it you will find many modern day examples of things that build on the truths the students have been exposed to in this work. Here's a quote from Brother Yun on pages 286 and 287:

"Once I spoke in the West and a Christian told me, 'I've been praying for years that the Communist government in China will collapse, so Christians can live in freedom.' This is not what we pray! We never pray against our government ...

God has used China's government for his own purposes, molding and shaping his children as he sees fit ....

Don't pray for persecution to stop! We shouldn't pray for a lighter load to carry, but for stronger backs to endure! Then the world will see that God is with us, empowering us to live in a way that reflects his love and power....

There is little that any of the Muslim, Buddhist or Hindu countries can do to us that we haven't already experienced in China. The worst they can do is kill us, but all that means is that we will be promoted into the glorious presence of our Lord for all eternity!

[Our] missionary movement is ... an army of broken-hearted Chinese men and women whom God has cleansed with a mighty fire, and who have already been through years of hardship and deprivation for the sake of the gospel. In worldly terms they have nothing and appear unimpressive, but in the spiritual realm they are mighty warriors for Jesus Christ! We thank God that he 'chose the foolish things of the world to shame the wise; God chose the weak things of this world and the despised things – and the things that are not – to nullify the things that are, so that no one may boast before him.'" I Corinthians 1:27-29

This book can be purchased at www.backtojerusalem.com. While it may be less expensive on Amazon, the recommended website will provide monies for China's missionary endeavors.

LESSON XXI:

The Afterlife and the Resurrection

Parent Note: This lesson contains both some disturbing images and some challenging ideas. Read in advance to determine if any omissions on your part will be necessary given the age of your children.

The Sumerians, Babylonians and Canaanites all believed some pretty frightening stories about the afterlife, and applying those beliefs resulted in terrible consequences for many innocent people. In this lesson, we will again compare and contrast pagan and Jewish beliefs and the truth revealed in the New Testament. Be prepared to learn some rather startling things about the Bible along the way.

The Mesopotamians believed that death or the afterlife was a place of despair and darkness, where people crawled on their bellies, eating dust until they eventually faded away. Does this sound similar to any ideas conveyed in the Bible? What about the curse of Satan in the garden? God said, "Because thou hast done this, cursed art thou above all cattle, and above every beast of the field; upon thy belly shalt thou go, and dust shalt thou eat all the days of thy life."[149] How typical of Satan to make men believe that his curse was theirs also. Now contrast Satan's deception with the powerful truth of God's word: "Christ redeemed us from the curse of the law, having become a curse for us; for it is written, Cursed is every one that hangeth on a tree."[150] The theme of this lesson is Satan's deception versus God's truth. As you work through it, keep in mind that the strategy of Satan is to induce men to fear death and trivialize life.

In the *Secret of the Scribe*, Tabni's mother was thrown into a state of frenzy after the queen's death as she tried to save her daughter's life. While both Tabni and her mother are fictional characters, the story they portrayed is rooted in history as verified by the discoveries of archeologists. The Tombs of Ur, discovered in the 1920s, are a memorial to the afterlife beliefs of the Sumerians. Since dead slaves were no longer useful to the Sumerian gods, they made no provision for the fate of humans after death. Thus rich men and women prepared for their own afterlife by requiring provisions and servants to accompany them to the grave. Royal attendants were forced to enter the burial pit dug for the dead king or queen. After drinking poison, they would join their masters in death to serve his or her needs in the afterlife. Can you imagine a slave's terror at the death of a king or queen? The

---

149 GENESIS 3:14
150 GENESIS 3:13

A Comparitive Study using *Secret of the Scribe* · **221**

actions of the rich and powerful rulers of Ur illustrate again the point that people become like what they worship. Thinking only of their own needs in view of such a depressing future, they did all that they could to provide for themselves – even when that included taking the innocent lives of servants, who had faithfully served them in life. Since the powerful gods and goddesses often demanded human sacrifices, powerful men and women justified these murders in modeling them after the actions of the gods.

DID THE FEAR OF DEATH JUSTIFY THE ACTIONS OF A RICH DYING SUMERIAN, WHO VIEWED A SLAVE'S LIFE AS TRIVIAL WHEN COMPARED TO HIS OWN NEEDS? SATAN WOULD LIKE MEN TO THINK SO.

Discussion Questions:

1. What words would you use to describe the actions of the ruling class in Sumer in preparing for death?

2. What does this practice say about the value given to human life in ancient Sumer?

3. What does it say about the power of fear?

Turning again to Israel, we begin with the observation that the Old Testament provides a very limited theology about the afterlife. There are references to the Book of Life, David seeing his dead child again, Job's statement to see God in the flesh, Enoch being "taken by God", and Elijah's chariot ride to heaven. But how did these specific examples apply to the average Israelite? It was not until late in Israel's history during the exile period that God revealed an end time resurrection of all the dead. The Israelites believed that God clearly controlled the eternal destiny of all men, but the prospects of the grave carried none of the victorious hope we find in the New Testament. The focus of Israel's life was her relationship with God in the here and now. The grave seemed to bring an end to all that, including man's ability to praise God. Thus the common plea of the psalmist was for God to extend a person's natural life, as his relationship with God seemed to come to an end with death.

> *"For in death there is no remembrance of thee: In Sheol who shall give thee thanks?" Psalm 6:5 "The grave cannot praise you, death cannot celebrate you, those that go down into the pit cannot hope for your truth." Isaiah 8:18 "If the only home I hope for is the grave, if I spread out my bed in darkness, if I say to corruption, 'You are my father,' and to the worm, 'My mother' or 'My sister,' where then is my hope? Who can see any hope for me? Will it go down to the gates of the grave? Will we descend together into the dust?" (Job 17:13)*[151]

---

151 SEE ALSO PSALM 30:9

Mark, David, Isaiah and Job all shared some sense of finality and hopelessness associated with the grave. The grave or place of the dead was also called "Sheol" or the pit. During circumstances of immense difficulty, like Job's affliction, David's flight from Saul, or Isaiah's persecution by Manasseh, Israel's poets described the grave as a place of darkness, dust and despair. For God's people to have such fear of the grave may surprise you. You may be even more surprised to learn that Old Testament poets and prophets borrowed language from their pagan neighbors, using Canaanite imagery for the grave. In the verses above, you see in the hopelessness, darkness, dust, and corruption a typical ancient Near Eastern understanding of the grave. In the verse below, David made an indirect reference to the Canaanite god of the dead, calling him "Sheol", and "Death".

> *"They [those who die] are appointed as a flock for Sheol; Death shall be their shepherd; And the upright shall have dominion over them in the morning; And their beauty shall be for Sheol to consume, That there be no habitation for it."*
> *Psalms 49:14 (ASV)*

The words "Death" and "Sheol" are references to pagan imagery. In Canaanite stories about the gods, the god of death (or the grave) was named Mot. He was pictured as a horrific monster, who consumed the dead like sheep. The gates of Hell were the jaws of Mot. In one of the more dreadful Canaanite myths, the god Baal gave a banquet and invited all the gods, never expecting his brother Mot to show up. But he came. Baal served his guests the choicest wine and bread. However, Mot, who fed only on the bodies of the dead, was so enraged by this insult that he demanded Baal to return with him to the grave. Even mighty Baal was powerless before the god of death, and he was taken to the underworld. Before continuing with this story, we should pause and ask a few questions:

Discussion Questions:

1. Why would biblical writers under the inspiration of the Holy Spirit use references to pagan gods?

2. Why wasn't Israel given a tangible hope for an afterlife?

3. While there is no such being as the god Mot, is there a real "god" of the dead? Who would this be?

4. In Psalms 49:14, what is the "shepherd" of the "sheep" going to do to those who enter the grave?

5. Stop for an moment and think about the New Testament: who is the "Shepherd of the sheep", and what does He do for his flock (See John 10:2)?

A Comparitive Study using *Secret of the Scribe* · 223

Isn't it quite remarkable that this same metaphor – involving sheep – would give Canaanite children nightmares, while giving Christian children such a beautiful picture of being loved and cared for? The Good Shepherd gave up his life for his sheep (John 10:11). But the Good Shepherd metaphor was not limited to the New Testament. What is the most famous Old Testament psalm written by David all about?[152] Ironically, this is the psalm most often read at funerals. The shepherd who leads us through the valley of death comforted Old and New Testament believers alike. Though the Old Testament saints had no idea how the Good Shepherd would lead His people through death, they still found comfort in knowing that He would, while the Canaanites had only despair. So while David and others used pagan imagery of death in Scripture, we see an amazing contrast between Satan, who would consume us in death, and Christ, who would give up his life for ours.

Let's think further on why the Bible contains pagan imagery. The Old Testament includes historical accounts and records, a collection of laws and wise sayings, beautiful poetry, and powerful prophecies. These various forms of writing serve important purposes in the Bible. It is noteworthy to point out that the Bible was not written down before false ideas about the world held sway, but afterwards. Paganism had been practiced for at least a thousand years before Abraham, and it was still another 400 to 800 years before Moses would write the Torah. The Bible was written as a polemic. This may be a new word for you, but it's important to learn the meaning in order to understand why God would allow the use of pagan imagery in His scriptures. A polemic is an argument that sets itself against a well-established idea. What was the "well-established idea" or worldview during the era in which the Bible was written? From Egypt to Babylon, Greece to Briton, people worshipped many gods. While the myths varied slightly and the names of the gods and goddesses changed, the essential idea that the world was comprised of a collection of nature gods and goddesses was ingrained in the minds and hearts of these ancient peoples. This being the commonly held notion, God's Word was written in such a way as to turn the "common notion" on its head.

For example, take the New Testament story of Paul, who traveled to the city of Athens as recorded in Acts 17. Before reasoning with the wise men of the market place, he walked around taking note of the religious objects of the Athenians. On display were exquisite Greek statues that represented each of their gods and goddesses. Paul was there that day to challenge the Athenians' ideas about the

---

152 PSALM 23

world. How did he start his challenge? In "walking around" the city square, he spied an alter which the city had erected to "An Unknown God." Paul proclaimed that this altar was unintentionally erected to the risen Christ. In the process of conveying this startling truth to his listeners, he also quoted Greek poets. Why, as a Hebrew scholar, didn't Paul quote David or Isaiah, instead of some pagan Greeks? The answer is that Paul's audience needed truth revealed in words they understood and valued. The words of their own poets, as well as the alter to the "Unknown God", stood as pointers to the truth of God – the truth Paul preached that day.

Like the Greek poets whom he quoted to the Athenians, Paul also used Canaanite imagery to write some of the Bible's most powerful language about Christ's victory over death. For you see, even though the Canaanites' story was false, it captured a poignant truth – human life is swallowed up by death. Can you imagine what a shock the story of Christ's defeat of death and His glorious resurrection would be to pagan ears? It was Paul who proclaimed that Christ had swallowed up the swallower:

> *"Death is swallowed up in victory."*
> *" O Death, where is your sting?*
> *O Hades, where is your victory?"*[153]

The Bible reveals the character and nature of God, but it also reveals the character of Satan and the forces of evil. Satan's ploy is always to wrap a piece of truth in a lie, but God unwraps the lie to reveal the truth! There was indeed a great deal of truth buried in pagan mythology. God's Word shoveled away the dirt. This is the purpose of a polemic: to expose what is false and reveal what is real. Using the language of the surrounding cultures, biblical writers provided a powerful testimony of the one true God by contrasting Him with the many false gods and goddesses of the ancient world.

Discussion Questions:

1. What do you think now about the Bible using pagan imagery?

2. What does this tell you about a God who would defeat paganism using the language of the polytheist?

---

153 1 CORINTHIANS 15: 55

A Comparitive Study using *Secret of the Scribe* · **225**

> It would be helpful as a future reference to note in your **Jacob Journal** some of the ideas you found interesting about the Bible's use of pagan imagery. Note the meaning of the word polemic and one of the Bible's purposes for using language common in the culture surrounding Israel.

This truth is quite remarkable, but what were the Israelites to do hundreds of years yet before Jesus Christ, when they stumbled across this language in the scriptures? While Israel was not given an explicit hope of heaven, she was given the covenant/promises between God and his people that established her special relationship with Him in this life. Israel's future hope was in her promised Messiah. By the time of Christ, there were two powerful groups in Israel: one who believed in an afterlife/resurrection (the Pharisees) and one who did not (the Sadducees). A scholar of the Old Testament could make a case for either view from scripture; However, largely due to the events of the period between the Old and New Testaments,[154] the average Jew did believe in a general resurrection. Martha expressed this when she said to Christ, "I know that he (Lazarus) shall rise again in the resurrection at the last day".

So let's get specific: during Old Testament times, would a faithful Israelite go to heaven when he died? Did Noah go to heaven when he died? Did Job? Both Noah and Job were called blameless men by God Himself; surely they went to heaven. What about those who were not blameless, such as Moses or David? Did sin keep men and women out of God's heaven? If Satan could come before the courts of God, surely Moses and David could. What about the Jewish exiles whom God expressly forgave for their sins? Surely they could go to heaven. Since God forgave their sins and proclaimed others righteous, why didn't He articulate that having his forgiveness meant they would go to heaven? Is forgiveness of sin all that is required to go to heaven? If that was the case, why didn't the Old Testament sacrificial system, which provided a means for forgiveness, promise eternal life?

The sacrificial system never promised eternal life because it couldn't give it. Israel, like all men, had to receive the very life of God in order to live eternally in His kingdom. Beginning with the sin of Adam and Eve, mankind chose death, and human access to the Tree of Life was barred by God. Through a Chosen People, God would lead mankind back to Himself. Beginning with the Law, God provided both a reflection of His character and the standard that revealed sin. Through sacrifice, God taught the Jews that life is in the blood, and that the blood of animal sacrifice could cover sins of repentant men and women. However, these sacrifices had to be offered over and over again, and they never granted eternal life. Then

---

154 During the reign of the Seleucid king, Antiochus IV Epiphanes, Jews were forced to submit to Greek ways. Jews suffered terrible religious persecution, including martyrdom. The belief that in the resurrection the wicked would be punished and the righteous rewarded helped Jews come to terms with such great injustice.

God the Son took on Jewish flesh, and, as the Lamb of God, shed his blood for the life of men. His sacrifice once and for all covered men's sins, gave eternal life, and at last restored the hope of an eternal kingdom of God. The resurrection and the hope of heaven was made possible only when the life of God was offered anew to mankind. God and God alone is our only source for life both in this life and in the next. Thus we remember the words of Christ: "I am come that they might have life, and that they might have it more abundantly."[155] "I am the way, the truth, and the life: no man cometh unto the Father, but by me."[156] Why only through Christ? Christ alone is God's provision, giving us access once again to the Tree of Life. "Oh taste, and see that the Lord is good."[157]

Discussion Questions:

1. What is the relationship of sin to death?

2. Why wasn't Israel promised eternal life in the Old Covenant?

3. What promises and provisions was she given that could give her hope?

4. What was the difference between the Old Testament sacrificial system and Christ's sacrifice on the cross?

5. In the Old Testament, Israel was taught to repent of her sins and to exercise that repentance through animal sacrifices. In the New Testament, the believer repents of his sin and expresses his _____ in the sacrifice of Christ upon the cross, which provides both life eternal and forgiveness for sins once and for all.

6. How is one's faith in the work of Christ expressed by a believer?

Let's return to the pagan myth discussed earlier and wrap up the story of Baal and Mot. You will recall that Baal was killed by Mot, the god of the dead. Mot hid Baal's body away without a proper burial ... a very bad thing in the ancient world. With Baal's death, the land went into a severe drought, and the fertility of animals and people came to a halt. So a goddess of fertility and war, the equivalent to the Ashereth whom the Bible refers to, went in search of Baal's body. Through divine intervention, she found the body, gave it a proper burial, and then sought

---
155 JOHN 10:10 (KJV)
156 JOHN 14:6 (KJV)
157 PSALM 34:8

revenge on Mot. Finding the god of death, she clove him in two with her sword, ground him to pieces, and scattered him across the earth. Then the great God El had a vision in which Baal was resurrected. He was – but later so was Mot. With Baal's return to life, the fertility of his land returned too. However, as Mot resumed his power over the dead, he demanded his rights to a dead Baal in the Netherworld. A compromise was worked out: another god became a stand-in for Baal and went to the realm of Mot six months of the year, while Baal and Ashereth provided fertility for the land. In the fall, Baal descended to Mot's dominion and was "resurrected" every spring.

You probably recognize some similarities in this story to Egyptian myths involving Isis and Osiris and his evil brother Set. Isis, Osiris and Set were all brothers and sister as were Baal, Mot, and the goddess who revenged his death. Osiris was also the god of agriculture. Every ancient pagan culture has a story that explains why the earth is fertile for some portion of the year and dormant for the rest. Given human dependence on food and the necessity of the seasons, dying and rising gods' and goddesses' myths were rituals that were central to these pagan cultures. Annual reenactments by the people of these powerful myths included terriblly immoral practices, but it was believed that these human actions were necessary to incite or provide the gods' renewed power. To the pagan mind, this "strengthening of the gods" was evidenced by the annual renewal of spring. Only one ancient culture lacked such a story with its corresponding fertility rites. God's Chosen People were the exception to the rule. In fact they had no rituals that they performed in hopes of their God imitating them or being strengthened by their reenactment; quite the opposite was true. Israel was to imitate her God and to rely on His strength and provision.

THE "DYING AND RISING" GODS STORIES EXPLAINED THE SEASONS, BUT THEY HAD NOTHING TO DO WITH ANSWERING QUESTIONS LIKE, "WHERE WILL I GO WHEN I DIE." THESE WERE NOT "SAVING" GODS.] ASSOCIATE WITH "... WAS "RESURRECTED" EVERY SPRING."

Discussion Questions:

(In contrast to other discussions, scripture references are not read in advance. They have been provided as footnotes which should be read after giving students an opportunity to answer the discussion questions first.)

1. Do you remember Israel's first annual ritual?[158]

2. What did Israel's annual reenactment represent?[159]

3. What future event did it foreshadow?

---
158 EXODUS 12:1-11,14
159 EXODUS 12:12,13

228 · Christian Theology & Ancient Polythesism

4. When Christ and his disciples reenacted this event on the night before he was betrayed, what new Christian "ritual" did he institute?

5. Christ offered his disciples bread and wine; what did they represent?

6. What do the broken body[160] and shed blood[161] of Christ represent?

7. In the reenactment of Communion, what is the Christian partaking of?

8. Do you remember the fourth commandment?[162]

9. What did Israel's weekly reenactment represent?

This discussion should have prompted many ideas and associations. But remember what promoted the discussion in the first place. Again it was something the pagans got right. Reenactments or rituals are necessary. What the pagans got wrong was their belief that these reenactments were intended to ensure the strength or potency of the gods. For God's Chosen People, reenactments renew our own strength and vitality in Christ. When the Pharisees questioned Jesus about the Sabbath, He said, "the Sabbath was made for man, not man for the Sabbath."[163] The Sabbath is God's gift to renew us and remind us of His provision. In the same way, our ability to accomplish our God-given purpose – to represent the life of Christ to the world – is renewed by taking that life into our bodies through communion. In contrast Baal's banquet, the "choicest bread and wine" of the Christian story carries a meaning that no pagan Canaanite could have ever imagined. The comparisons and contrasts are quite astounding.

While it should be rather evident where this lesson's comparisons are leading, it is necessary to read some actual text from another "dying and rising" story of a pagan god. ("Dying and rising" is the proper name for these stories rather than death and resurrection, as they are not about a single monumental event. Generally, "dying and rising" actions reoccur cyclically and sustain the course of life rather than alter it.) Below is the fertility myth told by Babylonians. This story stars Ishtar, the equivalent of the Canaanite fertility goddess Ashereth and the Sumerian goddess Inanna. (In the *Secret of the Scribe*, Inanna was the goddess whom the childless couple that befriended Tabni prayed to.) To aide your reading of this story, here's a little background and the basic plot: Ishtar, the goddess of life and fertility on the earth, grew discontent with her realm. Why should she be limited to the earth when she could control the afterlife, too? Only one small

---

160 JOHN 6:35,51
161 JOHN 6:54
162 EXODUS 20:8-11
163 MARK 2:27,28

problem stood in her way: her sister, the Queen of the Dead, had been given rule of the netherworld long ago. Full of pride and confidence, Ishtar challenged her sister's rule in a story commonly called "The Descent of the Goddess". (Note: Where the lines are in normal text, the story has been paraphrased.)

Read aloud the following story:

To the Land of No Return, the realm of Ereshkigal,[164]

ISHTAR, THE DAUGHTER OF THE MOON, SET HER MIND.
TO THE DARK HOUSE, THE ABODE OF IRKALLA,
TO THE HOUSE WHICH NONE LEAVE WHO HAVE ENTERED IT,
TO THE ROAD FROM WHICH THERE IS NO WAY BACK,
TO THE HOUSE WHEREIN THE ENTRANTS ARE BEREFT OF LIGHT,
WHERE DUST IS THEIR FARE AND CLAY THEIR FOOD,
WHERE THEY SEE NO LIGHT, RESIDING IN DARKNESS, ...
AND WHERE OVER DOOR AND BOLT IS SPREAD DUST.
WHEN ISHTAR REACHED THE GATE OF THE LAND OF NO RETURN,
SHE SAID TO THE GATEKEEPER:
"O GATEKEEPER, OPEN THY GATE,

---

[164] FROM ANCIENT NEAR EASTERN TEXTS TRANSLATED BY E.A. SPEISER AND GEORGE A. BARTON, ARCHAEOLOGY AND THE BIBLE, 7TH ED, PG 530F. ALSO AVAILABLE ON LINE AT: HTTP://WWW.GATEWAYSTOBABYLON.COM/MYTHS/TEXTS/CLASSIC/ISHTARDESC.HTM

OPEN THY GATE SO I MAY ENTER!

IF THOU OPENEST NOT THE GATE SO THAT I CANNOT ENTER,

I WILL SMASH THE DOOR, I WILL SHATTER THE BOLT,

I WILL SMASH THE DOORPOST, I WILL MOVE THE DOORS,

I WILL RAISE UP THE DEAD ...

SO THAT THE DEAD WILL OUTNUMBER THE LIVING."

THE GATEKEEPER OPENED HIS MOUTH TO SPEAK,

SAYING TO EXALTED ISHTAR:

"STOP, MY LADY, DO NOT THROW IT DOWN!

I WILL GO TO ANNOUNCE THY NAME TO QUEEN

ERESHKIGAL."QUEEN OF THE NETHERWORLD

THE GATEKEEPER ENTERED, SAYING TO ERESHKIGAL:

"BEHOLD, THY SISTER ISHTAR IS WAITING AT THE GATE, ..."

WHEN ERESHKIGAL HEARD THIS, HER FACE TURNED PALE

LIKE A CUT-DOWN TAMARISK,

WHILE HER LIPS TURNED DARK LIKE A BRUISED KUNINU-REED.

WHAT DROVE HER HEART TO ME?

WHAT IMPELLED HER SPIRIT HITHER?

LO, SHOULD I DRINK WATER WITH THE ANUNNAKI?

LESSER GODS OF THE UNDERWORLD

SHOULD I EAT CLAY FOR BREAD,

DRINK MUDDIED WATER FOR BEER?

SHOULD I BEMOAN [CARE ABOUT] THE MEN WHO LEFT

THEIR WIVES BEHIND?...

OR SHOULD I BEMOAN THE TENDER LITTLE ONE

WHO WAS SENT OFF BEFORE HIS TIME?

GO, GATEKEEPER, OPEN THE GATE FOR HER,

TREAT HER IN ACCORDANCE WITH THE ANCIENT RULES."

"LET HER ENTER MAKING SURE SHE BRINGS NOTHING WITH HER."

FORTH WENT THE GATEKEEPER TO OPEN THE DOOR FOR HER:

"ENTER, MY LADY, THAT [WE] MAY REJOICE OVER THEE,

THAT THE PALACE OF THE LAND OF NO RETURN MAY BE GLAD AT

A Comparitive Study using *Secret of the Scribe* · **231**

THY PRESENCE."

WHEN THE FIRST GATE HE HAD MADE HER ENTER,

HE ... TOOK AWAY THE GREAT CROWN ON HER HEAD.

"WHY, O GATEKEEPER, DIDST THOU TAKE THE GREAT CROWN
ON MY HEAD?"

"ENTER, MY LADY, THUS ARE THE RULES OF THE MISTRESS
OF THE UNDERWORLD."

WHEN THE SECOND GATE HE HAD MADE HER ENTER,

HE ... TOOK AWAY THE PENDANTS ON HER EARS.

"WHY, O GATEKEEPER, DIDST THOU TAKE THE PENDANTS
ON MY EARS?"

"ENTER, MY LADY, THUS ARE THE RULES OF THE MISTRESS
OF THE UNDERWORLD."

WHEN THE THIRD GATE HE HAD MADE HER ENTER,

HE ... TOOK AWAY THE CHAINS ROUND HER NECK.

"WHY, O GATEKEEPER, DIDST THOU TAKE THE CHAINS
ROUND MY NECK?"

"ENTER, MY LADY, THUS ARE THE RULES OF THE MISTRESS OF THE
UNDERWORLD."

At the gatekeepers biding, Ishtar passes through a total of seven gates each time
having to relinquish some object of her divinity or clothing until all are gone.
Humiliated, in the depths of Hell she meets its Queen.

AS SOON AS ISHTAR HAD DESCENDED TO THE LAND OF NO RETURN,

ERESHKIGAL SAW HER AND BURST OUT AT HER PRESENCE.

ISHTAR, UNREFLECTING, FLEW AT HER.

ERESHKIGAL OPENED HER MOUTH TO SPEAK,

"GO, NAMTAR, LOCK HER UP IN MY PALACE! NAMTAR IS

HUSBAND OF THE QUEEN OF THE DEAD

RELEASE AGAINST HER THE SIXTY MISERIES:

MISERY OF THE EYES AGAINST HER EYES,

MISERY OF THE SIDES AGAINST HER SIDES,

MISERY OF THE HEART AGAINST HER HEART,

MISERY OF THE FEET AGAINST HER FEET,

MISERY OF THE HEAD AGAINST HER HEAD -

AGAINST EVERY PART OF HER, AGAINST HER WHOLE BODY!"

[ISHTAR IS SLAIN! HER DEAD BODY IS LEFT TO DECAY.]

AFTER LADY ISHTAR HAD DESCENDED TO THE NETHER WORLD,

[ALL FERTILITY ON THE EARTH COMES TO AN END.]

THE COUNTENANCE OF PAPSUKKAL,

THE VIZIER OF THE GREAT GODS,

WAS FALLEN, HIS FACE WAS CLOUDED

HE WAS CLAD IN MOURNING, LONG HAIR HE WORE.

FORTH WENT [THE VISER] BEFORE EA, THE KING:

"ISHTAR HAS GONE DOWN TO THE NETHER WORLD,

SHE HAS NOT COME UP.

SINCE ISHTAR HAS GONE DOWN TO THE LAND OF NO RETURN,

Al renewal of life on earth has come to an end.
Ea in his wise heart conceived an image,

Crafty Ea hatched a plan and sent a eunuch (the Sumerian version has two flies instead of a eunuch) 165 to visit the Queen of the Dead. Being carefully instructed by Ea, the eunuch got along splendidly with the Queen until he asked for the life-water bag. Begrudgingly she had to comply with his request, but not until after spewing forth some nasty curses on the eunuch/flies. Then she commanded her husband, the vizier, Namtar, with these words saying:

"UP, NAMTAR, ... BRING FORTH THE ANUNNAKI,

seven judges of the underworld who controlled the life-water bag,

SEAT THEM ON THRONES OF GOLD

SPRINKLE ISHTAR WITH THE WATER OF LIFE AND TAKE HER FROM

MY PRESENCE!"

... THE ANUNNAKI arrived and were SEATED,

ISHTAR WAS SPRINKLED WITH THE WATER OF LIFE, REVIVED AND

TAKEN FROM HER PRESENCE.

WHEN THROUGH THE FIRST GATE HE[THE GATEKEEPER]

---

165 THE EUNUCH AND THE FLIES ARE PICTURES OF INFERTILITY AND DECAY. BOTH WOULD BE APPEALING TO THE GODDESSES OF THE DEAD.

A Comparitive Study using *Secret of the Scribe*

HAD MADE HER GO OUT,
HE RETURNED TO HER THE BREECHCLOTH FOR HER BODY.
WHEN THROUGH THE SECOND GATE HE HAD MADE HER GO OUT,
HE RETURNED TO HER THE CLASPS FOR HER HANDS AND FEET.

Through each successive gate, he returned the things he had taken

WHEN THROUGH THE SEVENTH GATE HE HAD MADE HER GO OUT,
HE RETURNED TO HER THE GREAT CROWN FOR HER HEAD.
"IF SHE DOES NOT GIVE THEE HER RANSOM PRICE,
BRING HER BACK."

These words were the parting shot of the Queen of the Dead. She required a ransom paid for her release; Ishtar must send someone to replace her in the underworld. Ishtar can't decide who to assign to such a fate until she sees her husband Tammuz (the god of agriculture) sitting on her throne wearing kingly garb rather than mourning clothes. Assuming that he did nothing for her while she was in the grave other than steal her throne, she ordered him to the grave. Thus Tammuz is forced to take her place. Only later does Ishtar realize that her judgment was too hasty, since the fertility of the earth still depended on them both. Tammuz' sister volunteers to take his place every six months out of the year.

Discussion Questions:

1. What was the purpose of both of the "dying and rising" god stories discussed thus far?

2. Why didn't Israel have such a story?

3. Do these stories have anything to do with the afterlife of their slaves?

This terrible story was annually reenacted by the Babylonian people, with kings and priests and temple prostitutes in star roles. These reenactments gave people "hope" and some sense of control that, although their winters were long, their gods or goddesses would rise again to bring productivity to the earth. As noted earlier, Israel, who had no such story, was told from the beginning that God made lights in the sky to govern day and night and seasons and years.[166] His great and bountiful creation was brought forth by His all-powerful Word, not by the begetting and birthing of gods and goddesses. God's Word provided everything man needed to experience life in Him. He sustains all things, including the seasons of productivity and rest, by the power of His Word.[167]

Unfortunately, knowing the truth and living it are two very different things. Israel fell into the cult practices of the Canaanite gods Baal and Asherah, and the Southern kingdom of Judah also fell into the Babylonian cult of Ishtar and Tammuz. In the Babylonian story, part of its reenactment started every summer solstice, when plants began to wither from the heat. This was seen as the dying of Tammuz, who would have to return to the Netherworld in just a few short months. The Bible records a scene in which Jewish women mourned for the forthcoming "death" of Tammuz. The Prophet Ezekiel wrote in disgust, "Then he brought me to the door of the gate of the LORD's house which was toward the north; and, behold, there sat women weeping for Tammuz." Ezekiel 8:14 (KJV) In fear, Judah was keeping a ceremony for this false god before the Temple of the Lord. Once again, God's people were caught in Satan's deception that explained the world in terms of nature gods and their slaves, a deception ending in death and exile from her God-given land. Finally, through Judah's suffering in Babylon, the very place where this false practice originated, she forsook her neighbors' idolatry and choose life – the very life Moses held out to her as obedience unto God. Thus in the Gospels, we find no mention of Baal, Asherah, or Molech and no more weeping for Tammuz. It was then that Israel was given a resurrection story, but it was not a Hebrew version of a "dying and rising" god. Israel's story had nothing to do with planting and harvesting – hers was a story that brought the renewal not of spring but of the very life of mankind.

Let's turn now to events leading up to that story. It was Christ who told his disciples that he would suffer, die and be resurrected, as recorded in the Gospels. The passage below was referenced earlier in contrasting the monster Mot, who ate dead people like sheep, with God's role as the Good Shepherd. Read it here, looking for its contrast with the story of Ishtar.

Read aloud John 10:7-18, and answer the questions below:

1. What imagery is common to both stories?

---

166 Genesis 1:14
167 John 1:1-5; Hebrews 1:3

A Comparitive Study using *Secret of the Scribe* · 235

2. Who controls the gate of the sheep pen?

3. What is the purpose of the gate?

4. Why did Christ give up his life?

5. Why did Ishtar lose hers?

6. Who is the thief in John 10:10?

7. Who is the thief in "The Descent of the Goddess"?

8. Who took the life of the shepherd?

9. Who took the life of the goddess?

10. John 10:18 says that Christ has authority over what?

All four Gospels provide eye witness accounts of the resurrection of Israel's Messiah and his victory over death. Read the one below from the Gospel of Mark.

Read Mark 16:1-8 and discuss the questions below:

1. Who was witness to the empty tomb?

2. What was the angel's message?

3. What was the women's response? Why do you think they were afraid?

4. The angel bore witness to the most awe-inspiring miracle that God had ever performed among men. Do you think their response of fear was appropriate? Why or why not?

In the addition to the eye-witness accounts of the empty tomb of Christ, there were those who were miraculously raised from the dead immediately after Christ's death on the cross.[168] This tells us clearly that these were holy people whose resurrection bore witness to the work of Christ through the cross. Later, Christians would look back on these resurrections and come to understand them as part of a "first fruit" offering – an offering of dedication and memorial to God prescribed in the Old Testament. This offering set aside the first portion of God's provision for man

---

168 MATTHEW 27:52-53

236 · Christian Theology & Ancient Polythesism

as sacred unto God; these resurrected believers displayed the power of Christ's resurrection through their flesh and blood.

The Bible gives us detailed accounts of Christ's death and resurrection. What is not clearly conveyed is what happened during the time Christ was in the tomb. The early Church interpreted several passages from the writings of Paul and Peter as the story of Christ's decent into Hell.[169] Today, Christians hold differing interpretations of the biblical references from which the story springs. Nevertheless, the early church's interpretation offers a powerful and dramatic contrast to the pagan myths, and it brings to resolution the fate of the Old Testament believers. The story is called the "Harrowing of Hell." Simply told, it goes something like this: Immediately after His death on the cross, Christ descended into Hades, where he stormed the gates of Hell and invaded Satan's domain of death to rescue fallen mankind. Hades is flooded with light, revealing Satan and his demons, cringing powerless before their Creator. Christ extends his nail-pierced hand to Adam and Eve and frees a rejoicing train of Old Testament saints from Satan's domain of death. Ephesians 4:8 describes Christ:

> "...When he ascended up on high, he led captivity captive, and gave gifts unto men. (Now that he ascended, what is it but that he also descended first into the lower parts of the earth? He that descended is the same also that ascended up far above all heavens, that he might fill all things.) (KJV)

Here those in captivity were under the domain of Satan and death. They were rescued or "captured" by their new master, the Lord Jesus Christ, who had "trampled down death by death."

Here are two artists' rendering of Christ, releasing Adam and Eve and the Old Testament saints from Satan's domain. Images of the "Harrowing of Hell" were painted throughout most of church history; many include the "jaws of Hell". The word "harrowing" describes something that is deeply painful. Ironically, harrowing is also a term used in agriculture and has to do with the farmer's final preparation of the soil before planting the seed. What "seed" is just about ready to be planted?[170] In this picture, who is experiencing pain as a result of harrowing? This first picture above comes from an illuminated manuscript called the Winchester Psalter created in the 1100's.

---

169 ACTS 2:23FF; ROMANS 10:7; EPHESIANS 4:8–10; 1 PETER 3:19–20; 1 PETER 4:6
170 THE SEED OF THE GOSPEL IN THE HEARTS AND LIVES OF MEN, WOMEN AND CHILDREN.

Observation Questions:

1. What is under Christ's feet?

2. What is around the demon's feet and hands?

3. What is forming the mouth of Hell?

4. Why do you think the artist used a "monster month" to depict the entrance into Hell?

5. What is in the top right corner of the picture?

This second image was a fresco painted in the 1400s by Italian artist Fra Angelico. It captures the beauty of the event, for as Satan is crushed under the gates of Hell, and the demons cower in terror in the corner; the light and victory of the Savior is clearly portrayed.

In contrast to the pagan story, Satan can demand nothing from Christ; it is Christ who frees from Satan's domain the victims of his treachery. Satan does not humiliate Christ; Christ has willingly taken on the shame of man's death. It is for needy men, not for His own power that Christ descended into Hell. In taking from Satan what he had previously claimed, Christ swallowed up the Devil's power over his domain. Christ is the doorkeeper to Hell, not Satan.[171] Ironically the claim of Satan's power over death was destroyed by death – the death of a God who took on human flesh so that He might cancel out the claims against us.

The meaning of Christ's death has scarcely been more beautifully explained than in the words of Aslan to Susan and Lucy, who witnessed the horrific ordeal:

"It means," said Aslan, "that though the Witch knew the Deep Magic, there is a magic deeper still which she did not know. Her knowledge only goes back to the dawn of time. But if she could have looked a little further back, into the stillness and darkness before Time dawned, she would have read there a different incantation. She would have known that when a willing victim, who had

---

171 Matthew 24:31-46

committed no treachery, was killed in a traitor's stead, the Table would crack and Death itself would start working backwards."[172]

The Old Testament, starting in Genesis 3, was like Narnia in the dead of winter. With the incarnation of Christ, the ground began to thaw. Calvary was the stone table where the power of the White Witch was broken. While Lewis's story looks back to the cross, the Prophet Isaiah looked forward to Christ's victory over death:

> "On this mountain he will destroy the shroud that enfolds all people, the sheet that covers all nations; he will swallow up death forever. The Sovereign Lord will wipe away the tears from all faces; he will remove the disgrace of his people from all the earth. The Lord has spoken." Isaiah 25:7

IN THE BEGINNING WAS THE WORD AND THE WORD WAS WITH GOD AND THE WORD WAS GOD ... IN HIM WAS LIFE AND THE LIFE WAS THE LIGHT OF MEN. ... –JOHN 1:1,4

When people in ancient Mesopotamia or Canaan died, their body was wrapped in a sheet or a shroud in preparation for burial. Prophetically, Isaiah was pointing to a mountain, where Satan's power over death would be destroyed. The ancient metaphor of death swallowing up human life would be turned on its head when "the Way, the Truth and the Life" swallowed up death. Unknown to Isaiah, that mountain would be Calvary, and the "man of sorrows ... assigned a grave with the wicked", as foretold in Isaiah 53, would be the very Son of God. Through death, Christ conquered Satan's domain. This truth was also reflected in the refrain of an ancient church hymn sung at Easter: "Christ is risen from the dead, trampling down death by death, and upon those in the tombs bestowing life."[173] We serve a risen Savior, who is man's only hope for eternal life – Jesus Christ, the Light and Life of the whole world.

The ultimate proof of Christ's victory over death is not the story called "the Harrowing of Hell"; it is His glorious bodily resurrection. As Christ foretold to Martha before raising Lazarus, "I am the resurrection and the life. He who believes in me will live, even though he dies; and whoever lives and believes in me will never die." John 11:25 It was the resurrected body of Christ that provided proof or assurance of that promise.

* * *

So what does this story mean to Christians? Consider again how the pagans of ancient times ascribed powerful importance to the annual cycle of the death and

---

172 THE LION, THE WITCH AND THE WARDROBE BY C. S. LEWIS
173 THIS REFRAIN IS STILL SUNG IN EASTERN ORTHODOX CHURCHES TODAY ON PASCHA (PASSOVER/EASTER).

resurrection of their fertility gods and goddesses. The pagans believed their very lives depended upon this cycle continuing year after year. If spring planting and fall harvesting and animal breeding were not renewed, the people feared they would die of starvation. While the death and resurrection of Christ has nothing to do with the springtime renewal of flowers and trees, it has everything to do with the renewal of life in man. We are the creation that He has brought back to life – but for what purpose? Unfortunately, if the average Christian young person today were asked, "What does the death and resurrection of Jesus Christ mean to you?" they would probably say, "My sins are forgiven so that I can go to heaven." If so, the story of The Lion, the Witch and the Wardrobe should have ended shortly after the stone table cracked, with Susan, Peter, Edmond and Lucy suddenly transported to Aslan's Country. But this is not how the story ended. Instead Narnia had to be put right. The sons of Adam and the daughters of Eve had battles to fight and lands to be reclaimed for the lion.

The apostle Paul talks about the purpose of Christ's work on the cross this way:

"... being dead through your trespasses ... he [made you] alive together with him, having forgiven us all our trespasses."[174]

"Therefore if any man be in Christ, he is a new creature: old things are passed away; behold, all things are become new. ... Now then we are ambassadors for Christ,... For he hath made him to be sin for us, who knew no sin; that we might be made the righteousness of God in him."[175]

Discussion Questions:

1. According to the first verse, what did Christ's forgiveness provide?

2. Based upon the second paragraph of verses, what has become new?

3. From the very last line above, what was the purpose of Christ taking our sins upon Himself?

---

174 Colossians 2:13
175 II Corinthians 5:17,20,21

4. What other important purpose are we given in Christ?

We are forgiven and made alive unto God so that we might be renewed and transformed by that life in the here and now. In making us new creations, Christ has restored to us the meaning we lost and the death we incurred when we chose to be gods unto ourselves. He has restored to us the ability to choose between life or death. Before coming to know Christ, people are walking dead men. Christ said "I came that they may have life and have it to the full"[176]. He didn't say, "I have come so they could go to heaven when they die". While Jesus makes our future hope abundantly clear[177], heaven is not the immediate goal of our salvation.

Christ came so that we might know the life of God living in us and that, through us, His life might be made known. God created people to live on this earth as His representatives. The unfolding story of scripture plainly reveals that human beings cannot accomplish this God-given purpose without the life of Christ within us.

This is life lived in the fullness of the love and life of the Trinity, beginning in the here and now. To be made alive in Christ is an astonishing gift; nevertheless this earthly life is not easy. We live in the midst of a spiritual war zone. Though mortally wounded, our enemy still roams and will stop at nothing to see our defeat. We live in a body with passions, desires, and a self-will that demands to be given first place. We live a life in which Christ promised that we would suffer. However, he also promised peace and comfort and joy and love. He promised never to leave us or forsake us. And yes, he promised a future eternal hope.

A great Christian pastor named Irenaeus living in the second century after Christ expressed a powerful truth when he wrote these words about being alive in Christ:

"The glory of God is a human being fully alive."

Discussion Questions:

1. What kind of life do you think he was implying by the words "fully alive"?

2. How is God glorified by such a life?

3. How is such a life made possible?

Perhaps your answers were something like this: Such a life is made possible only through the love of the life-giving Trinity at work in us. Through the love of

---
176 JOHN 10:10
177 JOHN 14:1-4

God, we are transformed to reflect His very life. When the life of God is revealed in His prized creation man, then God is glorified both by the man who is being transformed and by those who see God in him. The purpose of all creation is to reveal God, and that revelation always brings praise, glory and honor to His name, as well as joy, fulfillment and blessedness to the "Potter's clay".

> # For Christ plays in ten thousand places. Lovely in limbs, and lovely in eyes not his, to the father through the features of men's faces."
> ## ~Gerard Manley Hopkins

Your theme chart **TC-3** is ready for completion. Answer the final question under Lesson 19 noting that to choose life is to choose Jesus Christ, the only source of real life. Because so many of these comparisons took most of the lesson to develop, chart **CC-10 The Afterlife and the Resurrection** has been assigned at the end of this lesson. To help you with the task below is a summary of the pagan myths we discussed. You will be filling out the questions defined on the chart. The work involved can be spread out across the following course summary and student letter.

Babylonian Summary: Ishtar wants to rule Hell, so she challenges her sister's domain; instead she is humbled and killed by the goddesses of the grave. While Ishtar is dead, all fertility comes to an end. The great gods intervene, bringing her back to life, but she must send someone to take her place. In revenge, she sends her husband, Tammuz. However, because he is needed each spring, his faithful sister volunteers to take his place six months of every year.

Canaanite Summary: Baal gives a feast, which Mot (Baal's brother and god of the dead) attends and is insulted by the food of bread and wine. He demands that Baal return with him to the underworld. Mot kills Baal and gives his body no burial. All fertility comes to an end. Baal's lover finds his body, buries him, then finds and "buries" her sword in Mot. Mot is dead. Through a vision of the great god, Baal is resurrected. Fertility returns. Mot is also resurrected and demands Baal's life in the grave. Another substitution is arranged, and Baal spends only six months of every year in the grave, thus enabling the seasons of productivity to take place.

LESSON XXV:

A Course Summary of Christian Theology and Ancient Polytheism

So where have we been? We've compared and studied a view of the world and a way of life that flows from believing in one God versus what life looks like worshipping many gods. Specifically, we've compared the God of ancient Israel and the early New Testament with the gods and goddesses of ancient Mesopotamia and Canaan. To be sure, there are other religions that believe in one God, such as Islam, but Allah is not the God of the Bible.

It is not just a belief in "one God" that shapes our view of life; it is that one God's quality, character and purposes that shape what we believe about ourselves, what character we strive for and the purposes for which we live. How we answer the question, "who is God and what is He like" is the fount from which all other worthy questions of life must flow. He is the starting point of our existence, our meaning, our place within the universe. Without an anchor firmly grounded in a proper knowledge of God, we are adrift in the world. Thus through this study we've sought to know God better, not only in contrast to other gods, but more importantly through His unfolding biblical narrative and through the Bible's central themes that point to the Son of God. Hopefully, you have discovered that the Bible is both an invitation to "taste and see that the Lord is good" and a call to share in His goodness.

† † †

Let's review God's story as we compared it with the polytheistic stories: Our study centered around God's interaction with Israel in comparison with the gods of her neighbors. Whereas the ancient Sumerians believed that they were created as slaves for their needy greedy nature gods, ancient Israel believed that she was fashioned by the transcendent, benevolent Creator of all. God made Israel's first parents, Adam and Eve, and placed them in a garden where He provided everything needed for life in Him. Adam and Eve were entrusted with a high calling – to reflect their Triune Maker and take care of His creation. Deceived by one who hated both the Maker and His chosen representatives, Adam and Eve chose to become gods unto themselves. Death soon followed, for they were severed from the Life-Giver. But God's plan was not thwarted by their sin. Choosing a representative called Abraham, God promised to make a great nation through him whereby someday all the nations of the world would be blessed. Abraham's descendants, Israel, became a nation in Egypt, yet she was a nation of slaves. Through His awesome power, God freed Israel from bondage to worship Him in the desert. Like her first parents, Israel was given the

Christian Theology & Ancient Polytheism/Review · **243**

... A Course Summary continued

job of being God's representative. But for Israel this meant that she must bring judgment on the peoples of a land who had chosen death through the idolatrous worship of many gods. Unlike her neighbors, whose beliefs fostered immorality, murder, and sorcery, Israel was entrusted with God's Law, which was a reflection of His moral character. In contrast to her neighbors' seven-day week, in which they ceaselessly labored to meet the needs of their gods, Israel was given a sacred Seventh Day and Seventh Year of rest. Through resting, she commemorated God's creative work and expressed dependence on Him for all her needs. When Israel worshipped God and represented Him, she laid claim to her role as steward of the land, while Satan used his lies to beguile her neighbors into surrendering the lordship of the land to Baal. In the end, Israel did not bring judgment on the idolaters of the land. Instead, she became a slave herself, rejecting both God's moral law and her dependence upon Him. After much long-suffering by God, Israel was driven from the land into captivity, where at last through her own suffering Israel learned to be faithful to the love of God. To this remnant, God gave the promise of a New Covenant in which He would write his laws upon tablets of human hearts. Through His Son and His Spirit and through a daughter of Abraham, God enacted his promise to bless the whole world.

Separate from the story of Israel, but included in her canon of scripture, were the stories of Noah and Job. In contrast to Israel's account, the Babylonians told the story of a "Job" whose suffering was meaningless and who sought relief through a sorcerer with the power to appease the gods and drive away the demons. Job's suffering was anything but meaningless. The book opens with Satan's challenge that Job only worshiped God because He provided. God trusted Job and accordingly took away His gifts. When Job continued to faithfully worship Him, God revealed the significance of the role He gives trustworthy yet weak human beings – to thwart the claims of Satan and reclaim territory we had given away in the fall. Job both testified to the worthiness of God's worship and revealed that what the sufferer needs most is not health and prosperity, but a revelation of God's transcendent wisdom and power in the midst of the storm. The help of the Babylonian was a powerful man; the help of the Hebrew was a powerful God.

While the contrast in this story is between two men (the Babylonian and the biblical Job), the contrast between the Jewish and the Sumerian flood stories is between the deities. Sumer's flood story involved cranky gods, who justified the destruction of humanity for their own selfish desire to get a decent night's sleep. Israel's flood story was about a God who gave men free will, knowing they would run amuck. He knew that He would have to destroy almost all of His creation, even

244 · Christian Theology & Ancient Polytheism/Review

... A Course Summary continued

though man's destruction would cause Him great pain. He knew when He saved Noah that the ark would lead to the cross.. But it was worth the price of divine and human suffering for men to share the selfless love of a Triune God – to be able to freely and willingly receive and return that love.

In the stories of the afterlife, we saw the god of death and the goddess of life grasping for more power. Both ended up being violently destroyed, then brought back to life so that the seasons of fertility and barrenness could be maintained. Brothers, sisters and lovers were substitutes sent to Hell by the goddess of life and the god of the dead. In the story of the cross, God is the lover of mankind, who takes on the flesh of His "brothers" so that He can ransom and rescue those held captive by the god of Death. By His willing sacrifice, He triumphs over the grave and swallows up death in Life. His resurrection is the first fruit of His brethren, who have been called out of death and darkness into His glorious light and life. Through the price of His substitutionary death we have been given again the life our first parents traded away for a bite of forbidden fruit.

The stories of Israel, Noah, and Job and of Christ's resurrection reveal an all-powerful, all-good, all-wise God, who loves and provides for his creation. His character is all the more distinct when contrasted to the limited, self-centered, capricious gods and goddesses who made men to slave for their needs.

> *"He is not served by human hands, as if He needed anything, because He gives all men life and breath and everything else." Acts 17:25*

† † †

We have looked at the Bible as we would a great piece of literature that ultimately tells one grand story. What is its plot? Who are the main characters? What's the purpose of the story? What message does the author convey through its major themes? What's its central conflict? How is it resolved? The Bible tells the story of one main character, the protagonist – God. The supporting cast includes the antagonist – Satan, and man, who must choose a side. The community of people, through which God tells His story, changes throughout the narrative while man's God-given role stays the same. The community, which is the expression of man's special creation, begins by focusing on the husband and wife, then on the nation Israel, and then on the Body of Christ. However, the purpose for all three modes of relating to God remains the same: mankind is to

Christian Theology & Ancient Polytheism/Review · **245**

... A Course Summary *continued*

represent God in the flesh. Satan hates God and man. As Satan is God's antithesis, his darkness, ugliness and deceit stand in stark contrast to the light, beauty and truth of God. Satan is man's antagonist, who tempts him away from his creator and actually necessitates the greatest actions of the Hero – as Savior. In the story's plot, free-willed man is created both to share in the love of God and to represent Him upon the face of the earth. Worship, sacrifice and suffering all play major parts of His story and His process to make us like Himself. Worship is the scripture's central conflict, but it is not its central purpose. The central purpose is to provide a revelation of God, for it is through this revelation that we discover the One who is worthy of worship.

This brings us again to the adversary, who delights in stealing worship from God and dominion from man and imprisoning us as his slaves. His primary temptation in the Old Testament was idolatry, but both its ancient and modern forms transform people into the objects of their worship and bring about death. Satan's methods are all about power and entrapping men through physical desires and selfishness. Conversely, God uses weak, free-willed human beings and gives them His power through the Holy Spirit to enable victory over our enemy, our flesh and our self-will. Despite our weaknesses and vulnerability, God has made the actions of man central to His plan. He equips us (without obliterating our free wills) to play profound roles as co-laborers with Christ for His eternal glory and our eternal transformation. We have been given a high and noble calling – to share in the very life and love of the Trinity. Out of the overflow of that love, the Triune God provides us with all things. It is the "God who Provides" who is worthy of all our worship, honor and praise.

† † †

Throughout this course we examined four themes from the Bible that we tracked through the Old Testament and into the New – all are brought together in Christ. Moses' refrain to "Choose Life or Choose Death" is ultimately a call to choose Christ, who is the only life and light of men. In the theme, "God as Man's Provider", Christ is God's ultimate provision for mankind. In "Man as God's Representative", Christ clothed in human flesh is the ultimate representative of God to man, revealing God and bringing glory unto the Father. In "Suffering", it is again the Lord Jesus Christ, who as the suffering servant accomplished the plan of God upon the cross, making possible through his torturous death and glorious resurrection our very life. While there are other biblical themes that could have been chosen for this book, the reality is that all major

... A Course Summary continued

Scriptural themes directly or indirectly point to Jesus Christ. He is the Alpha and Omega, the beginning and the end, the Word made flesh. He is the revelation of God in bodily form. "For in Him dwelleth all the fulness of the Godhead bodily." He is the Providing, Suffering, Life-Giving God, who is alone to be worshipped. Glory to Him!

† † †

So we come at last to the invitation: Remember, the Bible was written to people who were surrounded by and at times immersed in gross paganism. Can you imagine how beautiful the God of the Bible must have sounded and how elevated biblical truths must have looked from the pit of paganism? The beauty, goodness and truth of Israel's God must have astounded a searching polytheist or the repentant Israelite, who had the courage to leave the lies and darkness behind. But there were some things that the polytheists rightly understood. People are called to imitate their gods. The annual festivals of the creation stories and the "dead and rising god" fertility rites were re-enacted each year in painstaking detail. These faithful reenactments, though corrupt and twisted, were central to the polytheist's religion and displayed to everyone around them exactly what they believed about the character and nature of their gods and goddesses. Not to testify to the potent reality of both their creation and spring "resurrection" myths was believed to have dire consequences for the entire community.

Here is where the pagan can challenge the Christian. Do we take seriously the call to imitate our God in His goodness, beauty and truth? Do we think intentionally about what it means to live according to the Bible's creation and resurrection stories? Do we think about the ramifications to our communities of family, church, or neighborhood when we sin and fail to live in the light of the Creation and Resurrection? Do we value others as unique pictures of God? Do we live in light of our God-given purpose to love like Him and spread His image across the earth? Do we sacrifice the desires of our flesh to do the will of the Father? Do we consider others as more important than ourselves? These are just some of the ways in which we can imitate or honor our Creator and Savior and show to the world what He is like. Indeed, we have been given a high and noble calling. You might be thinking, "Yes, but the pagans only did their big imitation thing once a year. Imitating God sounds like something we should be doing every day." Exactly. When you start thinking like this, then you've got it! The Bible is an invitation to come and see the beauty and goodness of the Lord and to be transformed by it.

a letter to my students

Dear Student,

I write this closing letter to you, boldly proclaiming that Christ is the Way, the Truth and the Life. In this last lesson, we focused on Christ as the Life, but I pray that you have seen through the Word of God and this course that Christ is also the Way and the Truth.

When I was your age, I wondered deeply how people could know for sure that the Bible is true. I thought, "How do I know Jesus is true; or that stuff about the Holy Spirit living inside me? If the Holy Spirit does live inside me, I can't feel him there." I wondered, "Why is it that most everybody around me is so sure about Christianity. Still other people are convinced that their religions are true... how do the people close to me really know Christianity is true"?

In my adult life, I have come to realize that the certainty of "knowing God is real" looks rather different for different people. If you ask your parents how they know God is real (assuming they are believers), each of them may give you an answer you can tell is very satisfying for them but may or may not be meaningful for you. The reality is that nobody can prove to others that God is real, no matter how compelling his or her personal experience is.

Here's the bottom line: If God really wanted to prove to you that He's real, He could write something like, "I am real" with his finger on your bedroom wall. Unfortunately, I've come to realize that God isn't much interested in proving that He is real, regardless of what people may tell you. Rather, God's Word says that our relationship with Him is based on faith. We must choose to believe that God is God without seeing the "writing on the wall". Even so, God is kind, and He doesn't ask for blind faith; He doesn't ask you to believe in a God you know nothing about. His Word was written with the explicit purpose of telling you and me about Himself. The Bible was originally written to Israel, a group of people who were constantly told by the neighboring nations around them that, "Anybody who believes in one God is a fool". But God wasn't interested in proving Himself to Israel either. Instead, He just kept choosing authors to write and reveal more about Himself to His chosen nation. The people of Israel finally believed Him – later rather than sooner, but they walked through a lot of painful stuff first.

Your journey may look more like Israel's or you may have a good deal of faith in God now, which may or may not waiver in the future. Please always remember, that in choosing your faith you are choosing what kind of God you will trust in. As you have seen, the God of the Bible is not like the gods or goddesses of the ancient pagans. While we didn't study other gods, believe me ... He's not the god of Islam, nor of the Hindus. He's not the god of the Aztecs, nor

Brigham Young, nor Joseph Smith. He's not the god of Buddhism (Buddhists don't really have a god). God is certainly not the god of the atheist; the atheist is the god of the atheist. In choosing Christianity, you choose to love and serve the God whom you've been studying throughout this course. Perhaps He's the God you've been learning about all your life. He's the God who loves, and if the Bible is true, He has proven His love through the cross. However, He will never force His love upon you. You'll have to choose to believe and to keep believing that He is your Creator and Savior. Always remember that when people choose their religion that the choice they make ultimately determines the kind of God they will worship. You can worship goddesses, you can worship yourself or you can worship the Lamb that was slain to give life to mankind.

In the time you have spent reading the Bible's testimony about who this God is – a testimony that many refer to as His "love letter" to us – I hope you have moved closer towards truly "knowing" for yourself that Jesus is the Way, the Truth and the Life. If not, I hope you'll keep writing down your questions in your Jacob Journal, because wrestling with God can result in some amazing blessings. Despite the length of this course, we have only cracked the surface of God's book, so keep reading, keep questioning and keep searching for the Way, the Truth and the Life. You will find Him if you seek Him with all of your heart.

A fellow seeker and finder,

Mrs. Brim

Jacob Journal

...wrestling with God, Jacob was blessed.
—Genesis 32:28-29

Jacob Journal

...wrestling with God, Jacob was blessed.
—Genesis 32:28-29

Jacob Journal

...wrestling with God, Jacob was blessed.
—Genesis 32:28-29

CC-1: The Nature and Works of the Gods*

Comparison Chart 1 Parent/Teacher Copy	Pagan Gods and Goddesses	The God of the Bible
CHARACTER QUALITIES OF THE CREATOR(S)	Capricious, self-centered, quarrelsome, lazy, immoral	Steadfast, unchanging provider, good, transcendent (separate from his creation), all-powerful, Trinitarian, self-giving, creates and controls all things.
HOW THE WORLD WAS CREATED	The co-habiting of the gods and goddesses births each new aspect of nature.	By God's spoken word – "And God said, 'Let there be'..."
HOW MAN WAS CREATED	From clay, Enlil made an initial lifeless form. Goddesses shaped the clay, put it in a womb, and eventually birthed a slave called Man.	Out of the dust of the earth God formed man, and out of man's rib God formed Eve and gave both the breath of life.
WHY MAN WAS CREATED – HIS PURPOSE	The gods needed slaves to do their work.	To reflect the image and likeness of the triune God. Man is relational, man is steward of God's creation; as one flesh man creates new life and fills God's world with His image.
WHAT IS THE VALUE OR WORTH OF MAN	Because man makes it possible for the gods to live at ease and in peace, human value is rooted in his or her usefulness.	Man's value is rooted in the worth ascribed to Him by His maker.
WHAT DO BABYLONIAN AND HEBREW LAWS REVEAL ABOUT THEIR GODS? (LESSON 15)	The laws of Hammurabi reveal that pagan gods and pagan culture value property and controlling things. The morality of pagan gods and goddesses is often lower than the standard of the Babylonian law.	God is all-powerful. The power of Satan is no threat to His power. Rather, God directs His power to weak men and women who depend upon Him in their struggles against Satan, e.g. Elijah and the prophets of Baal.
IN THE PAGAN AND BIBLICAL ORIGIN STORIES, WHAT ROLES DOES POWER PLAY? (LESSON 18)	The sustaining and ensuring of the power of the gods/goddesses was provided for by the work of man. The forces of chaos always threatened to overcome the gods of order, so renewing the gods' power was essential.	The Laws of Moses reveal the holiness of God's character, based in love, mercy, justice and goodness. Obedience to His standard brought life and holiness to His people. Disobedience brought death for those who choose to mock Him or His representatives or harm those made to represent him. The Law reveals the value God places on relationships over things.

*Please note: these charts are for parent reference. The summaries provided here are more elaborate than what a student will be able to synthesize on his or her charts.

Comparison Chart · Parent/Teacher Copy · **253**

CC-2: View of Nature*

Comparison Chart 2 Parent/Teacher Copy	Polytheism	Monotheism	Naturalism	Pantheism
WHAT IS NATURE?	Each aspect of nature —water, moon, harvest, sun, rain, air—are specific gods or goddesses, both natural and supernatural.	An orderly, good, natural creation of a supernatural God		
HOW DOES MAN RESPOND TO EACH VIEW OF NATURE?	Man fears nature, as it is comprised of the gods who control his fate.	Man cares for the world as God's steward and uses its resources as God's provision for his physical needs.		
IS NATURE MORE IMPORTANT OR LESS IMPORTANT THAN MAN?	Man is less important than nature because he was made to serve the gods of nature. Man is a mere slave, while nature is comprised of the gods and goddesses.	Man is more important than nature because God has placed him over nature, yet nature like man has value because it is a reflection of the glory of God. Man is to care for nature like God cares for man.		

*Please note: these charts are for parent reference. The summaries provided here are more elaborate than what a student will be able to synthesize on his or her charts.

254 · Christian Theology & Ancient Polythesism

CC-3: The Great Flood*

Comparison Chart 3 Parent/Teacher Copy	Gilgamesh's Flood	Noah's Flood
WHAT SIMILARITIES DO YOU SEE BETWEEN THESE TWO STORIES?	God/gods destroy the world with a great flood. Only one man and his family survive. They build a boat to save both the family and animals. When the boat comes to rest, they release several birds to see if they can find dry land. Both Noah and Utnapishtim offer sacrifices to God/gods after safely leaving the boat.	
WHY WAS MANKIND WIPED OUT?	They annoyed the gods by disrupting their sleep. People were made to meet the needs of the gods. When they inconvenienced the gods, the most powerful god (Enlil) decided to do away with them.	People were made to represent the all-good Creator God. They were warned that, if they disobeyed, they would die. Rather than becoming like God, they became utterly evil and deserving of destruction. Sending the flood was God's righteous judgment. Yet the same God who brought judgment showed mercy to the righteous and made a way of escape. Noah was greatly blessed by God for his obedience. God saved both people and the animals through Noah.
WHY WERE UTNAPISHTIM'S AND NOAH'S FAMILIES SAVED?	Ea liked Utnapishtim for some undefined reason. Perhaps this was a way of foiling Enlil's plans.	Noah walked with God. He obeyed God and was fulfilling his purpose to represent God on the earth.
WHAT DO THESE STORIES REVEAL ABOUT THE CHARACTER OF THE GODS/GOD?	Some gods are neither merciful nor just. They need rest and get irritable when they lose sleep. Some are crafty like Ea. They contradict one another. They instruct people to lie. They can be frightened by the power of the other gods (Enlil was the storm god) Some were sympathetic like Ishtar. They could make mistakes like Enlil, who was chastened by Ea for being angry that some humans survived. They were a mixture of good and evil, power and weakness.	God's character is just and merciful, compassionate and full of love. God grieves over the destruction of man, whom He made out of and for love. (He loves mankind, but He holds him responsible for his evil.) Knowing Noah's descendents would reject and disobey Him again, God nevertheless chose to save Noah. God chose to suffer because of man's sin. He gives man hope (the rainbow) and is Himself man's hope.

*Please note: these charts are for parent reference. The summaries provided here are more elaborate than what what a student will be able to synthesize on his or her charts.

Comparison Chart · Parent/Teacher Copy · **255**

CC-4: Worship: Seven Days a Week*

Comparison Chart 4 Parent/Teacher Copy	Ancient POLYTHEIST	Old Testament Monotheist
WHY DID THEY PRACTICE A 7-DAY WEEK?	Their 7-day week revolved around the worship of the seven heavenly bodies , who represented the 7 most powerful Sumerian gods/goddesses.	God made the world in six days and rested on the seventh. Israel's 7-day week was a sign of her relationship with the one true God, whom she represented to the world.
WHAT DID THEY DO EACH DAY OF THE DAY THAT EXPRESSED THEIR WORSHIP?	Each day was spent bowing down and praying to idols that represented the "god of the day." Every day was spent working since man was the gods' slave. This worship is called idolatry, because it is worship of idols that represent the forces of nature.	Israel was worshipping God by imitating his act of creating the world and resting on the seventh day. Resting showed their dependence upon God.
WHAT BEARS THE IMAGE OF THE GODS/ GOD?	Idols made of wood, stone or clay.	Man and woman
DEFINE IDOLATRY AND REST IN THE CORRECT COLUMN. (LESSON 6)	Idolatry: Depending on and worshipping things made by God rather than worshipping and depending on the Maker.	Rest: Trusting in God's provision by obeying His Sabbath Laws and worshipping and imitating Him alone. In the Old Testament, when Israel kept the Sabbath Laws, she was representing the Lord Who will Provide to a lost world.
WHY WOULD A TRUE POLYTHEIST NEVER REST AND A TRUE MONOTHEIST NEVER COMMIT IDOLATRY?	Man was made to work as a slave of the gods. Slaves did not get days off in ancient Mesopotamia, since their gods depended upon their labor.	God strictly forbade worshipping idols, because they represented things that were made rather than the Maker. Man was made to represent the Maker on whom he depended.

*Please note: these charts are for parent reference. The summaries provided here are more elaborate than what a student will be able to synthesize on his or her charts.

256 · Christian Theology & Ancient Polythesism

CC-5: Worship Through Sacrifice*

Comparison Chart 5 Parent/Teacher Copy	Ancient Polytheist	Old Testament Monotheist	New Testament Monotheist
REASONS FOR SACRIFICE: (LESSON 7) FOR POLYTHEISTS, LIST THE GENERAL REASONS WHY THEY OFFERED SACRIFICES. FOR MONOTHEISTS, SUMMARIZE THE REASON FOR EACH OF THE BIBLE'S EIGHT GREAT SACRIFICES. NOTE SACRIFICES SEVEN AND EIGHT UNDER N.T. MONOTHEISTS. (LESSON 7)	To meet the needs of the gods To ensure their strength and the stability of nature To gain the favor of the gods To make amends for some offense against the gods To avoid suffering	1. God covers man's shame. (Gen. 3:7,21) 2. Sacrifice is offered on God's terms. (Gen. 4:2-6) 3. Sacrifice is man's grateful response to God's salvation. (Gen. 8:15-21) 4. The Lord Will Provide the sacrifice man needs. (Gen.22:1-19) 5. The blood of the lamb saves from slavery and death. (Ex. 12:1-14,21-32) 6. God established the O.T. sac. system to provide for the forgiveness of sin, thanksgiving, provision for the priests, and for fellowship. (see L. 8 for ref.)	7. Christ is the Lamb of God who takes away the sins of the world, covering our shame and freeing us from slavery to sin; through His blood we are given life eternal. He is God's ultimate provision for man. His sacrifice is the only means of salvation. Through Christ we have fellowship with God. (see L. 8 for ref.) 8. Christians sacrifice the desires of our flesh in grateful response and in imitation of Christ's sacrifice of his flesh. A Christian sacrifices his sinful desires daily as he strives to be like Christ. These daily sacrifices are an act of worshipping God. (see L.8 for ref.)
HOW IMPORTANT ARE REPENTANCE AND OBEDIENCE IN RELATION TO SACRIFICE? (LESSON 8)		Sacrifices never gave Jews an excuse for disobedience; in fact, sacrifices were meaningless if man did not repent first. (Ps. 51)	The forgiveness of Christ's sacrifice is only available to those who repent. The Christian's sacrifice is daily obedience.
SUMMARY: SUMMARIZE THE REASONS FOR MONOTHEIST SACRIFICE. (LESSON 8)		Since man's first sin, God has been sacrificing for man's needs and teaching us about the importance of sacrifice in our relationship with Him. God is not needy; we are. We humbly acknowledge our need for forgiveness and by faith accept His sacrifice on the cross. Then we sacrifice in response to the God on Whom we depend to meet all our needs. These sacrifices include denying our sinful desires and instead choosing obedience. This is an act of worship unto God and a reflection of His good work in us.	

*Please note: these charts are for parent reference. The summaries provided here are more elaborate than what a student will be able to synthesize on his or her charts.

Comparison Chart · Parent/Teacher Copy · **257**

CC-6: Worship Through Prayer*

Comparison Chart 6 Parent/Teacher Copy	Ancient Polytheists	Hebrew Monotheists
WHAT DID BOTH ANCIENT POLYTHEISTS AND MONOTHEISTS BELIEVE ABOUT PRAYER THAT WAS TRUE? INCLUDE THE TYPES OF PRAYERS THAT BOTH GROUPS PRAYED.	Both rightly understood that all of life depended on the supernatural. Prayer was the means of bringing to the gods/God requests for help and repentance and for exalting the gods/God they served. Pagans and Hebrews knew that prayer was a vital form of worship – through prayer they were communicating with their personal gods or God and expressing their dependence. The gods were/God was their source of provision and help. Both monotheists and polytheists extolled the greatness of their gods/God as more powerful than themselves, and they recognized that displeasing their gods/God was sin requiring repentance.	
NOTE THE FIRST MAJOR DIFFERENCES IN THEIR BELIEFS ABOUT PRAYER: WHO THEY WERE PRAYING TO.	In praying to nature gods and goddesses they were actually praying to demons. They were presenting their needs, asking for forgiveness and giving the praise due only to God to Satan and his demons.	They were praying to the one true Creator God – the only one who has the power to forgive, the only one who is the source of man's provision and the only one who should receive man's praise and adoration.
NOTE THE SECOND MAJOR DIFFERENCE IN THEIR BELIEFS ABOUT PRAYER: WHAT DID EACH BELIEVE ABOUT THE POWER OF PRAYER?	Some prayers held magical powers. The power of the words themselves could bring about or sustain reality. Prayers were the containers for the power of the words. These powerful words were called incantations. They believed incantations held supernatural power both as curses and as sources of renewing life.	The Israelite believed in the power of prayer, but the power to effect prayer resided in the One to whom the prayers are raised. The effectiveness of the Israelites' prayer was not in the words being said, but in the life being lived according to God's design. Obedience or repentance prompts God to answer prayers.
WHY WERE PAGAN PRAYERS IDOLATROUS?	They expressed dependence upon and directed to created things that which belongs only to God. Pagan prayer and praise robs from God the glory due His name.	

*Please note: these charts are for parent reference. The summaries provided here are more elaborate than what a student will be able to synthesize on his or her charts.

258 · Christian Theology & Ancient Polytheism

CC-7: Consequences of Idolatry vs. True Worship*

Comparison Chart 7 Parent/Teacher Copy	Polytheism		Monotheism		Modern Idolatry	
HOW AND WHY IS HUMAN SEXUALITY IMPACTED BY EACH WORLDVIEW?	**Consequence (how)**: Gross immorality was central to worship of the gods and goddesses.	**Reason (why)**: The acts of gods and goddesses that birthed new life were imitated by pagan worshippers.	**Consequence (how)**: Marriage union is sacred. Marital love produces life. That life and love is sacred.	**Reason (why)**: Marriage represents the One Triune God, who is the source of life and love.	**Consequence (how)**: Immorality becomes a lifestyle which you as a "god" are entitled to.	**Reason (why)**: When self is god, personal pleasure justifies behavior.
HOW AND WHY IS THE VALUE OF HUMAN LIFE IMPACTED BY EACH WORLDVIEW?	**Consequence (how)**: child sacrifice	**Reason (why)**: The value of human life was determined by its usefulness towards serving the good of the community.	**Consequence (how)**: All human life is priceless, both because of Who made us and Whom we were made to be like.	**Reason (why)**: God in love made all people to represent Him.	**Consequence (how)**: Abortion on demand	**Reason (why)**: When self is god, whatever gets in the way of personal fulfillment must go.
HOW AND WHY IS ONE'S VIEW OF DEMONIC POWER IMPACTED BY EACH WORLDVIEW?	**Consequence (how)**: witchcraft	**Reason (why)**: Canaanite gods struggled for power, so humans emulated them by trying to seize divine power for their own purposes.	**Consequence (how)**: Seeking demonic power is a grave evil. Christians seek the supernatural power that comes from the Holy Spirit.	**Reason (why)**: The purpose of supernatural power is for our transformation –becoming like God. His power enables us to resist the devil and produce the fruit of the Holy Spirit.	**Consequence (how)**: Witchcraft as entertainment, or witchcraft as power	**Reason (why)**: When self is god, whatever gives power and control over life's circumstances is valued.

*Please note: these charts are for parent reference. The summaries provided here are more elaborate than what a student will be able to synthesize on his or her charts.

Comparison Chart · Parent/Teacher Copy · **259**

CC-8: Hammurabi's Code and Mosaic Law*

Comparison Chart 8
Parent/Teacher Copy

Instructions: *Due to the volume of information, answer all questions in paragraph form.*

1) COMPARE HAMMURABI'S VIEW OF HIS GODS AND HIS ACHIEVEMENTS TO MOSES' VIEW OF GOD AND HIS ACHIEVEMENTS.	Hammurabi was a proud man who wanted to proclaim his own glory and success; Moses was a humble man concerned with God's glory rather than with his own. The Law directed people's attention to God and His great works rather than what Moses had done.
2) RECORD THE PURPOSES OF BOTH LAWS.	H: to provide justice, eliminate evil-doers, protect the weak, further the rule of Hammurabi, and promote the good of humanity. M: To reveal the one true God, to love, obey and fear God, to keep Israel from sinning and forsaking God, to have a long life, good land, and much prosperity, to make a holy people, a royal priesthood, God's treasured possession.
3) NOTE WHAT TYPE OF LAWS DO NOT EXIST IN HAMMURABI'S CODE AND THE REASON WHY.	Babylonian law does not include anything about how the people were to relate to their gods, because pagan gods were not interested in relationships with humans who were mere slaves. The only human representative of the gods was the most powerful king, Hammurabi. Without the purpose to create relationships or representatives nothing like the Ten Commandments exists in Babylonian Law.
4) WHAT SIMILARITIES AND DIFFERENCES EXIST BETWEEN THE LAWS DEALING WITH MARRIAGE, MURDER, AND THIEVES?	Both sets of laws call for death as the penalty for adultery, since even pagans saw how crucial it was to protect the institution of the family. Murder in both laws was also punished by death. The main differences arose in the laws about theft. Theft in Israel received the lesser punishment as property is less valuable than human life. In Babylonian both theft and murder received the death penalty because both people and things were viewed as property. Property was the highest value of Babylonian law. Murder was like just another form of theft, since it deprived the gods of their laborers. But in the eyes of God, murder was doing away with a picture of Himself and a member of His family. As such, murder and theft were punished differently.
5) HOW WERE "AN EYE FOR AN EYE" LAWS IMPLEMENTED DIFFERENTLY IN BOTH CULTURES?	Both systems of law upheld the idea that the punishment ought to be proportionate to the crime committed, but as the Babylonian law viewed some persons as more valuable than others, justice was determined by the "worth" of the victim. Punishment, assigned by judge, was equal to the crime only when the criminal was an equal to his victim. Slaves were never personally compensated or given personal rights in Babylon as they were in Israel. In Israel, all people, slave and free, Israelite and foreigner were viewed as having equal value in God's eyes and entitled to justice under the law.
6) BRIEFLY DEFINE HOW THE REBELLIOUS CHILD WAS DEALT WITH AND WHY ISRAEL'S LAW HAD SUCH SEVERE PUNISHMENTS FOR THAT SIN.	Rebellious youths had their hands cut off under Babylonian law but were killed under Old Testament law. The harsher punishment was due to the seriousness of this sin in God's eyes. Rebellion is like the sin of witchcraft in that it steals power that belongs to the supernatural. Rebellion steals the power and authority God gave to His representative - the parent. Sin is never a purely private matter; it affects the community. As Israel was a people called to obey the Law of God and become a nation of priests, dealing with sin that threatens the communal understanding of the necessity of obedience was imperative. Honoring parents is loving both God and man. Dishonoring parents is hating both God and man. Such a drastic consequence for rebellion would also produce fear, another motivator not to sin.

*Please note: these charts are for parent reference. The summaries provided here are more elaborate than what a student will be able to synthesize on his or her charts.

260 · Christian Theology & Ancient Polytheism

CC-9: Suffering of the Babylonian and Biblical Job*

Comparison Chart 9 Parent/Teacher Copy	Babylonian "Job"	Biblical Job
DESCRIBE THE CHARACTER OF THE SUFFERER.	He offered sacrifices and prayed to the gods. He celebrated the gods festivals and worshipped their images and revered their names and taught others to do the same.	There was no one on earth like Job. He was blameless, upright and feared God. He turned away from evil and had great integrity despite his affliction. (Job 1:8, 2:3) And he was a priest. (1:5; 40:8)
WHAT IS THE REASON BEHIND HIS SUFFERING?	The god Marduk caused the suffering for some unknown reason.	Job knows that God is behind his suffering, but he is unaware that his suffering is due to the accusations of Satan.
HOW IS THE SUFFERER RESTORED?	Marduk sends a sorcerer who knows how to appease him and the spells and incantations to drive away the harmful demons.	In His time, God brought an end to Job's suffering and restored his wealth and family after giving him an audience with His maker.
WHAT DOES SUFFERING TEACH HIM ABOUT THE GODS/GOD?	The sufferer learns nothing about his gods in the Babylonian story. The goodness of the sufferer matters little or not at all. Mere human beings have no way to learn the ways of God. (v.35)	Suffering teaches Job to humbly submit to a God who is all-wise and all-powerful. The value of being taught the incomprehensible ways of God enabled Job to cease his striving, to rest in God's trustworthiness, and to repent of challenging the ways of God.
COMPARE THE PURPOSE OF AND USE OF POWER BY THE SORCERER WITH GOD'S POWERFUL WORDS TO JOB.	The sorcerer uses supernatural power to send a message to appease Marduk and powerful words of incantations and spells to cause a wind that drives away the tormenting demons.	God does not use his power against Satan, Job's response to his suffering drives Satan away. Out of the storm God displays his astounding power to Job as the creator and sustainer of all. God gives purpose, life and power to all things. All are dependent upon Him and are created for his pleasure.

*Please note: these charts are for parent reference. The summaries provided here are more elaborate than what a student will be able to synthesize on his or her charts.

Comparison Chart · Parent/Teacher Copy · **261**

CC-10: The Afterlife and The Resurrection*

Comparison Chart 10 Parent/Teacher Copy	Polytheists	OT Monotheists	NT Monotheists
WHAT OR HOW DID THE GODS/GOD PROVIDE FOR THE AFTERLIFE FOR EACH GROUP?	The gods make no provisions for man's afterlife. Any provisions are made by man with a few exceptions. Men do not join the gods in death. Confined to a separate netherworld, they crawl on their bellies and eat dust until they disappear.	O.T. teachings on the afterlife are very vague. The emphasis of the O.T. is man's need to live life in obedience to God, to worship Him and enjoy the blessings of Abundant life, here and in eternity, is only available through the shed blood of Jesus Christ.	After man choose death, God the Redeemer paid the ultimate price to buy man back from sin and eternal death.
WHAT IMPORTANT STORIES DID EACH HAVE INVOLVING "RESURRECTION"?	Canaanite: Baal the fertility/land god is killed by the god of death. All fertility of land, animals, and men comes to an end. Baal is resurrected for six months each year so the cycle of spring/harvest can take place. Babylonian: Istar attempts to conquer the realm of Hell, only to be killed by the goddesses of Hades. Crafty gods save her because all fertility has come to an end. She is resurrected and in anger sends her husband to the grave. But Tammuz returns every six months for the cycle of spring/harvest.	Ancient Israel had no "resurrection" stories that explained the seasons. The creation story says that the lights in the sky were given to control the seasons.	The NT resurrection story is about the renewal of life in mankind through Christ giving up his life on the tree, so that mankind may once again eat of eternal life. The early church interpretation of Christ's descent into Hell is the story of God going to rescue his beloved children from the power of Satan. Christ conquers death by death. Satan is powerless before the Savior. The gates of Hell are broken down and the righteous OT saints are taken to heaven.
WHAT WAS RESURRECTED THROUGH EACH STORY?	Gods and goddesses and Spring.	The chapter of God's story that restores immortality to man has yet to be told. Man lost his immortality, only the Son of Man can restore it.	Christ and mankind
THROUGH WHAT RITUALS WERE THESE STORIES REENACTED, AND WHO RECEIVED RENEWED POWER OR STRENGTH THROUGH THEM?	Annual spring and harvest fertility rites. These reenactments gave strength to the gods and ensured the renewal of spring.		The Lord's Supper/Communion/Eucharist, whereby people celebrate Christ and his death, when his body was given up for our great need. Easter is the celebration of Christ's resurrection and His victory over death and the grave. Mankind can now experience life now and in eternity.

*Please note: these charts are for parent reference. The summaries provided here are more elaborate than what a student will be able to synthesize on his or her charts.

262 · Christian Theology & Ancient Polythesism

TC-1: A Grand Theme of Scripture – God as Man's Provider*

Theme Chart 1 Parent/Teacher Copy	Instructions: Note examples of things God provides as directed by the scriptural reference and corresponding lesson.
LESSON II Genesis 1&2	God provides food, a unique identity and purpose, meaningful work, a beautiful garden home, a spouse, and freedom to choose while providing warnings of the consequences of disobeying God.
LESSONS III-IV Genesis 6-8	God provided for Noah and his family through the ark. The story of Noah is actually the first great salvation story – God saves one man and his family from death and destruction. God saved Noah's family, knowing full well the price He would pay for the salvation of Noah's sinful descendents. If God were like the pagan gods, who wanted to avoid suffering, we would never know life or love.
LESSON VI Genesis 2:2	Sabbath is the O.T. sign of God's provision and of Israel's covenant with God. God's rest symbolized that He had provided all man needed for love and life eternal.
Exodus 20:8-11, 31:12-17	God provides animal skins to cover Adam and Eve from the shame brought on by sin.
LESSON VII Genesis 3:21 Genesis 22:1-1	God provides a ram for Abraham and is called "The Lord Will Provide" – looking forward to the ultimate Provision of Christ. (The ram/lamb is another O.T. symbol of God's provision.)
Exodus 12	Through the blood of the lamb, God provides delivery from slavery and death.
Lev. 1-4, 11-18	God provides a sacrificial system by which His people were forgiven of their sins.
John 1:28, 29	The Cross is the N.T. symbol of God's provision (the lamb is the symbol that bridges both O.T. and N.T.) Jesus, the Lamb of God provided for salvation from sin and death. The provision of Christ is God's greatest demonstration of love for humankind.
LESSON XV Titus 2:11-15	God gives us grace through the salvation provided in Christ and through the spiritual energy provided by the Spirit to obediently love Him and our neighbors. In doing so, we represent the love of God to the world.
LESSON XIX Jeremiah 31	God provides hope for the captives through promised forgiveness, redemption, restoration and a new covenant. God provides rest for the land, enabling Israel to keep her covenant with God.
LESSON XXIII Job 38-42:6	God provided a revelation of himself, teaching Job that the Giver is worth more than all His gifts.

*Please note: these charts are for parent reference. The summaries provided here are more elaborate than what a student will be able to synthesize on his or her charts.

Theme Chart · Parent/Teacher Copy · **263**

TC-2: A Grand Theme of Scripture – Man as God's Representative*

Theme Chart 2
Parent/Teacher Copy

Instructions: *With each corresponding lesson and scripture note where this theme begins, and give examples of how man represents God. With each new reference note repetitions or new applications of this idea. For each scriptural reference, give examples for how or why man represents God.*

Lesson & Reference	Summary
LESSON II Genesis 1&2	Man's purpose is to reflect the image and likeness of the Triune God. Man is relational; man is a steward of God's creation, having dominion over God's creation. People are to spread the image and dominion of God across the whole earth. As one flesh, man and woman create new life in reflection of the life-giving Trinity.
LESSONS III-IV Genesis 9:1-7	God re-establishes that man is made in His image. People are to multiply and fill the earth, spreading His image and dominion across creation. The plants and now animal meat are given to man for His provision from God. The life of man is precious. Man or animal cannot take it without forfeiting their own. By implication, only God can justly take the life of man.
LESSON V Exodus 20:8-11 Genesis 2:2,3	Man worships God by imitating Him, thereby reflecting His image. The Israelites worshipped God through practicing a seven-day week. Just as God worked six days and rested on the seventh, so did the Israelites. Sabbath rest, both weekly and every seventh year, was her act of trust in and covenant with the God who provided everything for her life.
LESSON VI Colossians 1:15 Ephesians 4:22-24	The way Christians bear God's image is through imitating Christ, who is the very image of the invisible God. We imitate the sacrifice of Christ through dying to ourselves and living unto God. This sacrificial life of Christ in us transforms us, through the power of the Spirit, to reflect God more and more closely.
LESSON XVII Genesis 1:26,27	God gave the first glimpse of His Trinitarian personhood through the creation of man. God reveals Himself to the world in and through people. This includes the writing of the Word of God, the Incarnation, and the three communities through which man was intended to bear His image —marriage, Israel, and the Church.
LESSON XVII 1 Kings 18:16-40; I Corinthians 1:27-29	As God's representative, the prophet Elijah prayed, asking God to withhold the rain (a power falsely attributed to Baal). On Mount Carmel, the most powerful demonic forces of the day were defeated by a weak man through whom God displayed His mighty power.
LESSON XIX Rev. 3:15-16	Go to TC-2 and note the implications of Revelation 3:15-16 for those who strive to represent God. Whole-hearted worship transforms the heart of the worshipper. To reflect the image of God, God and God alone must have 1st place in the temple of our hearts. Divided hearts reflect a distorted image of God to the world.
LESSON XIX Jeremiah 50:17-20 II Chronicles 36:15-23	As God's representative, the prophet Jeremiah convicted king and people of their idolatry. He preached God's judgment — the destruction of Jerusalem — and future hope to the exiles.
LESSON XXI Job 1 and 2	Man's role as representative is put to the ultimate test when God allows Satan to "take away all that he has provided. Job's continued worship of God in the midst of being deprived of the goodness of the Lord as a testament both to the worthiness of God's sole right to worship and man's worthiness to be his representative on the earth.

Please note: these charts are for parent reference. The summaries provided here are more elaborate than what a student will be able to synthesize on his or her charts.

TC-3: A Grand Theme of Scripture – Choose Life or Choose Death*

Theme Chart 3 Parent/Teacher Copy	Instructions: *Note examples of the choice for life or death directed by the scriptural reference and coorresponding*
LESSON IV Why is free will necessary? (Gen. 2:16) How was man using his free will in Noah's day? Genesis 6–8	While free will made sin possible, it also made it possible to love – the highest form of love based on choice. While man could choose to disobey, his choice to obey is his expression of his love for God. God made man to share in the very love and life of the Trinity. Most had said no to God's life and love. They chose instead the death God had promised to those who rejected Him. All died in the destruction of the flood save Noah. Noah chose to walk with God and to obey his laws. The salvation of Noah was the salvation of humanity and all living things.
LESSON VII How does what we worship bring us life or ultimately death? How was idolatry the choice for death as seen in the O. T. and in modern culture?	We were made to worship God. Worshipping God transforms us into His likeness which is life. Worshipping what is not God degrades us. Our personhood shrivels, becoming used up by our objects of worship until eventually we die. God gives us life. False objects of worship suck life from us. Pagans believed that human life only had value if it served the purposes of the gods. Serving the purposes of the gods led to man's death and destruction through immorality, child sacrifice and witchcraft. Modern culture in the name of self worship is walking the same destructive path. The ideas of God elevated Western culture; the idolatry of modern culture corrupts, degrades and ultimately destroys.
LESSON XVI Summarize Israel's two options. Deuteronomy 30:11-20	Israel must choose between life and prosperity or death and destruction. Her decision was a reflection of whether or not she loved God or her neighbor's gods. Obeying God would result in blessing. God is life. The gods of her neighbors would bring death to her and her children.
LESSON XVII How does man's free will relate to the Bible's ultimate?	Like our obedience, we have the freedom to choose who or what we will worship. When we obey and worship God, we are choosing life and love.
LESSON XVIII What was the choice and outcome of Elijah's offer? I Kings 18:16-40	Believing he was the only prophet of God left, Elijah asked the people to choose between his God or the Baal of 450 pagan prophets. When God displayed his power in response to Elijah's prayer, the people cried, "The Lord – he is God!" 450 prophets of Baal were put to death.
LESSON XXIV What is the ultimate and only choice for life? John 10:10; 14:6	To choose life is to choose Jesus Christ, man's only choice for real life here and in eternity. The gift of eternal life could not be offered to O.T. saints until the Giver of Life had willingly sacrificed and exchanged His life for the life of the whole world.

*Please note: these charts are for parent reference. The summaries provided here are more elaborate than what a student will be able to synthesize on his or her charts.

Theme Chart · Parent/Teacher Copy · **265**

TC-4: A Grand Theme of Scripture – Suffering*

Theme Chart 4 Parent/Teacher Copy	
Instructions: *Note the examples of suffering for each reference or lesson below. Begin with the name of the sufferer and whether they suffered justly or unjustly. Add the suffering they experienced. Each example may have more than one sufferer.*	
LESSON IV Genesis 6-8	• Mankind suffered justly. They died in the terrible destruction of the flood, because of their utter evil. • God suffered unjustly. He grieved over the destruction of His special creation. Through saving Noah and his family, God knew full well the price He would pay for the salvation of Noah's sinful descendents. If God was like the pagan gods, who wanted to avoid suffering, we would never have known true love –a love that willingly suffers for the beloved.
LESSONS XIX Book of Jeremiah	• God suffered unjustly. Judah, like Israel before her, behaved like an unfaithful wife. She rejected God's life and love and prostituted herself before false gods. • Judah suffered justly. She received the punishment that God had warned her about in the days of Moses. Nevertheless God used her suffering to purify Israel. God in his mercy would redeem a remnant, who would be forgiven and experience the fulfillment of God's promises. The destruction of God's temple would mar His reputation before a pagan world. • Jeremiah suffered unjustly. He suffered ridicule, beatings and imprisonments. He had to endure watching the wretched suffering of his people and the destruction of the Temple of Jerusalem. Jeremiah never saw the exiles return, the temple rebuilt, or the rest of God's promise fulfilled. However, he believed that God was faithful, despite his personal experience.
LESSON XXI Book of Job – Prologue	Job suffered unjustly. To worship God when suffering is one of the highest expression of man's trust and acknowledgement that God alone is God.
LESSON XXII Book of Job – Epilogue	Job suffered unjustly and is never told why. What God gave him were questions about His knowledge, wisdom, and power, enabling Job to see an all-wise, all-powerful God who was worthy of man's trust no matter what circumstances bring.
SUMMARY:	There are many examples of unjust suffering in the O. T. and N. T. The unjust suffering of God is the highest expression of His love for mankind. This suffering climaxes at the cross. Those who bear the image of God also suffer unjustly, but in doing so they offer the highest form of worship unto God and spread the image of God across the earth. The suffering of both God and man is the path leading towards the day in which God will restore his righteous rule across the face of the entire creation.

Please note: these charts are for parent reference. The summaries provided here are more elaborate than what a student will be able to synthesize on his or her charts.

266 · Christian Theology & Ancient Polythesism

BSC-1: The Bible's Story – Scripture's Three Main Characters*

Bible Story Chart 1 Parent/Teacher Copy	*Instructions: The letters next to each question correspond to a direction found within the instruction boxes in the lessons.*	
A	Who is the main character of the Bible?	God
A	Who are the two supporting characters, and what are their relationships to God?	Man and Satan – both are creatures created by God.
A	Name the Three Persons of the One Triune God:	Father, Son and Spirit
A	Name the three communal human relationships that were established to represent God to the world:	Marriage, Israel and the Church
B	In calling the Church the "Bride of Christ" what does this title tell us about the relationship God has offered us? (Think about the contrast to the polytheistic title for man – slave of the gods.)	God is offering mankind a relationship of love as His beloved. He is inviting us to share in the very life and love of the Trinity for all eternity.
B	As those who accept God's proposal of love wear no wedding ring, how do we display to the world that we are "betrothed" to the King of Kings and Lord or Lords?	Through His life and love being seen in us and shared with those around us.

*Please note: these charts are for parent reference. The summaries provided here are more elaborate than what a student will be able to synthesize on his or her charts.

Bible Study Chart · Parent/Teacher Copy · **267**

BSC-2: The Bible's Story – Scripture's Primary Purpose & Central Conflict*

Bible Story Chart 2 Parent/Teacher Copy	Instructions: *The letters next to each question correspond to a direction found within the instruction boxes in the lessons.*
B What is the main purpose of the Bible's stories and of all creation?	To reveal the character and nature of God
B How do the two supporting characters serve the story's purpose?	Man was made to be like God, to represent and spread His image across the face of the earth. Satan, as the antithesis of God, contrasts the light, beauty, and truth of God with his darkness, ugliness, and deceit. Satan, as the antagonist, tempts men into rebellion against God. This necessitated the greatest actions of the Hero.
B Out of jealousy, pride and hatred, what does Satan endeavor to steal from God and man?	The worship of God and the dominion of man over the earth.
C In challenging God's sole right to worship, God could have crushed Satan by his power. What did he do instead?	He made weak human beings with the freedom to choose whom they would worship. God would woo them to Himself through love, thereby defeating Satan's challenge with love rather than power.
C What question is at the heart of the Bible's central conflict?	"Who should be worshipped?"
D Give a biblical example of Satan attempting to steal the worship of God and the dominion of man:	Satan's invention of the Baals was a direct affront to God and man by directing into idols the worship belonging only to God and making man the slave of the Baals rather than rulers of God's earth.
D How does the Bible's primary purpose resolve the main conflict?	The Bible's revelation of the character and actions of God shows that He is the only one worthy of all worship, honor, and praise. The character of God, rather than the power of God, settles the question of whom should be worshipped.
E Out of jealousy, pride, and hatred, what ploys does Satan use in his efforts to steal from God and man?	Two things: Satan tries first to discredit the worship Job offers to God and then he tries to claim the rule of the earth by roaming across it.
F When Satan challenged God's right to worship, God could have crushed Satan with his power. What did he do instead?	God trusted Job to disprove Satan's claims. His confidence in Job's integrity was such that He allowed Job to face the enemy at a severe disadvantage in his affliction.
F Why are people "filling the earth" central to God's plan.	In God's image bearers filling the earth, they proclaim that He is Lord of all Creation. God entrusted the earth to man's stewardship and will enable man to fulfill His commission. Man must defeat his enemy Satan who deceived him into forfeiting His life and rule

*Please note: these charts are for parent reference. The summaries provided here are more elaborate than what a student will be able to synthesize on his or her charts.

268 · Christian Theology & Ancient Polytheism

CC-1: The Nature and Works of the Gods

Comparison Chart 1 Student Copy	Pagan Gods and Goddesses	The God of the Bible
CHARACTER QUALITIES OF THE CREATOR(S)		
HOW THE WORLD WAS CREATED		
HOW MAN WAS CREATED		
WHY MAN WAS CREATED – HIS PURPOSE		
WHAT IS THE VALUE OR WORTH OF MAN		
WHAT DO BABYLONIAN AND HEBREW LAWS REVEAL ABOUT THEIR GODS? (LESSON 15)		
IN THE PAGAN AND BIBLICAL ORIGIN STORIES, WHAT ROLES DOES POWER PLAY? (LESSON 18)		

Comparison Chart · Student Copy · **269**

CC-2: View of Nature

Comparison Chart 2 Student Copy	Polytheism	Monotheism	Naturalism	Pantheism
WHAT IS NATURE?				
HOW DOES MAN RESPOND TO EACH VIEW OF NATURE?				
IS NATURE MORE IMPORTANT OR LESS IMPORTANT THAN MAN?				

270 · Christian Theology & Ancient Polythesism

CC-3: The Great Flood

Comparison Chart 3 Student Copy	Gilgamesh's Flood	Noah's Flood
WHAT SIMILARITIES DO YOU SEE BETWEEN THESE TWO STORIES?		
WHY WAS MANKIND WIPED OUT?		
WHY WERE UTNAPISHTIM'S AND NOAH'S FAMILIES SAVED?		
WHAT DO THESE STORIES REVEAL ABOUT THE CHARACTER OF THE GODS/GOD?		

Comparison Chart · Student Copy · **271**

CC-4: Worship: Seven Days a Week

Comparison Chart 4 Student Copy	Ancient POLYTHEIST	Old Testament Monotheist
WHY DID THEY PRACTICE A 7-DAY WEEK?		
WHAT DID THEY DO EACH DAY OF THE DAY THAT EXPRESSED THEIR WORSHIP?		
WHAT BEARS THE IMAGE OF THE GODS/GOD?		
DEFINE IDOLATRY AND REST IN THE CORRECT COLUMN. (LESSON 6)		
WHY WOULD A TRUE POLYTHEIST NEVER REST AND A TRUE MONOTHEIST NEVER COMMIT IDOLATRY?		

272 · Christian Theology & Ancient Polythesism

CC-5: Worship Through Sacrifice

Comparison Chart 5 Student Copy	Ancient Polytheist	Old Testament Monotheist	New Testament Monotheist
REASONS FOR SACRIFICE: (LESSON 7)			
FOR POLYTHEISTS, LIST THE GENERAL REASONS WHY THEY OFFERED SACRIFICES.			
FOR MONOTHEISTS, SUMMARIZE THE REASON FOR EACH OF THE BIBLE'S EIGHT GREAT SACRIFICES. NOTE SACRIFICES SEVEN AND EIGHT UNDER N.T. MONOTHEISTS. (LESSON 7)			
HOW IMPORTANT ARE REPENTANCE AND OBEDIENCE IN RELATION TO SACRIFICE? (LESSON 8)			
SUMMARY: SUMMARIZE THE REASONS FOR MONOTHEIST SACRIFICE. (LESSON 8)			

Comparison Chart · Student Copy · **273**

CC-6: Worship Through Prayer

Comparison Chart 6 Student Copy	Ancient Polytheists	Hebrew Monotheists
WHAT DID BOTH ANCIENT POLYTHEISTS AND MONOTHEISTS BELIEVE ABOUT PRAYER THAT WAS TRUE? INCLUDE THE TYPES OF PRAYERS THAT BOTH GROUPS PRAYED.		
NOTE THE FIRST MAJOR DIFFERENCES IN THEIR BELIEFS ABOUT PRAYER: WHO THEY WERE PRAYING TO.		
NOTE THE SECOND MAJOR DIFFERENCE IN THEIR BELIEFS ABOUT PRAYER: WHAT DID EACH BELIEVE ABOUT THE POWER OF PRAYER?		
WHY WERE PAGAN PRAYERS IDOLATROUS?		

274 · Christian Theology & Ancient Polythesism

CC-7: Consequences of Idolatry vs. True Worship

Comparison Chart 7 Student Copy	Polytheism	Monotheism	Modern Idolatry
How and why is Human Sexuality impacted by each worldview?			
How and why is the Value of Human Life impacted by each worldview?			
How and why is one's view of Demonic Power impacted by each worldview?			

Comparison Chart · Student Copy · 275

CC-8: Hammurabi's Code and Mosaic Law

Comparison Chart 8
Student Copy

Instructions: Due to the volume of information, answer all questions in paragraph form.

1) COMPARE HAMMURABI'S VIEW OF HIS GODS AND HIS ACHIEVEMENTS TO MOSES' VIEW OF GOD AND HIS ACHIEVEMENTS.	
2) RECORD THE PURPOSES OF BOTH LAWS.	
3) NOTE WHAT TYPE OF LAWS DO NOT EXIST IN HAMMURABI'S CODE AND THE REASON WHY.	
4) WHAT SIMILARITIES AND DIFFERENCES EXIST BETWEEN THE LAWS DEALING WITH MARRIAGE, MURDER, AND THIEVES?	
5) HOW WERE "AN EYE FOR AN EYE" LAWS IMPLEMENTED DIFFERENTLY IN BOTH CULTURES?	
6) BRIEFLY DEFINE HOW THE REBELLIOUS CHILD WAS DEALT WITH AND WHY ISRAEL'S LAW HAD SUCH SEVERE PUNISHMENTS FOR THAT SIN.	

276 · Christian Theology & Ancient Polythesism

CC-9: Suffering of the Babylonian and Biblical Job

Comparison Chart 9 Student Copy	Babylonian "Job"	Biblical Job
DESCRIBE THE CHARACTER OF THE SUFFERER.		
WHAT IS THE REASON BEHIND HIS SUFFERING?		
HOW IS THE SUFFERER RESTORED?		
WHAT DOES SUFFERING TEACH HIM ABOUT THE GODS/GOD?		
COMPARE THE PURPOSE OF AND USE OF POWER BY THE SORCERER WITH GOD'S POWERFUL WORDS TO JOB.		

Comparison Chart · Student Copy · **277**

CC-10: The Afterlife and The Resurrection

Comparison Chart 10 Student Copy	Polytheists	OT Monotheists	NT Monotheists
WHAT OR HOW DID THE GODS/GOD PROVIDE FOR THE AFTERLIFE FOR EACH GROUP?			
WHAT IMPORTANT STORIES DID EACH HAVE INVOLVING "RESURRECTION"?			
WHAT WAS RESURRECTED THROUGH EACH STORY?			
THROUGH WHAT RITUALS WERE THESE STORIES REENACTED, AND WHO RECEIVED RENEWED POWER OR STRENGTH THROUGH THEM?			

278 · Christian Theology & Ancient Polythesism

TC-1: A Grand Theme of Scripture – God as Man's Provider

Theme Chart 1 Student Copy	**Instructions:** *Note examples of things God provides as directed by the scriptural reference and corresponding lesson.*
LESSON II Genesis 1&2	
LESSONS III-IV Genesis 6-8	
LESSON VI Genesis 2:2 Exodus 20:8-11, 31:12-17	
LESSON VII Genesis 3:21 Genesis 22:1-1 Exodus 12 Lev. 1-4, 11-18 John 1:28, 29	
LESSON XV Titus 2:11-15	
LESSON XIX Jeremiah 31	
LESSON XXIII Job 38-42:6	

Theme Chart ·Student Copy · **279**

TC-2: A Grand Theme of Scripture – Man as God's Representative

Theme Chart 2 Student Copy	Instructions: With each corresponding lesson and scripture note where this theme begins, and give examples of how man represents God. With each new reference note repetitions or new applications of this idea. For each scriptural reference, give examples for how or why man represents God.
LESSON II Genesis 1&2	
LESSONS III-IV Genesis 9:1-7	
LESSON V Exodus 20:8-11 Genesis 2:2,3	
LESSON VI Colossians 1:15 Ephesians 4:22-24	
LESSON XVII Genesis 1:26,27	
LESSON XVII 1 Kings 18:16-40; I Corinthians 1:27-29	
LESSON XIX Rev. 3:15-16	
LESSON XIX Jeremiah 50:17-20 II Chronicles 36:15-23	
LESSON XXI Job 1 and 2	

280 · Christian Theology & Ancient Polythesism

TC-3: A Grand Theme of Scripture – Choose Life or Choose Death

Theme Chart 3 Student Copy	Instructions: Note examples of the choice for life or death directed by the scriptural reference and cooresponding
LESSON IV Why is free will necessary? (Gen. 2:16) How was man using his free will in Noah's day? Genesis 6-8	
LESSON VII How does what we worship bring us life or ultimately death? How was idolatry the choice for death as seen in the O. T. and in modern culture?	
LESSON XVI Summarize Israel's two options. Deuteronomy 30:11-20	
LESSON XVII How does man's free will relate to the Bible's ultimate?	
LESSON XVIII What was the choice and outcome of Elijah's offer? I Kings 18:16-40	
LESSON XXIV What is the ultimate and only choice for life? John 10:10; 14:6	

Theme Chart ·Student Copy · **281**

TC-4: A Grand Theme of Scripture – Suffering

Theme Chart 4 Student Copy	Instructions: Note the examples of suffering for each reference or lesson below. Begin with the name of the sufferer and whether they suffered justly or unjustly. Add the suffering they experienced. Each example may have more than one sufferer.
LESSON IV Genesis 6-8	
LESSONS XIX Book of Jeremiah	
LESSON XXI Book of Job – Prologue	
LESSON XXII Book of Job – Epilogue	
SUMMARY:	

282 · Christian Theology & Ancient Polythesism

BSC-1: The Bible's Story – Scripture's Three Main Characters

Bible Story Chart 1
Student Copy

Instructions: The letters next to each question correspond to a direction found within the instruction boxes in the lessons.

A Who is the main character of the Bible?

A Who are the two supporting characters, and what are their relationships to God?

A Name the Three Persons of the One Triune God:

A Name the three communal human relationships that were established to represent God to the world:

B In calling the Church the "Bride of Christ" what does this title tell us about the relationship God has offered us? (Think about the contrast to the polytheistic title for man – slave of the gods.)

B As those who accept God's proposal of love wear no wedding ring, how do we display to the world that we are "betrothed" to the King of Kings and Lord or Lords?

BSC-2: The Bible's Story – Scripture's Primary Purpose & Central Conflict

Bible Story Chart 2
Student Copy

Instructions: The letters next to each question correspond to a direction found within the instruction boxes in the lessons.

B	What is the main purpose of the Bible's stories and of all creation?	
B	How do the two supporting characters serve the story's purpose?	
B	Out of jealousy, pride and hatred, what does Satan endeavor to steal from God and man?	
C	In challenging God's sole right to worship, God could have crushed Satan by his power. What did he do instead?	
C	What question is at the heart of the Bible's central conflict?	
D	Give a biblical example of Satan attempting to steal the worship of God and the dominion of man:	
D	How does the Bible's primary purpose resolve the main conflict?	
E	Out of jealousy, pride, and hatred, what ploys does Satan use in his efforts to steal from God and man?	
F	When Satan challenged God's right to worship, God could have crushed Satan with his power. What did he do instead?	
F	Why are people "filling the earth" central to God's plan.	

Marcia Harris Brim

has been writing and publishing for the broader homeschool market for six years. This is the first major work she has written specifically for Christian homeschool families and private Christian schools. It combines her love of history and worldview with her educational degree in Theology from Multnomah Bible College. While her previous curricula help students develop thinking skills, this work encourages students to think Christianly about their world and the life they lead within it.

Marcia has been uniquely equipped to provide a framework for teaching Christian theology as a necessary foundation for a Christian worldview. She did not learn to read until her mid-thirties. Severely dyslexic, her learning disabilities are in part due to an inability to retain knowledge without a contextual framework – the big picture. This has driven her to seek to understand the scope of Scripture. Thus this work is born out of her own great need to see God's Word as a whole, set within a framework that puts the parts of Scripture together. For many, this framework will be unnecessary, as it is simply the sum of the parts. For others, it will be life changing, as the messages of God's Word will cohere in ways they have never seen before.

May this work be a blessing to your family,
as it was born out of weakness and dependence
on our great God and Savior, Jesus Christ.